DECONSTRUCTING
MACBETH

DECONSTRUCTING
MACBETH

The Hyperontological View

H. W. Fawkner

Rutherford • Madison • Teaneck
Fairleigh Dickinson University Press
London and Toronto: Associated University Presses

© 1990 by Associated University Presses, Inc.

All rights reserved. Authorization to photocopy items for internal or personal use, or the internal or personal use of specific clients, is granted by the copyright owner, provided that a base fee of $10.00, plus eight cents per page, per copy is paid directly to the Copyright Clearance Center, 27 Congress Street, Salem, Massachusetts 01970. [0-8386-3393-5/90 $10.00+8¢ pp, pc.]

Associated University Presses
440 Forsgate Drive
Cranbury, NJ 08512

Associated University Presses
25 Sicilian Avenue
London WC1A 2QH, England

Associated University Presses
P.O. Box 488, Port Credit
Mississauga, Ontario
Canada L5G 4M2

The paper used in this publication meets the requirements
of the American National Standard for Permanence of Paper
for Printed Library Materials Z39.48-1984.

Library of Congress Cataloging-in-Publication Data

Fawkner, Harald William, 1946–
    Deconstructing Macbeth : the hyperontological view / H.W. Fawkner.
    p.   cm.
    Includes bibliographical references.
    ISBN 0-8386-3393-5 (alk. paper)
    1. Shakespeare, William, 1564–1616. Macbeth. 2. Deconstruction.
I. Title.
PR 2823.F38   1990
822.3'3—dc20   89-45784
                                                                                 CIP

PRINTED IN THE UNITED STATES OF AMERICA

CONTENTS

Acknowledgments 7
A Note on the Text 9

1.1 Tracing *Macbeth* 19
1.2 The Question of Presence 27
1.3 Staging Contexts 38
1.4 Theatrical Servitude 44

2.1 The Questioning of Identity 52
2.2 Vanishings 59
2.3 Cuttings 68

3.1 The Assassination of Intentionality 77
3.2 Soliloquy 85
3.3 The Daggers of Absence 90

4.1 Horror and Pseudohorror 98
4.2 The Active Phase of Servitude 108
4.3 The Botcher 115

5.1 Ontological Relief 123
5.2 Deconstructing Character 129
5.3 The Traitor Man 138
5.4 Thickening Brightness 147

6.1 The Notion of Expenditure 155
6.2 Sovereignty 164
6.3 Tragic Simulacrum 173
6.4 Cosmetics 181

7.1 The Ontological Fallacy 188
7.2 The Desire of Apollo 198
7.3 Shakespeare's Other 204

Notes	219
Terminological Usage	233
Bibliography	237
Index	257

ACKNOWLEDGMENTS

It is a pleasure to acknowledge the assistance I have received in preparing this book from David K. Roberts, Michael Koy, Maurice Charney, B. Sandmark, C. Schaar, and Thomas Yoseloff. Grateful acknowledgment is also made to Cambridge University Press for the use of material from John Dover Wilson, Introduction to *Macbeth*; from Dennis Bartholomeusz, *Macbeth and the Players*; and from G. I. Duthie; "Antithesis in *Macbeth*"; to Sheed & Ward, Ltd., for Hans-Georg Gadamer, *Truth and Method*, translated by P. Christopher Smith; to The University of Toronto Press for Thomas F. van Laan, *Role-Playing in Shakespeare*; to The University of California Press for Marvin Rosenberg, *The Masks of Macbeth*; to Oxford University Press for Hegel, *The Phenomenology of Spirit*, translated by A. V. Miller; for Hegel, *Logic*, translated by William Wallace; and for Samuel Johnson, *Johnson on Shakespeare*; to Methuen & Co. and Routledge & Kegan Paul for Jean-Paul Sartre, *Being and Nothingness*, translated by Hazel E. Barnes; for Marjorie Garber, *Shakespeare's Ghost Writers*; for P. Parker and G. Hartman, *Shakespeare and the Question of Theory* (including "Telmah" by T. Hawkes, "Tongue-Ties Our Queen?" by H. Felperin, and "*Hamlet*: Letters and Spirits" by M. Ferguson); for Jonathan Culler, *The Pursuit of Signs*; for Robin Grove, "Multiplying Villainies of Nature" in John Russell Brown, *Focus on* Macbeth; and for John Bayley, *Shakespeare and Tragedy*; to Hackett Publications, Inc. for Charles B. Guignon, *Heidegger and the Problem of Knowledge*; to The University of Nebraska Press for Jacques Derrida, *Glas*, translated by John P. Leavey, Jr. and Richard Rand; to Princeton University Press for Michael Goldman, *Acting and Action in Shakespearean Tragedy*; and for Sigurd Burckhardt, *Shakespearean Meanings*; to Yale University Press for Stephen Booth, *King Lear, Macbeth, Indefinition, and Tragedy*; to The University of Massachusetts Press for James L. Calderwood, *If It Were Done*; to Ohio University Press for John L. Murphy, *Darkness and Devils*; to The University of Chicago Press for Jacques Derrida, *Writing and Difference*, translated by Alan Bass; to Humanities Press, Inc. and The Athlone Press for R. S.

White, *Let Wonder Seem Familiar*; to Harvester-Wheatsheaf and Simon & Schuster for Stevie Davies, *The Idea of Woman in the Renaissance*; to Random House, Inc. for Friedrich Nietzsche, *The Birth of Tragedy*, translated by Walter Kaufmann; to Basic Books for Alexandre Kojève, *Introduction to the Reading of Hegel*, translated by James H. Nichols, Jr.; and for Jonathan Culler, *The Pursuit of Signs*.

A NOTE ON THE TEXT

If this text had a point of origin, it would perhaps be a moment in the early eighties, when I was struck by the relevance for *Macbeth* of a Hegelian notion: that a "master" who receives an infinite amount of dialectical recognition (what Shakespeare calls "golden opinions") arrives at an existential impasse. Precisely by being recognized in an unlimited fashion, he does not get recognized at all. Dialectical recognition depends not only on the materialization of admiration but also on our recognition of the worth of those recognizing us; but in *Macbeth,* the hero is so far ahead of his peers in terms of heroic status that they fail to function in a satisfying way as dialectical equals. Or rather: it is impossible to imagine a future where their dialectically organized "golden" opinions any more would impress the hero as golden. Thus, although other plays, including *Coriolanus,* are more centered than *Macbeth* on heroic dialectic itself, it is only in *Macbeth* that the real structural paradox of dialectical mastery is examined. From the viewpoint of my own private prejudices, therefore, Shakespeare seems to be concentrating on a paradox at the beginning of *Macbeth* that is disturbingly similar to the paradox energizing Hegel in the opening sections of the *Phenomenology of Spirit.* What impresses me here is not the topical similarity, the sharing of a common ground of inquiry into the nature of human desire, but the similarity of the "analytical" moves: the ability of each analyst, working in his own medium, to delineate the vulnerability of the "master." The master is "cornered" in *Macbeth,* and so is he in Hegel. This cornering seems in both cases to be a strangely impersonal mechanism—as if the subject could from the outset anticipate the futility of his heroic future.

The dialectical process where the "master" quickly exhausts the energies of his own golden identity has been famously explicated in Kojève's sometimes lucid and sometimes reductive reading of the *Phenomenology.* For those not familiar with the theoretical apparatus of this model of "desire for desire" a short list of Hegelian and post-Hegelian terms is provided at the end of the main text.

The other point of departure, as the title suggests, is deconstruction. This is partly so because *Macbeth* naturally lends itself to deconstructive analysis (it is a patently self-deconstructing play), partly so because the dialectical and Hegelian problematic of the play spontaneously slides over into a postdialectical and postphenomenological one. Certain supplementary directions of inquiry were provided by Jacques Derrida on the matter of this transition during a private encounter where the deconstructive program for *Macbeth* was the main topic of conversation. The Hegelian framework was very much in the foreground during this discussion: *Glas*, the various phases of mastery and servitude, and finally the essay on Bataille subtitled "A Hegelianism without Reserve."

It might be said, then, that the critical enterprise focuses the triangle Shakespeare–Hegel–Derrida; yet my immediate objection to such a premature pigeonholing would be that dialectical phenomenology and deconstructionism are here essentially operative in terms of analytical frames—not as systems or ideologies. To be familiar with the analytical potentials available within a certain intellectual apparatus does not to me seem to be the same thing as belonging for life to the particular "school" bred by that apparatus. The heretical impulse, I trust, is nowhere more effective than inside systems that once and for all have decided that they themselves are the essence of the heretical.

Interpretative penetration is no doubt a function of some process of interaction between three distinct phases or states: those of (1) familiarization, (2) overfamiliarization, and (3) defamiliarization. This of course goes for the drama, the text: one needs to be familiar with it, indeed overfamiliar with it; and then one needs some "jolt" to bring oneself out of the torpor of automatized response—to restore oneself to that "primitive" state of exceptional alertness, where one (like Shakespeare's first audience) is naive enough to be ready for just about anything. But perhaps these three stages also can be applied to the critic's attitude to his own theoretical assumptions: that one first needs to self-consciously select certain lines of intellectual approach, that one then needs to follow these lines to their logical limits— and that one finally needs some "jolt" in order to distance oneself from the securities of one's own premises. From that viewpoint, this book is the retrospective attempt to deal intellectually with a series of such jolts and to conceive the otherness of such an alien and unexpected pattern as possibly carrying some signifying power of its own. The "inverted" Macbeth extracted from this investigation is that alien pattern—and "he" seems to be capable of some power of signifying.

Sometimes, no doubt, the various "jolts" encountered en route serve the purpose of clarifying the locus of a problem, not the ideal manner of solving it. All explications of individual passages are from this viewpoint tentative. What is ultimately at stake in these pages is thus in a sense not the promise of final knowledge about the play (a notion that would repeat the hero's own tragic error) but the willingness to ask a set of new questions about *Macbeth*. In that event, the critical emphasis is on the nature of that asking itself.

Finally, something needs to be said about value judgements. Deconstruction, as we know, tends to generate an emotional type of reactivity in several quarters. Sometimes these emotional overtones are caused by the difficulty of the deconstructionist viewpoint, the person at the receiving end turning the frustrations of the reading process into the anger of theoretical hatred. Sometimes, in addition, deconstructionist praxis itself is responsible for such types of emotional breakdown, for there are obviously times when deconstructors, including Derrida, are more self-mystifying and "obscure" than they need have been. Value judgements are of course operative in these types of friction between critics and readers; yet the value judgements I wish to focus here for a moment are those that are more sweepingly ideological in their structure. I am not thinking of the banal distrust that the simpleminded "humanist" turns toward deconstructionism, the phony idea that deconstructions are the end of humanist civilization, or the work of the devil. Instead I am thinking of the cultural clashes that are created when deconstruction, as in the case of the opposition between Judaism and Christianity in *Glas*, focuses controversies of a quasi-theological or spiritual nature. Here, it is not only emotions that are stirred and troubled, but our entire philosophies of life: our commitment or noncommitment to a specific existential credo.

My attitude to this deeper-running type of ideological and emotional conflict is a twofold one. *On the one hand*, I do not think it is possible to work a thorough deconstruction on a text without considering the text's ability to itself negotiate the spacing(s) between such ideological poles. In other words, the "Christian" issue in a drama like *Macbeth*—the reasons for and against viewing the play primarily in terms of Christian humanism—

cannot be swept under the carpet during the process of deconstructing the play as a whole. Deconstruction does not neutralize ideologies, bypass them and set up its own "purely academic" questions in the impersonal space of logical abstractions of a merely theoretical kind. On the other hand, I do not hold the view that deconstruction itself is an ideology, that it could or should be ideological. From that viewpoint, I resent certain tendentious slidings within the deconstructionist movement itself, slidings where deconstructions work in propagandistic fashion to secretly impose a specific theological or philosophic view on the world. In those circumstances, the text simply becomes a tool in the hands of the propagandist, and the "reading" we get retains no element of usefulness from the perspective of critical science.

This fact that deconstruction by nature is and is not ideological is of considerable importance for us as we eventually move into the final stages of inquiry in this book. I am thinking here of a figure that will be foregrounded in those concluding pages: that of reversibility. Reversibility is on my view something that preoccupies Shakespeare with increasing intensity during the final years of dramatic compilation, and reversibility is also something that is often foregrounded in deconstructionist theory. Yet there is a type of reversibility that deconstruction usually never discusses: and that is the reversibility that can affect deconstruction itself. It is precisely in this perspective that we can best study the paradoxical nature of the relationship between deconstructionism and ideology. *Glas*, with its Christian/Judaic conflict, is a case in point. Here, by overemphasizing Hegel's "Christian" prejudices, Derrida seeks to *reverse* the philosophic hierarchization effectuated by dialectical phenomenology: what is "Christian" is said to be sacrificial only in a spurious sense, for the sacrificial impulse in Hegel's allegedly Christian philosophy is quickly prepared to sacrifice itself too. Sacrifice sacrifices sacrifice, putting an end to the sacrificial impulse and instead establishing the reign of philosophic self-completion and spiritual salvation. (We will be discussing the final act of *Macbeth* in relation to this important notion of the sacrifice of sacrifice.) Hegel (or the philosophic superstructure of Christian humanism) thus reverses the sacrificial current; and Derrida/*Glas* reverses that reversal: "permits" sacrifice to go on, affirms the notion of a sacrificial remainder that escapes from the centristic aspirations of philosophic salvation and salvational philosophy. In the holocaust, burning goes on; at no point does the burning process completely burn up burning, completely efface the horror and sacrifice of (the idea and trace of) the burn. ("Cinders," as the recurring leitmotif of Derrida's later writings, is the notion that focuses this "remainder" and trace of all sacrifice, what itself must not be sacrificed.) Yet if we read Hegel's *Phenomenology of Spirit* carefully, and with special reference to section B.B., "Freedom of Self-Consciousness: Stoicism, Scepticism, and the Unhappy Consciousness" (§§ 197–230), we see not only that Hegel has anticipated the "pessimistic," Derridean viewpoint (that there is no end to sacrifice, no end to otherness) but also that he from the outset has understood the radical reversibility of the entire problematic: that if *in theory* you can reverse the "optimistic," salvational notion of sacrificial otherness into its opposite (the pessimistic outlook of the Unhappy Consciousness delightfully agonizing over the unreachability of the beyond), then *in theory* you can reverse this reversal too. Hegel sees the reversibility of this theoretical dilemma as a factor that gives him (and the "optimistic" philosophy of the Happy Consciousness) a crucial advantage over his unhappy opponent. The Unhappy Consciousness, Hegel argues, is caught in the web of his own theory of sacrifice and contradicts himself absurdly. The Unhappy Consciousness wants to practice a philosophy of sacrifice and self-renouncement (unalleviated by philosophic salvation), but he does not want to embrace the ultimate sacrifice, the highest level of renouncement and self-renouncement: that of sacrificing sacrifice (and unhappiness) too, that of *renouncing* the philosophy of renouncement. Hegel thus opposes to the Unhappy Consciousness what he considers to be the most extreme and absolute form of sacrifice: the sacrifice of the privilege of being a man of sacrifice.

These comments serve the purpose, as we have seen, of calling attention to the complexity of the relationship between Derridean deconstruction and Hegel's speculative phenomenology. This complexity is first of all connected with the problem of ideological and theoretical reversibility. From this perspective, the emphasis on various Hegelian notions in this review of *Macbeth* does not at all reflect a desire to move "backwards" in the intellectual history of the West—to situate the inquiry in some early nineteenth-century space of idealist speculation; on the contrary, the aim is to clarify a space of possible analysis where Hegel and Derrida are *logically speaking* coeval—the space, in many ways, of *Glas*. As the problem of intellectual reversibility demonstrates (the logical reversibility between the Happy Consciousness and the Unhappy Consciousness), Hegel's phenomenology is not merely a "source of influence" for Derridean thinking of the deconstructionist kind, not a platform that is in the "past" of deconstructive theory, not a derelict and antiquated foundation partly discarded, partly "overcome," and partly recognized as being of limited usefulness. The agony of returning to Hegel is for Derrida (even more than for Bataille) not simply the pain of confronting a thinker with an altogether different outlook on life, but the pain of recognizing that the various "escapes" from Hegelian phenomenology are already inscribed inside it as "steps" or phases in its own processes of initiation. Thus, as Bataille observes, it is not enough to be familiar with Hegel in the Nietzschean manner of merely knowing some popularized version of the conflict between "master" and "slave." It is one thing to wave slogans about the "Unhappy Consciousness" in a general, propagandistic way; it is another matter to understand the logical precision of such notions as they work against a background of detailed knowledge of Hegel's precise thinking. If *Glas* tells us anything about Hegel, it tells us something about precision.

Since the processes of intellectual reversibility (outlined above) often afflict deconstructionism itself, opening it up to the risk of being defeated by its own logical mechanisms, it is evident that deconstructive theory cannot work on Shakespeare in a prescriptive fashion. You cannot turn everything in Shakespeare into signifying verities that will conform to deconstructionist dogma. As I have already suggested, *Macbeth* through its very structure *asks* to be deconstructed; but it also asks for other, supplementary types of critical performance. Thus each individual work by Shakespeare has its own unique deconstructive potential; and the art of deconstructing Shakespeare is not primarily that of merely identifying that potential, but the greater challenge of identifying its limits—and, above all, investigating the special territory, different in each play, glimpsed beyond those limits.

If Friedrich Nietzsche's deconstructive heritage, as currently revitalized by Jacques Derrida, in the final analysis amounts to a radical perspectivism, and if this perspectivism always entails the desolidification of the imaginary conceptual durability of metaphysical universals (such as "ontology") and ideological truths (such as those of academic deconstructionism), then the rigid and quasi-imaginary line of metaphysical demarcation between ontology and deconstruction must itself be questioned. If a hyperontology became part of such a process of unmasking, and if it itself could have a provisional conceptual outline, it would therefore define itself in the "space" between ontology and its refutation—*as* the crumbling of the wall between ontological imagination and imaginary ontology.

DECONSTRUCTING
MACBETH

1

1.1 Tracing *Macbeth*

This book is not an interpretation according to deconstructionist "method." As Rodolphe Gasché points out in *The Tain of the Mirror*, much academic deconstruction has simply chosen to ignore the philosophical levels of Derridean thought (*TM*, 3), and the reductive treatment of deconstruction as a method (*TM*, 123) is one of the sad consequences of such an academic attitude.[1] Deconstructionism in its superficially "clever" guise vanishes into truth of an ordinary propositional kind (*TM*, 77), thus making a further unhappy contribution to that sweeping technologization of thought that Hegel dismissed as "mere reflection" (*Verstand*) and that Heidegger turned into a principal enemy of deep meditative thinking (*TM*, 123). Such deconstructive cleverness on a merely reflexive (i.e., "logical") level of academic action leads to what Gasché correctly identifies as "the metaphysics of reflection" (*TM*, 32)—the very type of Western intellection that Hegel, Heidegger, and Derrida from the outset reject in clearing an opening for their own projects. This reflexive or reflective type of deconstructionism tends to emphasize tricks and games that will not be played in the current venture: the inward collapse into indifference of conflicting strata of writing (*TM*, 138), the predictability of "aporias" (*TM*, 142), and so on. Our aim in this book will not be to annul or neutralize opposites, but to deconstruct them. In studying discrepancies in *Macbeth*, we will not simply be deconstructing "logical contradictions"; for the contradictions that a deconstruction interests itself in are not merely logical (*TM*, 135).

The temptation to work a weak deconstruction on *Macbeth* is of course considerable, since weak deconstruction is reflexive and since *Macbeth* is a manifestly self-deconstructing play: that is, a text that lays a trap for every critic by situating the scene of reflexive deciphering within itself.[2] From the viewpoint of weak deconstruction, virtually nothing can be done to *Macbeth* that *Macbeth* has not already done to itself, explicitly.

In moving away from such a weak notion of deconstruction into a strong one, our task is basically that of acknowledging Derrida's persistent concentration on the critique of ontological issues, issues about the ultimate foundation of reality (TM, 7). As he critiques such ontological notions, Derrida does not simply move away from them in dismissive manner; on the contrary, he lingers in those regions where the shadow of the ontological problematic always can be felt: as a notion, but also as a sensation, a philosophical mood. Critics who do not bother to participate in this mood, or even realize that they need to come to know it, are not in the final analysis performing deconstructions; instead they are often extending the claims of the philosophy of reflection.

It must be seen, then, that Derrida in an important sense extends Heidegger's inquiry into the question of being (TM, 313). As Derrida himself points out in *The Truth in Painting*, the Heideggerian questioning of Being in its turn presupposes a critique of Western (i.e., Cartesian) subjectivity: our culture's obsession with the idea of trying "to secure for itself, in subjectivity, a *ground* of certainty (an unshakable rock or pedestal on which this time the adhering sole no longer slips)."[3] As I shall argue, the Macbethian dilemma brings its forces of rupture into this very notion: "Then comes my fit again; I had else been perfect; / Whole as the marble, *founded* as the rock" (3.4.20–21). To be perfect is for Cartesian (thus modern) man to be founded; and the foundational drive is postheroic rather than heroic. If one's battle is ever abated, writes Bataille, the desire to be everything breaks one into pieces. In the heroic era, man is the plaything of nothingness; in the postheroic era, nothingness is the plaything of man.[4]

Once it has been recognized that Derridean deconstruction typically lingers inside the very region of the ontology it critiques, it becomes clear that deconstruction is no simple negation of ontology. On the contrary, Derridean thought in a sense effectuates its disruption of ontology by deepening the very issues that ontology forwards for the benefits of its own cause. In this way, as I will be arguing in a forthcoming work on *Antony and Cleopatra*,[5] the force of what lends itself to deconstruction in Shakespeare gradually shades off (or brightens!) into the force of what I try to focus in terms of a "hyperontology." Any attentive reader of Derrida will of course already have noticed that much of Derrida's later writing is dominated by hyperontological rather than directly deconstructionist issues.

It might be said, then, that this current study situates itself in a somewhat indefinite borderland between deconstruction and hyperontology. It is a territory where deconstructionist issues are primary, but only in the sense that they are the mere conditions of possibility for what, beyond deconstruction, already slides abysmally out of reach.

Looking at the deconstructionist side of this deconstruction/hyperontology issue, I might first like to emphasize that my main target is not only the play "itself" but also what it has become in modern Cartesian consciousness: what *Macbeth* now *is* once academic criticism of the reflective kind has completed (and exhausted) its work. Of course it is nowadays impossible to make a firm distinction between a "real" or originary *Macbeth* and a "secondary" *Macbeth* as a product of what modern culture has turned it into. Indeed, the action of the play itself shows how such a process of ontologization is always already on its feet. I nevertheless think it is significant to formulate questions that address themselves to the role played by criticism in deciding what *Macbeth* is all about. Thus, insofar as deconstruction involves creating a total reversal (especially of binary opposites), my main purpose will not be to let the play play a game against itself, but to let the play play a game against what criticism has turned it into. The hierarchies I am interested in deconstructing, then, are not strictly internal ones belonging exclusively to the "inner reality" of the actual drama; for me, this inner drama is already always outside the play, troubling those that observe and judge it.

When it comes to the inner drama of the play, I will be using a number of Derridean "concepts" in relation to the question of Being as it gets asked and opened in the drama. This is mainly how I conceive deconstructive power: *relating* nonontological "concepts" to the ontological ones that already stand in full view.

Any attentiveness toward the question of Being immediately involves some process of slowing: we see this in Macbeth himself, who "slows down" as soon as the Weird Sisters enter his field of attention. A switch of wavelength occurs, a change of gear. If, as Heidegger argues, Being is always intuitively preunderstood in terms of light and lighting (he tends to speak of "the lighting of Being"), and if, as he also argues, the transition from weak reflective thinking to strong meditative thinking involves some necessary slowing of our intellectual faculties, then the sense of the luminous thickening of things in *Macbeth* ("Light thickens," 3.2.50) may itself be perceived in a slightly new light.

In the modern world, writes Baudrillard, "light is slowing down": travelling below its own right speed, as it were, light (indistinguishable from our minds perceiving it), depletes a world of full meaning. As in *Macbeth*, the sense of such deceleration is the twin partner of its opposite: "Ever since acceleration has become our common condition, suspense and slow motion are the current forms of the tragic. Time . . . is no longer illuminated by a will; nor is space any longer defined by movement." But with this loss of ordinary (and full) meaning through the loss of movement and acceleration, there is the strange acquisition of something else: "the slow emergence of another meaning . . . So slow that light would curl up on itself and even come to a halt."[6]

Destiny, it seems to me, is itself caught in this process of slowing. This is no doubt partly caused by the hero's ability to concentrate on the fixed image of his own fate—to make that fate itself curl back on him. As slowness, *Macbeth* is from this viewpoint a study of the process of the infinitely extended deferral of destiny. In such a condition, to follow Baudrillard once more, the evasion of one's fate itself becomes fate; what "observes" this evasion (not one's fate but the "ecstasy" of one's fate) would then not simply be the subject, but language itself. Perhaps only language.[7]

What Derridean "concepts" would be deconstructively active in facilitating the sighting of the "slowing" in *Macbeth*? First of all, and precisely because academic deconstructionism is tempted to settle down into the domestication of otherness promoted by the Western metaphysics of reflection (*TM*, 101), one would need to recognize the force of what Gasché calls "Derrida's Other," "the *general* Other" (*TM*, 103). Otherness is *in general* originary and quasi-foundational in Derridean thought. This in its turn means that we are dealing with a *general* theory of originary duplication (*TM*, 225). Things actually start with (their) doubling. This doubling is at once their own and not their own. The relation to the other is somehow anterior to selfhood (*TM*, 192) and to phenomenological intentionality (*TM*, 281)—so that pure self-reference becomes as unlikely (*TM*, 227) as soliloquy without traces of alterity (*TM*, 191).

This kind of thinking, going back to Hegel's notion that each pole (in a bipolar opposition) constitutes itself through the work of the anti-pole that it seems to cancel and negate, radicalizes itself in the more elusive areas of Derrida's thought into the notions of arche-trace (*TM*, 187), arche-writing (*TM*, 193), and arche-violence (*TM*, 193): all suggesting the quasi-foundational work of an "originary trace" (*TM*, 192). Spacing, as initial duplication (*TM*, 225), engages with the tragic "slowing" (recently discussed) by breaking up the pointlike instantaneity of the origin, which becomes delayed in relation to itself (*TM*, 196). As I will try to demonstrate, Shakespeare's entire conception of the tragic movement is logically built on this notion of the origin as (its own) aftereffect (*TM*, 209). The tragic status of the weird "supplement" (in Shakespeare, in Derrida) depends on this "slowing" of the origin in relation to itself. At once completely necessary and completely unnecessary, the "supplement" is a nondialectical middle that endlessly has to mock the hero before he finally intuits *its* treachery.

The "slow-motion" quality of Macbethian awareness, furthermore, is directly related to the work of what Derrida calls "the trace." Coeval with the (double) origin, indeed as the very energy that splices it into duplicity, the "trace" does not follow things as a latecomer. It is on the contrary what from the outset turns the origin into a "smear." As such a smudge, such a smudging of pointlike presence, Murder (like Truth) will accost Macbeth in terms of a trace that has no origin, in terms of an origin that never properly arrives. No understanding of *Macbeth* is at all possible without insight into this coimplication between tracing and effacing (*TM*, 189). Such "originary effacement" (*TM*, 216) forces us to think the drama *Macbeth* as the impossible. It is this difficult activity that I believe the hero himself undertakes: to think himself as impossible, in terms of the impossible, in terms of the possibility of the impossible, in terms of *some* possibility that somehow, strangely, is and is not possible. Macbeth, I would argue, seems to be thinking this impossibility of himself from a point that is both inside and outside his own drama. This point, at once double and single, is what he tries to focus in the play, and it is what I hope to focus in this book. The venture, then, is doomed from the outset as being impossible as well as possible. As Derrida puts it, "no one has ever said that deconstruction, as a technique or a method, was possible; it thinks only on the level of the impossible and of what is still evoked as unthinkable."[8]

This idea of thinking the impossible is already fully operative in Shakespeare criticism. To think the impossible, here, is not an empirically oriented effort to erect some utterly implausible extradramatic context; rather, it is the straining of the mind to capture some elusive suggestion that the play itself attempts to think—perhaps without quite succeeding to. This "failure" of the play to quite think out the logic of its own powers of suggestion need not necessarily be seen as a "lack" in the play, some shortcoming on the part of articulation, author, or design. Rather, such a lack of full articulate plenitude attests to the ability of all articulation to deliver more than it proposes to. This "more," we know in the poststructuralist era, is also necessarily a "less"—and it is this deviation of *Macbeth* from *Macbeth* that awaits exploration.

An interesting example of this critical evocation of the "unthinkable" is Terence Hawkes's "backward" reading of *Hamlet* as *Telmah*. It is not the reversal itself that affirms the "unthinkable," but the ability of Hawkes's criticism to focus the critical *experience* of the unthinkable in the controversy between W. W. Greg and John Dover Wilson on the issue of the failure of *The Mousetrap* to trap Claudius.[9] When Dover Wilson first realizes the subversive potential of Greg's reading, he is suddenly at once able and unable to think *Hamlet* in terms of the unthinkable. On the one hand, for Wilson, nothing is but what is not; no part of *Hamlet* is not contaminated by *Telmah*. On the other hand, for Wilson, what is now to be continued to be thought is not the interface *Hamlet-Telmah* (an impossible thought, a thinking leading away into the impossible) but ways of quickly neutralizing this new potential, ways of getting back to scratch. But there is a moment for Wilson, finely delineated by Hawkes, when the critic is poised on the kind of brink that shapes Macbeth's destiny: he is shaken to the ground by the possibility of the unthinkable, and this possibility, or in fact the unthinkable as such, darkly inaugurates a "spell" or "insanity" that stays with the critic for the remainder of his life as a "disturbing" and "mindblowing" state of latent excitement.[10]

In *Macbeth*, of course, this poise on the brink of the unthinkable is eternalized—for as I will be suggesting, the experience of being on the verge of the unthinkable does not leave Macbeth simply because he murders, simply because he transforms the unthinkability of murder into the thinkability of murder (its material effectuation). Although "the unthinkable" is logically tied to murder, it is not reducible to murder. Indeed, *thinking out murder*, rather than decreasing the element of "the unthinkable" in Macbeth, increases it.

Normative critics have traditionally made consistent attempts to think around this "unthinkable" core of *Macbeth*—and this pattern of behavior is not only predictable but also understandable, "rational": Who, after all, wants to think into the unthinkable? Who, after all, wants to see thought vanish into the unthinkable? Yet the task of ascertaining the reality of the "unthinkable" Shakespeare is not as "dangerous" as it may first seem, the main reason being that the "unthinkable" Shakespeare only can be glimpsed from a perspective where the thinkable Shakespeare has already stabilized himself (historically, hermeneutically, and so forth). The "counter-reading" only becomes operative against the background of its opposite, just as the normative reading only becomes possible (as a theatrical event in "dramatic" space) for one who is already familiar with an extra-dramatic world of real princes, real mothers, real fathers, real murders, real revenges, and real jealousies. From this viewpoint, as Hawkes correctly argues, the "counter-reading" cannot become a fully stabilized "alternative reading," a slickly present negative opposing a slickly present positive. The "counter-reading" cannot just present itself as the "real play."[11] And the reason, I might add, is that the "counter-reading" cannot *present* itself at all. Insofar as the "counter-reading" unbalances the normative reading by questioning the legitimacy of presence, by questioning presence as the (normative) ground for stabilizing "meaning," it cannot itself fall into the very trap it is dismantling: presence. "A thing, we are taught, cannot be both what it is and another thing. But that is precisely the principle challenged by *Telmah*."[12] This notion, with all its obvious relevance for *Macbeth*, destroys the possibility of "thesis" versus "antithesis" as formula for the understanding of the space negotiated by "reading" and "counter-reading." The "counter-reading" is at once outside the normative reading *and* inside it. What is opened up by this type of deconstruction is not the dialectical other of the text, but "a sense of an everpresent potential challenge."[13]

For me, this means that we can never be bluntly dismissive in our dealings with the critical tradition. In fact, the only time when dismissiveness is a critical necessity is the moment when we see that the normative critic has dogmatically and unilaterally organized his discourse so that the road toward the deconstructive horizon is utterly blocked. In this situation of premature and absolute closure, the deconstructionist has no alternative but to force an opening.

But if I agree with Hawkes that the "topsy-turvy" counter-reading cannot replace the normative reading, substitute itself as transcendental signified, I am not sure that I hold this view for the same reasons. Hawkes fears anything that is smoothed-over, "offered, gift-wrapped, as the truth."[14] Instead he favors a jazzy notion of subversion, the erratic being more important than the homogeneous, interpretative improvisation being more vital than the coherent consistency of the oppositional force.[15] I would instead like to suggest that the counter-reading in a sense *has* to be coherent and consistent: it has to build toward some kind of logic of its own. Why assume that deconstruction must be a bit scatterbrained, fuzzy, anarchistic, pluralistic, disjointed, and unorganized in order to truly engage with its opponent and become a critique of presence?

The architectonic way of envisioning deconstruction is a further source of confusion.[16] A defective "cornerstone" is looked for in the "architecture of the work," and the deconstructionist sees himself discovering this unique cornerstone and then bringing the whole building down by unloosening it. Such architectural rhetoric, somewhat overspatialized as it is,[17] has the disadvantage of suggesting to us that irreducible contradiction in a text must be located in a certain spot, identified in a particularly crucial and unique locus. This locus, now itself a kind of transcendental signified (for deconstruction), becomes a privileged place in the text—so privileged, in fact, that the critic can dispense with the bothersome and laborious task of examining the remaining 99% of the literary work. Once this marvelous transcendental signified has in this way been identified, the rest of the text can be appropriated in its name. The remaining parts of the text now have to point at this privileged site.

There are numerous drawbacks in this type of "Achilles' heel" deconstruction. First, as most readers recognize, it is fairly easy to find *some* contradictory (or "loose") cornerstone in any text. Second, it is not all that difficult to suggest that this particular spot of weakness radiates its type of vulnerability into other parts of the text. Third, normative critics are reassured by the fact that the onslaught of critical subversion in the final analysis restricts itself to a very limited portion of the text.

In the current enterprise I have not privileged any unique cornerstone in this traditional manner, for, to extend (and perhaps finish off) the architectural rhetoric, the play *Macbeth* consists *only* of cornerstones. All of its building blocks are in a sense cornerstones, things subject to deconstruction and self-deconstruction. It worries me little that this situation, conspicuous throughout the text, might displace the "genuine" force of the deconstructive potential. For me, there is no "genuine" deconstruction, and I will therefore be happy to find the critical enterprise categorized according to a variety of conflicting sets of ideological evaluation. What interests me is the consistency in

Macbeth of a certain force of uncanny suggestion, and if I inquire into the nature of the challenge of its unthinkability, I do so because the line of rupture is central. What deconstructs *Macbeth* is not in a corner, least of all in a hidden one.

1.2 The Question of Presence

A few words need to be said about presence, since I will be discussing *Macbeth* in terms of a deconstruction of presence. We saw, some time ago, how Derrida identified deconstruction as something that "thinks only on the level of the impossible and of what is still evoked as unthinkable."[18] This Derridean "unthinkability" relates itself directly, especially with reference to a "metaphysics of presence," to Martin Heidegger's attempt to think "what is unthought in all metaphysics."[19] For Heidegger to open this question, one that he opened in the name of presence, he had to think presence: that is, he had to first conjecture presence as that which was crucially unthought in Western thinking, and then he had to lay upon himself the burden of trying to think this "unthinkable" thing, presence. While Derrida follows suit here, working in his own quite different way through what needs to be thought out concerning presence, an entire set of "deconstructive" critics have interpreted the question of presence as an epistemological issue. This development is somewhat odd, indeed, for the main impact of Heidegger/Derrida has been to bracket the epistemological type of inquiry and dismiss its solemn issues (from Descartes up to Nietzsche) as pseudo-problems. This epistemological type of deconstruction tends to end up or (what is the same) commence in a mood of epistemological pessimism. We are told that we are eternally removed from reality as well as art, from nature as well as self—and we are told that language, as mediation and intervention, engineers this "absence" of everything. From the epistemological viewpoint, "presence" is simply what is missing on account of the work that language/thought performs in the name of absence. This epistemologization of deconstruction can be observed, typically, in an essay called "The Deconstruction of Presence in *The Winter's Tale*." Here, Howard Felperin consistently uses the word "presence" in the epistemological (i.e., commonsensical) fashion,[20] clinching the matter by referring to the fact that "literature is never really 'there' or fully present, but is always mediated action, action estranged by the linguistic medium."[21] My purpose, however, is not to argue that one type of deconstruction is better than the other, but simply to point to the difference between a postontological conception of presence (as discussed by Derrida) and an epistemological one. This difference is fairly crucial in the current enterprise, for it is the former alternative that I will promote at the expense of the latter. In other words, I am not at all interested in the "deferral of presence" as a function of linguistic "mediation," but interested instead in the deferral of presence as a function of ontological illusion.[22] Language, far from being less important in the latter problematic, is more so.

In his work on Heidegger, *De l'esprit* (1987), Derrida discusses a "yes" "preceding" the binary opposition *yes/no*; this "yes," following Heidegger, amounts to a response or responsiveness that is the condition of possibility for all language. "Being," as it were, calls us on the phone, and as we pick up the receiver saying "yes," or "yes?", we find ourselves—already—engaged in the attentiveness/responsiveness that *is* language.[23] Moreover, in his work on Joyce, crucially centered on the word "yes," Derrida confesses that the question of the "yes" has for a long time crossed and animated all of his significant thinking, writing, reading, and teaching.[24] This interest in the trivial word "yes" on the part of Derrida is in itself interesting, and it is of course directly related to the way in which Heidegger attends to language. Heidegger believes that we must "attempt to give heed to [the] game of language and to hear what language really says when it speaks."[25] No word is trivial. In fact the most trivial words (like the word "man" in *Macbeth*, like the word "yes" in *Ulysses*) are in a sense the most risky and potentially playful ones. The "familiar carries an air of harmlessness and ease, which causes us to pass lightly over what really deserves to be questioned."[26]

For me, the question of presence in *Macbeth*, and indeed the question of deconstructing that presence, is not simply a matter of locating points of "absence" in a "Shakespearean language of presence"; on the contrary, it is a question of attending to the presencing of presence itself in *Macbeth*. It is in that presencing of presence itself that I find the deconstructive potential, the secret work of the unbalancing of presence and self-presence. When, toward the end of this book, I focus an inconspicuous and rare word like "geese," I do this in order to "listen" to language in a way that itself promotes the possibility of a deconstruction of presence. Words, as Derrida shows with the word "yes" in *Ulys-*

ses, have a tendency to surprise us, to move across a particular textual situatedness that suddenly unloosens them from ontological self-presence. From this viewpoint, what we must learn is not how to "get" at words; instead, we must learn how to let words get at us—*come* at us much as Birnam Wood comes at Macbeth. Once this type of sensibility is operative, we may recognize with Heidegger that "it is not we who play with words, but the nature of language [that] plays with us."[27] The modern intellectual has a (culturally conditioned and historically determined) tendency to be "clever" with language, to be "witty"; but this reflex, superficially an affirmation of the gaiety and playfulness of language, in a sense amounts to a deadening of language. By appropriating what Heidegger calls "the gambling game of language, where our nature is at stake,"[28] we neutralize the uncanny element of risk and uncertainty in language, transforming it into an entirely canny type of conversational mastery.

"Most textual interpretations," writes Heidegger, "remain at the level of a conversation,"[29] and Derrida's apparently phonocentric use of the "telephone" and its "calling" is from this viewpoint somewhat surprising. The beginning of everything is a phone call, the phone call. "*Au commencement fut le téléphone.*"[30] Being, the world, is as it were created and set awake by a calling: as if God one morning decided to call us up, make things begin to happen. This call is imagined as taking place "before" action, "before" the word[31]—and therefore before the division act/word, reality/language. But this rather odd notion perhaps becomes more poignant (and less phonocentric) once we understand it in relation to some text—for instance *Macbeth*. The witches, very much in the *tele*phonic sense, call Macbeth up: "call" him (in both senses), make a call to him. This, most emphatically, is a long-distance call, one where there is a characteristic sense of wonder at being at all connected to something so far off, *so absent*. There is a certain amount of "crackling" on the line, a certain fragility in the process of transmission. But in terms of "absence" what is most significant is not simply the distance between caller and receiver but the distance between the receiver and the call. The Weird Sisters have called Macbeth, called him up, and he has answered, saying (as we often do on the phone) "yes(?)." But by pronouncing this "yes," which is at once an answer and *not* an answer (an absent answer, a mere recognition of attentiveness), Macbeth has already opened himself up to the risk of the call. To the calling. This calling that calls him through the call *connects* Macbeth to the call/calling, but also to what is absent in the call, what, already, is absence in it (for instance "Macbeth," the word "Macbeth" as the Weird Sisters sound it, speak it, and call it).

The (reassuring) conversational aspect of (telephone)calling is not operative here—for the simple reason that it has not yet been given a chance to start. Macbeth would *like* to turn the long-distance call from the Weird Sisters into a conversation (and this is precisely what he and Duncan first try to do, this is precisely what he *remains* trying to do throughout the play); yet the Weird Sisters disconnect Macbeth as soon as this long-distance calling in any way threatens to degenerate into a conversation. They maintain their impact as a long-distance impact, as one fraught with absence and "crackling."

The distance, now, can already be felt between a logocentric phone call (promoting presence) and a nonlogocentric phone call (promoting the unsettling of presence). In fact, Derrida conceives the call as a violent "coup," as a blow/alarm/intervention/violation/intrusion that somehow "strikes" into the tranquil and unwoken.

When presence (in the sense of the tranquil composure of being, the reassuring composure of one who is self-present) is disturbed in this way—by a weird (phone) call—there is opened (as I just indicated) a distance between the receiver and the call. The call calls from afar. The callers call from afar. But most important, too, language calls from afar. Or from the (unpresent) intimacy of an absolute proximity. It depends on where you stand. If your perspective is that of "conversation," then the calling calls from an infinite distance. But if you attend in the site where language already *is* the ongoing engagement with its own risk, then the "call," even while startling you into an unprecedented wakefulness, does not descend upon you as the utterly alien. Macbeth, whose silhouette sometimes merges with that of his creator, emerges immediately as one who is actual in both of these sites—and therefore as one who can negotiate their spacing.

The point, of course, is that Macbeth can negotiate the space between the two "poles" of language (conversation and risk) but that he can never neutralize this space by an act of appropriation or reconciliation. The distance and absence that the call affirms in its capacity as *long*-distance call can never be totally erased. Macbeth can become *present* to the call, but that presence will never be able to free itself from the risk of the call, the disconnectedness that is built into it as a structural necessity, that empties "the line" of the reverbatory plenitudes of present speech. In becoming gradually *present* to the call (to his calling) Macbeth thus also has to become evermore present to his a priori absence in it. Language thickens here. It thickens, becomes more "linguistic," in proportion to the fragility of "the line"—in proportion to the absence of full resonance in the transmissional apparatus. Macbeth, constantly, has to try to *pick up* what is being spoken: and in doing so he has to stage his comprehending resources in the theater of the most demanding linguistic engagement ever devised. Shakespeare's. In fact, by having to strain his attention so dramatically, Macbeth situates himself close to us, "the spectators." For the language of the Weird Sisters, what they disseminate in terms of their disruption of linguistic composure, is what radiates, as language, throughout the entire play. Their radical language, as it expands endlessly through the substance of the drama, becomes the language that we ourselves are getting used to attending to, to experience. We too run the risk of being disconnected; and, paradoxically, the risk increases as we listen, the risk heightens as our attention heightens.

Curiously, and precisely because "language" is both inertia ("conversation") and risk (a long call), the word in itself does not really "help" Macbeth. It unhelps him when it is supposed to help him and (to his astonishment) helps him when it is used to express what is beyond help. Language (generally), like action (generally), cannot "save" Macbeth—for the call, as the originary abyss of language and its opening, has submitted the two sides to a radical instability. *"Avant l'acte, ou la parole, le téléphone."* *Avant.* Before. Macbeth sometimes escapes violently into the unilateral affirmation of words: only to find them full, already, of violence/action. So also he flees desperately into the "exterior" world of acts: only to find writing there too, writing (as we shall see) in the form of what "speaks" directly from the call.

Deconstruction, I am saying then, insofar as it solicits presence, very much amounts to questioning what is unthought in discourse. This "unthought" dimension, precisely by not being fully thought, displaces a text from full presence. This absent presence—which is not an absence—is also an absent self-presence: the text cannot become fully self-present to itself (even in criticism) since the point of what is "unthought" tends to recede infinitely. Heidegger only moves halfway toward this idea, stating that the "unthought" in a text would increase (rather than decrease) in the really great text. "What is unthought in a thinker's thought is not a lack inherent in his thought. What is un-thought is there in each case only as the un-*thought*. The more original the thinking, the richer will be what is unthought in it. The unthought is the greatest gift that thinking can bestow."[32] It is clear that in deconstructing Heidegger, Derrida is turning this very idea against his master: there remains something crucially unthought and unquestioned in Heidegger, and Derrida wishes to dig into "what in this way remains unquestioned."[33] Derrida can work a deconstruction on Heidegger through a single word, *Geist*, by showing how this word—through the undecidable opposition *geistlich/geistig*—fails to be fully present to its "right" position inside the Heideggerian effort to question what so far has not been questioned. Questioning, again, is not here doubting, but on the contrary the act of thinking through something untouched by vital thought.

If Heidegger endeavored to work a deconstruction [*Abbau/Destruktion*][34] on the spirit of the West, he nevertheless (for Derrida) remains blind to crucial dimensions of his own questioning. His interest in "presence" is by no means as subversive as Derrida's. In fact, Heidegger is not conscious of how he himself privileges the word spirit *(Geist)*—with all its pre- and post-Nazi overtones—in the efforts to evade Europe's "spirit." The very idea of "questioning" becomes a transcendental signified in the Heideggerian enterprise, and Derrida wishes to dismantle also the privileged site of the sacred "questioning"—to ask, indeed, what gets smoothed over as this special "questioning" becomes the be-all and end-all for Heideggerian thought.[35]

In fact—and this is crucial for the business of deconstructing *Macbeth*—there remains in Heidegger's thought a gigantic assumption about presence that he shares with nearly all philosophers, with the notable exception of Nietzsche. This is the assumption that ultimate issues narrow down to a site of comprehension where things are felt to be centripetal. Heidegger *focuses* "Being" as the place where presence and self-presence are gathered into significant meaning, and this very inward movement (poeticized in metaphors about "dwelling," "earth," "belonging," "guarding," and so forth) is itself stifling. Heidegger forces us *into* a comprehension of being, *into* the cores of various esoteric words, *into* a domecile where thought abides. We get a feeling of burrowing, almost of hibernation. (The animal Heidegger "survives" in the West by hibernating in it. Forever.) At the opposite extreme from this would stand the aspirations of Nietzsche: the idea of creative affirmation and new values. In fact, beyond the conspicuous differences between Hegel and Heidegger, there are (for Derrida) "troubling affinities" that should not be overlooked.[36] These affinities, to a large extent, are a function of the "centripetal" issue discussed a moment ago. While being affirmatively interested in Hegel (witness *Glas*), Derrida (following Bataille) discovers a "centripetal" inclination in him that in the final analysis is unbearable. This inward-moving aspect of Hegelianism, which is what permits system and totality, neutralizes all the exhilaratingly affirmative moves that Hegel undertook as he shaped his philosophical inquiries into daring intellectual adventures. Hegel gave only to retain. What he gave was only there to enchain: we end up in a metaphysics of presence where our *final* move is "to guard, to keep: guard the present [gift/presence]."[37] Desire is placed "in orbit,"[38] and the present created by this ring/gift is the presence to itself of a perfect circle. This circle is the circle of presence and self-presence, the circle of presence *as* self-presence. The system, because one can only circulate in it, is in the final analysis a closed system. Its economy is a "circulating economy," what Bataille will refute as a "restricted economy"—one opposing a "general economy," free from the circle. Derrida: "The contraction, the economic restriction forms the annulus of the selfsame, of the self-return, or reappropriation. The economy restricts itself; the sacrifice [the giving in the gift] sacrifices itself [turns back into a-present-I-have-given]."[39]

It is *this* "metaphysics of presence" that interests me in *Macbeth* for the simple reason that the text so obviously stages the drama of its possible deconstruction. Insofar as deconstruction solicits subjectivity, a conspicuous solicitation in *Macbeth*, it must engage with the question of self-presence,[40] and it must also engage with the above-mentioned notion of meaning as sacrifice. Macbeth, precisely by being thrown into sacrifice from the very beginning of the play, carries meaningful sacrifice as a heroic banner. When the Weird Sisters, by *calling* Macbeth ("Hail!" etc.), interrupt this sacrificial production of Meaning, Macbeth tries to overcome this interruption by interpreting it too as meaning. His tragedy, in a sense, is that he in this undertaking is at once infinitely unsuccessful and infinitely successful.

Since a deconstruction of presence (in the Derridean sense) subsumes a critique of Hegelian presence, and since Hegelian presence takes its beginning in the *absencings* of presence in the famous parable of the "struggle to death for recognition" (between master and slave),[41] we might briefly look at this important relationship between "recognition" (the production of heroic meaning) and the metaphysics of presence. Some understanding of this relationship is necessary in a deconstruction of presence in *Macbeth*, for it is not only evident that Macbeth first shows himself as one directly emerging from such a struggle and that he refers to its meaningful heroic products as "golden opinions," but also that he yearns for a return to its duel-like premises as soon as he gets into really deep trouble. Dialectic becomes the site for a crucial nostalgia, one centered on the memory of the transcendental production of meaning.

As Derrida observes in *Glas*, however, the "struggle to death" (for recognition) is not only of interest as the source of transcendentality and meaning, but also as the source of the vanishing of empirical truth. Thus, what is interesting in any "struggle to death" (as *Macbeth* 1.3 shows) is not only what is gained (meaning, transcendence, recognition) but also what is lost (empiricalness, naive biological positivity, material presence). It is also important to observe that the outcome of the "struggle to death" affects neither of these two extremes (what is gained, what is lost). Something crucial is lost in the struggle even if one wins, something is won even if one loses—even if one dies, indeed especially if one dies. The work of absence in the "struggle to death" is thus not the absencing of life per se, but what the absencing of life itself absences. Death, in such a struggle, absences presence. *Glas:* "The struggle to death . . . is not a matter of just death, but of the annihilation of the characteristics of singularity, of every mark of empiricalness. . . . [What] remains when all of the empiricalness is abolished? Nothing, nothing that may be present or existent. . . . One fights to death . . . for nothing."[42]

Shakespeare, of course, takes great pains to drive home this very point in the first act of *Macbeth*. The hero is carefully and extensively shown as being one who has situated his manner of living (of attaining recognition) beyond the level of empirical presence. Macbeth, as he fights for "Scotland," is fighting for something that is transcendentally absolute: and it is this heroic faith in the meaning of this transcendentality that makes Macbeth absolutely careless about his own empirical status in and after the fight. We feel that he enjoys himself absolutely in the struggle, because the fight in itself provides him with the sense that something absolute is being produced (recognition, ideality). He is very much like the sportsman who extends himself beyond the normal limits of pain and suffering in order to win something that from the viewpoint of empiricalness is absolutely nothing.

This idea that the "struggle to death" is at once (as action) the annihilation of presence *and* (as telos) the perpetuation of presence is more crucial than we might first think: for when Shakespeare scrupulously delineates the military status of his hero, he does so with both of these extremes clearly in view. We feel, as we see Macbeth fighting, that he is one who cares, but also that he is one who does not care. We feel that he is the foremost and exemplary producer of meaning/presence in his society, but we also feel that—as athletic movement—he embodies annihilation itself. This "annihilation" is no such banal thing as his mere ability to finish off enemies, but on the contrary his desire to affirm annihilation itself. Structured in this manner by the "struggle to death" *in two opposite ways*, the hero is from the outset made to appear in a potentially *double* relation to a metaphysics of presence. From the very beginning he holds all the forces for the preservation of presence and all the forces for its displacement.

In sum, then, the strategy for working a deconstruction on presence in *Macbeth* will shape itself in this book in relation to thinking what remains unthought in the play. This realm of the "unthought"—which belongs to no particular corner of the text but which instead is present everywhere and nowhere—drives the deconstructive enterprise into an engagement with some types of Shakespeare critics and away from an engagement with others. It may be clear by now that in promoting the relevance of deconstruction in the Heidegger/Derrida tradition, I am seeking to enhance the appreciation of a crucially sensual dimension in deconstructive thinking—or deconstructive "desire." It seems to me that this sensual dimension, so conspicuous in Heidegger and Derrida (and so important there), is entirely missing in many criticisms belonging to what I have referred to as the epistemological version of deconstruction. There, the act of deconstruction has been reduced to a textual chess game, situated safely in purely cognitive space. All "moves," brilliant as many of them are, take place in a strictly cerebral environment, the wide Sargasso Sea of purely intellectual titillation.

In a sense, this difference between sensual and epistemological deconstruction corresponds to the tension between Continental philosophy and "analytical" philosophy: the former being, as it were, less thoroughly programmed by the dissociation of sensibility institutionalized during the early neoclassical era. Nietzsche, profoundly important for Derrida, of course attacked the antisensual philosophizing of the West by referring to it as ascetic; but the entire tradition of Continental thought (and not only Nietzschean discourse) is more sensually responsive and sensually affirmative than its rigid partner. When Hegel startles us with his unpredictable conceptual interfoliations, we feel that he is enjoying himself sensually: that he shifts his battery of concepts over into a slightly permissive playground where the various individual items begin to nudge, tease, caress, and fondle one another. Indeed, alarmingly, "worse" things happen. But this permissiveness is of course a salient feature of the discourse of Derridean deconstruction too—according to a freedom of mind that is at once more and less calculated than the one that is evident in Hegel. Astonishing things happen here, and they "happen," in particular, to concepts. Concepts are not only breaking down (under the strain of the deconstructive pressure), but they are breaking down in a way that is conceptually interesting, conceptually affirmative.

Now I cannot possibly imagine that Shakespearean deconstruction can become significant (beyond a certain limit) if it is not engineered, precisely, by a sensually alert type of review—for Shakespeare's language as conceptual playfulness is surely one of the most sensual things on earth. It follows from this bias in my attitude that I find myself closer to critics who attend to the quasi-erotic "feel" of Shakespearean displacements than to critics who perceive and analyze such displacements as purely cognitive happenings in cerebral reality. The surface appearance of logical purity in the latter type of critique tends to conceal the fact that logic indeed has reduced its sphere of interpretative action to those narrow and arid tracts where Shakespearean language is cognitive language and where Shakespearean drama is a cognitive experience. Deconstruction, for me, is not an exercise in logic or an experiment in language theory.

As a general study in Shakespearean indeterminacy, therefore, this critique might helpfully be seen as compatible with work of the type exemplified by Stephen Booth. Here it is not the (minute) deconstructionist aspect that marks the point of contact, but instead the sensual level of attentiveness that I have recently been referring to. Booth is sensitive to the way all kinds of entities in *Macbeth*, once sensually touched, give way to contact, retreat, and thus demand more daring forms of seduction. "Categories will not define. Words, notably the word *man*, whose meaning characters periodically worry over, will not define."[43] "What is true of words, sentences, and speeches is also true of the characters in *Macbeth*; they will not stay within limits either."[44] "In *Macbeth* no kind of closed category will stay closed around any object. The validity of that general assertion can be demonstrated in the details of almost any scene in the play."[45] Equivocations accumulate in the descriptions of fighting.[46] In the discourse of the bleeding Captain, "the doers of good sound either like or worse than the evildoers,"[47] and "[f]inality is regularly unattainable" in the play.[48] Worst of all, perhaps, it is "impossible to find the source of any idea in *Macbeth*; every new idea seems already there when it is presented to us."[49] Hence beginningness is curiously withheld in the drama, giving us the impression that the beginning is in the middle, or that the beginning only starts in the middle. Since the end, in the sense of finality, is also destabilized, one might say that "*Macbeth* is all middle."[50]

Remarks such as these, while not in themselves effectuating any deconstruction of presence in *Macbeth*, suggest important aspects of its condition of possibility. The main intuition, here, is that binary opposites do not work in *Macbeth* as they should do. This fact does not only apply to good-versus-evil and beginning-versus-end; most of the other axiomatic truths of classical thought are questioned, for instance causation: "Cause and effect do not work in *Macbeth*."[51] I will be returning to discuss the Shakespearean unbalancing of such classical oppositions, since what interests me (for the purpose of deploying a deconstruction of presence) is not the breakdown itself but the peculiar characteristics of each particular breakdown and the way these individual peculiarities suggest a specifically Shakespearean intuition of dialectical ruination. At this point, however, Booth's remarks may serve the purpose of clarifying the contrast between criticism conscious of the dialectical fallacy and criticism unconscious of the dialectical fallacy. In James Calderwood's *If It Were Done* (1986), Derridean terms like "supplement," "*pharmakos*," and "presence,"[52] although used in an un-Derridean fashion, are relevant for the type of mildly deconstructionist suggestion that the critic is forwarding; yet by turning the difference between *Hamlet* and *Macbeth* into a pure opposition, the critic seems to be working away from the possibility of a deconstructionist reading. In basing his entire introduction on the binary opposites reactive-versus-active, past-versus-future, interior-versus-exterior, and play-versus-reality, and by deciding that *Hamlet* forwards the former part of each symmetrical opposition, *Macbeth* the latter part, Calderwood sometimes overlooks the fact that the play *Macbeth* is based on the deconstruction of these binary opposites, and that the hero has to endure their collapse as the condition of possibility for his dramatic reality. Perhaps, after all, Shakespeare is not reversing his new play into an anti-*Hamlet*, but instead deepening the very problematic that *Hamlet* has opened. Perhaps Macbeth in an important sense is *more* reactive than Hamlet, *more* interiorizing than Hamlet, and also *more* play-oriented than Hamlet. Perhaps, indeed, this type of inwardization is all the more effective in that it is now concealed and staged in the form of its opposite. Perhaps the "exteriorizing" process (into ostentatious "action") that Shakespeare inaugurates here and carries yet farther in his tragic end game *Antony and Cleopatra* betokens (below a level of mere "showing") an unprecedented type of interiorization: of "self-comparison." Calderwood holds that Macbeth is future-oriented,[53] hypnotized as he is by the Weird Sisters. "The Witches solicit no one; they merely reveal the future."[54] But it could also be argued that it is futile and reductive to discuss Macbeth as being *either* for the future *or* for the past, since it is precisely the deconstruction of the opposition past/future that the play (through the Weird Sisters) from the outset implements. Calderwood speaks of the "either/or-ness of Macbeth," which he says is "consistent" with the hero's "world."[55] As my reading of the play will show, I think instead that Macbeth is at the farthest possible point from an "either/or" mentality, and that this very fact gives him his dramatic outline in whatever "consistency" his world can sport.

1.3 Staging Contexts

Deconstruction, I have argued, should not be dismissive. The point is not to think "around" the facts of history, but to think their reality in contexts of play that are inexhaustible. In this section, I will discuss some aspects of the traditional "background" to *Macbeth* in order to situate the deconstructive enterprise in relation to the realities it has to recognize and hold in view.

Tragedy always moves toward what Jaspers called "boundary situations" because the tragic vision impels heroic man toward the limits of human action.[56] The tendency of the tragic hero to defy destiny and to push himself to the limits of action somehow gets reflected in the attitude of the tragic writer himself. He too takes action, is taken to a "boundary situation" where his own sphere of action—writing—reaches and transgresses the horizon of what seemed possible; thus, in the greatest tragedies, we feel the poet's own involvement, a crucial immediacy that is not to be found in comedy and satire.[57] But in Shakespeare the "boundary situation" is even more acute than in ordinary tragedy; as Norman Rabkin observed, the innermost contradictions are of a "special sort" in Shakespeare, and it is indeed only by apprehending this "special" strain in the peculiarly Shakespearean tensions that we discover what is unmistakably Shakespearean.[58] In the extraordinary tragedy *Macbeth*, one might add, this ability of Shakespeare to exceed ordinary "tragic tension" is carried extremely far—so that, as Bernard McElroy remarks, the *Macbeth*-world is one of Shakespeare's most distinctive dramatic universes, with an atmosphere entirely its own.[59] *Macbeth*, writes Chaudhuri, is possibly Shakespeare's most breath-taking achievement, perhaps even surpassing *King Lear*.[60]

Yet in spite of the extremeness of *Macbeth*, the peculiar boldness of its conception, an entire tradition of criticism wants to think around the difficulty of the play and avoid an absolute confrontation with its core of darkness. As Graham Bradshaw remarks, one shows us how to make trifles of the terror in *Macbeth*.[61] *Macbeth* is really frightening, while the drama that critics discuss is not.[62] *Macbeth* is perhaps not the relatively simple play identified by standard criticism.[63] Timid criticism tries to "edit" the hero just as Duncan "edits" him—that is, by trying to overlook what is "obscene" in Macbeth's violent engagement with negativity.[64] As Chaudhuri argues, it is hard to understand how the traditional reading of the drama as a morality play can create the rich impact actually produced by the play.[65]

Several prejudices have contributed to the general simplification of *Macbeth* into a banal drama about the triumph of good over evil and to the simplification of the hero into a stage-villain with poetical outbursts. To begin with, there is of course Tillyard's influential "Elizabethan World Picture," an important notion in itself but dangerous in facilitating a trivialization of history. Perhaps, as Michael Bristol argues, there never was a single such World Picture, and in that case this monolithic notion obscures the "heterocosmic" nature of reality.[66] Stoll's "dramatic conventions" are subject to the same type of criticism, for they are based on the assumption that Shakespeare sacrificed "reality and psychology" in order to create dramatic figures quite different from the people "we know."[67] It could be argued, contra Stoll, that no firm line of demarcation can be drawn between "convention" and "psychology," for the simple reason that psychology "itself" is full of conventions—indeed quite "dramatic" and "theatrical" ones. Our existence is not just "there"; it is something "staged" as being there—staged for others, but also for ourselves.

This coimplication between psyche and convention is analogous to the coimplication between psyche and history. As Stephen Greenblatt points out, the deconstruction of the opposition history-versus-text has dismantled the positivist certainties of a nonliterary reality, the privileged sphere of historical fact.[68] This new perspective does not reduce the signficance of history but problematizes it. Frank Whigham has shrewdly demonstrated the relevance of this problematization in his discussion of the rhetoric of power at the Elizabethan court.[69] Yet if we interpret all of *Macbeth* in terms of "power," we risk creating precisely the kind of self-deception that Macbeth learns to develop in our play. Macbeth is from the outset not motivated by "power" at all (as I shall presently argue); but he gradually learns to rationalize his dilemma by using "power" as an explanation. "Power" comes to "explain" what a moment ago was pure otherness. To discover "power" as an explanation for what cannot be explained is a strategy that can be applied to *Macbeth* by critics who fail to realize that this very reductionism is what the play is staging as one of its centermost dramatic features.

Michael Manheim suggests that the secret aspirations and unspoken desires of the Elizabethans are discoverable inside the plays rather than outside them.[70] Indeed, given the fact that Elizabethans had a great capacity for experiencing what they did not believe,[71] it could be argued that the main condition of possibility for Shakespeare's drama was not any fixed World Picture to be grandly promulgated but a huge sense of freedom. Shakespeare, in an important sense, set his own standards. The "historical forces" were there alright, and no inch of "Shakespeare" is untouched by them; yet Shakespeare's dramas are not reducible to these "historical forces." I tend in other words to favor the simple notion favored by Herbert Howarth: that Shakespeare was an explorer.[72] Working inside the framework of certain historical possibilities, Shakespeare created something totally new—something radically different, daringly suggestive, and absolutely original. The reason why Shakespeare's audience

Staging Contexts 41

could appreciate and digest this absolute novelty is not that dramatist and audience shared certain belief-structures in an absolutely uniform way, but that the special spirit of discovery in the Renaissance permitted the two sides (Shakespeare and his spectators) to come together inside the imaginative freedom of dramatic innovation. Had the common denominator been simply passive, the mere sharing of certain "historical" structures, then the situation would have been that of closure. As it is, this closure was radically broken up by the affirmative violence of Renaissance creativity. It is interesting, of course, that this Elizabethan readiness to experience things "beyond" the now of history is itself a historical fact, something historically conditioned.

Rejecting closure, deconstruction thus perpetually needs to fight itself out of structure-thinking: the idea that texts can be "functions" of specific structures. As such, a "structure" is always a closed system, something that exhausts possibilities, including its own. But if "the historical condition" tends to crop up as one such structure promising premature closure, "the stage" is another. In every generation of Shakespeare critics there is someone bullying us into the belief that Shakespeare falls short of being a literary man, a poet. Instead, we are told, he is "a dramatist." We are meant to believe that Shakespeare's plays, far from being literary texts, are "theatrical scripts."[73] The main objection to this is not only the reversed argumentation forwarded by Harry Berger and others,[74] but the general absurdity of positing the relationship between text and performance as a pure opposition. I refuse to admit that there is any significant opposition between a "stage" Shakespeare and a "text" Shakespeare. I think the spectator performs the kind of "reading" operations that the literary man completes, and I think that the reader effectuates acts of visual and auditory participation that correspond to the ongoing responses of an actual spectator. In addition, as Felperin perceptively argues, the "impossibility of rendering theatrically the suggestive force" of certain volatile Shakespearean words limits the relevance of the thesis of the primacy of performance over text.[75] Close reading, far from being a specialist activity confined to the academies, is a procedure internal to the dramatic craft. Sigurd Burckhardt puts this in a nutshell:

> I am ... convinced that to be understood [Shakespeare] must be *read*—with attention to sometimes minute detail. There is an odd superstition abroad that nothing can be part of Shakespeare's intention that cannot be communicated directly across the footlights. First

and foremost, we are told, he was a "man of the theatre"; the implication is that what we see when we see a play of his acted is the unmediated thing itself. Of course this is nonsense; what we see is an interpretation, derived (it is to be hoped) from a very careful reading of the text by the director and the actors.[76]

For me, Shakespearean drama is very much a linguistic drama: what is staged is not simply the actions and feelings of men and women, but also the drama of language itself. Language, in Shakespeare, explores itself. And in performing this exploration, language is constantly pushing what is to be explored in front of itself. As Shakespeare explores language, he writes, and this creation of "new" language perpetually defers the possibility of closure in the process of discovery.

Now since this absolute Shakespearean pressure on language is also an absolute pressure on the signifying potential of language, the highest forms of dramatic language inevitably stir the major philosophical questions in our culture. (That Shakespeare can transgress "signification" and therefore also "philosophy" is another kettle of fish). In other words, Shakespearean tragedy engages with the various ways in which reality might (or might not) signify. Because, in this way, philosophical or quasi-philosophical issues in fact are *linguistically staged* in Shakespearean tragedy, close reading becomes absolutely necessary. Interpretation, hanging in the balance, can depend on minute linguistic details, the tiniest shift of emphasis or rhythm.

Deconstruction, of course, has a precarious relationship to philosophy. Insofar as philosophy amounts to closed systems of absolute truth, structures of stable cosmic meaning, or foundational faith in ontological "ground," philosophy has to be rejected by deconstruction. But deconstruction cannot be dismissive toward philosophy in general, since philosophical discourse is one of the major contexts that deconstruction carries along with itself as a condition of possibility. This double attitude to philosophy is also conspicuous in all the thinkers who in different ways have tried to "end" philosophy, from Hegel, through Nietzsche and Heidegger, to Derrida. To finish off philosophy, paradoxically, you have to develop it, take it one step further along, extend the reach of its discourse. This type of paradox also hits back on Shakespeare critics determined to rid Shakespeare of philosophical implication: they have to construct elaborate theories that in themselves are full of philosophical assumptions and that gradually come to look exquisitely philosophic.

It is clear, however, that once we agree not to define "philosophy" too rigorously (not to think of it as "philosophical system"), Shakespeare quickly emerges as a philosophically poignant artist. It is "somewhat daring," writes Virgil Whitaker, to argue that Shakespeare was a careful philosophic thinker; yet the "philosophic aspect" of the plays is unmistakably there, alongside what is purely dramatic or purely poetic.[77] It is in fact likely that each individual spectator attending *closely* to the language of Lear, or Macbeth, or Hamlet is really activating an individually subtle philosophic response. Why? Not because Shakespeare had "a philosophy"; but because the sheer intellectual intensity of Shakespeare's tragic discourse affirms a level of response where philosophical issues are already within view—and overwhelmingly so. When Macbeth slips into his "to-morrow" soliloquy, when Hamlet contemplates the bare bodkin, when Lear roars in the tempest: at these moments we do not witness unphilosophic figures momentarily slipping into quasi-philosophic discourse; on the contrary, we experience the vitality of humans who from the outset are endowed with that type of human alertness where philosophic difficulty is internal to tragic awareness. As Rabkin remarks, what makes a play like *Hamlet* a problem is also exactly what makes it Shakespearean.[78] When the problematization of the play is removed, the typically Shakespearean feeling evaporates. In fact, this level of problematization, always philosophically experienced, is internal to the basic appreciation of Shakespearean drama. M. D. H. Parker argues that we evaluate a certain work better than another not simply through an aesthetic judgement, but through a metaphysical one: we are (consciously or unconsciously) looking in the tragic vision for what is permanently and universally true.[79] This notion holds, it may be added, also when the conclusion might be that there is no permanent or universal truth. To arrive at such a conclusion, or intuition, one must have contemplated things suggested by the drama in the light of universality, or potential universality.[80]

Other factors contribute toward the "philosophic" texture of much Shakespearean discourse. To begin with, there is the typical preoccupation with truth: first through the conspicuous "seeming-being problem," which turns up everywhere in Shakespeare, second through the ever-present critique of hypocrisy as truth-deviation.[81] As Anne Righter showed in her important criticism, we have reasons to believe that Shakespeare's audience could respond in a sophisticated manner to questions about truth—about appearance and reality, semblance and authenticity; for the Elizabethans the relation of illusion to reality was by no means simple.[82] Another important "philosophic" factor is the tendency, inherited from Neoplatonism, for Renaissance thought to unify image and concept—to treat these as the two sides of the same coin.[83] This habit of mind is radically different from the one that Kant came to institutionalize for the modern mind when he declared that an "aesthetic idea" stretched beyond the ken of the conceptual mind.[84] Thought and air coimplicated one another in the medieval theory of "correspondences,"[85] and as the Neoplatonically influenced Elizabethan apprehended this "space" of the mind as the realm of intellectual suggestion, he or she did not normally divide image from idea—the "concrete" (as we say today) from the "abstract." And this lack of such division of labor is important for *Macbeth*, since the pivotal moment of tragic suggestion is the one where murder as image and murder as idea are one single unbroken entity for the horrified hero. Modern critics, so used to the neoclassical tendency to separate image and idea, tend to overlook the absolute coimplication of the two sides of imaginative space. I will be returning to this issue when we discuss Macbeth's hallucination of the idea/image of murder. What I am saying at this point is simply that it is absurd to say that Shakespeare, as an artist dealing with the "concrete," is opposed to philosophy (said to deal with the "abstract"), since the very division concrete-versus-abstract is something of a post-Renaissance construct institutionalized by neoclassical science, and since Shakespeare is everywhere working with precisely those troubled regions of human suggestion where image and idea intersect. Thus, when Shakespeare permits his heroes to slip into intellectual reverie, where images *are* the burgeoning substances of ideas and where ideas *are* the images of their own intellectual reality, then he is not writing outside the philosophic tradition of the West, but on the contrary digging at its very roots. To say that much is neither to say that Shakespeare is "a philosopher," nor to say that his discourse in the final analysis cannot subvert philosophy.

1.4 Theatrical Servitude

I will now be closing my introductory remarks by saying a few words about the highly complex issue of the relationship between meaning and theatricality in *Macbeth*. This relationship may also be understood negatively: as one between the negation of the theatrical and the negation of meaning. The question is in a sense finalized in the to-morrow soliloquy at the moment when the "poor player" recognizes the end of the epoch of meaning, a world "signifying nothing." It is not a matter, here, of discovering in any way that Macbeth *negates* the fully present player (the "good player"), or that nonsignification in the play *negates* its meaning. It is of course instead a question of finding the point in the good player where the transgression into the "poor" takes place—still—in *terms* of the good; of finding the point in the accumulation of meaning where the transgression of meaning itself has been promoted by meaning.

The reason why Macbeth's displacement from theatrical self-presence is so complex and contradictory is that theatricality itself is a fundamentally two-sided thing in *Macbeth* (and elsewhere). On the one hand, the theater is the place where meaning is produced; on the other hand, the theater is the place where meaning is subjected to equivocation. On the one hand Shakespeare situates himself firmly inside the tragic West, forwarding its project to turn negativity into meaning, suffering into tragic self-presence; on the other hand Shakespeare situates himself close to the twentieth-century world where the sublation of suffering is beginning to be questioned as a source of human truth. (This latter, "twentieth-century" feeling is perhaps most conspicuous in *King Lear.*) Macbeth, who from the outset seems strangely distanced from the drama of his own tragic fall, can in a wonderful way ride on *both* of these forces unleashed by the displacement of theatrical truth. Insofar as theater is an arena for the production of meaning, Macbeth's disenchantment is the withdrawal of his imagination from meaning and self-presence; but insofar as theater is the scenario for the staging of equivocation, Macbeth's increasingly anxious withdrawal from its premises betokens a fear of the loss of meaning. This is the really crucial point in my introductory remarks, one that is an unconditional prerequisite for the further understanding of what deconstruction will be taking for granted in the critical enterprise: that Macbeth is a man working simultaneously in two opposite directions, toward meaning and away from meaning. Macbeth is one who narrows himself down to an interest exclusively in meaning; but at the same time, and precisely on account of this obsession with meaning, he drifts—almost consciously—toward the horizon where foundational meaning is intuited as an impossible opium dream. Not only is there an absolute and constantly expanding contradiction between a Macbeth who clings to a metaphysics of presence and a Macbeth who obscurely anticipates the perfect emptiness of this metaphysical presence; also, the former side of the issue is directly instrumental in completing the latter. The metaphysics of presence *itself* voids metaphysical presence, itself uncovers its own logical precariousness. By throwing himself into a quest for metaphysical presence as absolute self-presence, Macbeth produces the opposite of that absolutely metaphysical self-presence: a full presence "signifying nothing." (This nonsignification of the fulness, incidentally, is conspicuous long before the time of empirical and moral fatigue in Macbeth.) Possibly, also, a converse situation may be faintly suggested: that Macbeth from the outset intuits the emptiness of metaphysical presence, and that he passively goes through the mechanical drama of presencing that metaphysical presence just to get his worst suspicions confirmed. But this is getting ahead of ourselves, so let us just for the time being briefly review the two basic issues discussed a moment ago: theatricality and its double relation to meaning.

Sidney Homan persuasively discusses Macbeth in terms of a "mania for certainty."[86] This expression could in fact be used as the crucial depth-formula for the current deconstruction of *Macbeth*. Macbeth does indeed develop a "mania for certainty"— what, following the terminology of Continental thought, I shall call "servitude," or "metaphysical servitude."[87] It is not here a question of a metaphysics that happens to be servile, but a question of grasping the *essence* of all metaphysical quest as, precisely, a "mania for certainty." This certitude/servitude, as the absolute foundation of truth as self-truth (perfectly limpid self-presence) first hypnotized the modern West through the creation of the Cartesian cogito. This cogito, emerging as the very *seeing* of modern man, crystallized in the general epoch when Shakespeare was active—in that special age when the West was poised between the premodern and the modern, between a socially determined selfhood and a self-determined "I." Although metaphysical presence first becomes visible in the metaphysics of Socrates/Plato, the process of institutionalizing its claims through scientific and political doctrine only really materialized in the seventeenth century. As numerous critics have recognized, also, the Shakespearean centering of the tragic hero as self-preoccupied cogito is historically determined by this very emergence of modern man. The individual, or modern self, only comes into

Theatrical Servitude 47

view, only comes into view for itself, insofar as there is a feeling of rupture with the ancient, socially determined self. It would be naive to argue that *Macbeth* is not related to this type of rupture in the name of individual freedom and self-definition.

The question of self-confidence is crucial in this context—for like most other significant things solicited by *Macbeth* it is two-sided. Macbeth is somehow caught in a play between absolute self-confidence and absolute loss of self-confidence. This is the basic plight of modern man. On the one hand he has been self-confident enough to do away with all the socially fixed certitudes of the "order" society and its hierarchical compartmentalizations of man; on the other hand, precisely because the old certainties are gone and the new ones discoverable only inside the self that has posited them, the abyss of absolute uncertainty is always only an inch away. Scepticism, the basic credo of modern man, always risks being annihilated by itself: modern man founds his existence on a platform that is in itself self-unbalancing.[88] In this way, by developing his self-confidence anxiously, sometimes hysterically, modern man is quite different from the heroic individual of classical antiquity. The classical hero is not guided by the "mania for certainty."

One may perhaps begin the task of tying this new type of self-confidence to the question of theatricalness by touching Kent van den Berg's discussion of the idea of the globe. He argues that the circular shape of the playhouse, of *The Globe*, "epitomizes an important moment in the history of consciousness: the separation of the mind as subject from the world as object."[89] The globe-making interest of Renaissance cartography does not simply reflect new knowledge and scientific advance "but also a new confidence in the human ability to stand outside of the entire macrocosm and comprehend the totality of existence as the reflection of subjective wholeness and self-sufficiency."[90] Here then, in the globe, in *The Globe*, we see two suggestions: there is the completion of cosmic comprehension as circular fulness, the filling of the classical circle that now fulfills itself as globe and globular self-presence; but there is also the sense of withdrawal and disenchanted detachment—the globe is seen, out there, as "object" and exterior "fact." The subject is suddenly outside, marooned in the vacuum of cognitive space.

Van den Berg argues that this new subject-versus-object feeling promoted by metaphysical withdrawal has bearings on Shakespeare's insights into the nature of role-playing and theatrical subjectivity. "When the self is distinguished from the world, it becomes internally divided in a way that corresponds to the distinction between the actor and his role. This self-division is attended by an ambivalence about human freedom."[91] But the problem is that the "premodern" self that existed "before" this metaphysically implemented split itself was full of role-playing. This is so because the *staging* of the self, far from being a latecomer, is an originary aspect of selfhood. Van den Berg himself recognizes as much when he speaks of history as being "staged" in terms of festivals, tournaments, banquets, royal entries, stately progresses, and so forth.[92] "Theater" was very much internal to everyday life in the premodern world, in a world with very little modern privatization of emotion, in a world still not dominated by "inner life." Thus, if the metaphysical creation of "the globe" (as reality firmly placed outside the cogito) is significant in relation to role-playing and theatrical acting, this significance was somehow to involve some kind of displacement or unbalancing of theatrical reality. It could indeed be argued that this was the case—that there was a radical strain on theatrical representation in Shakespeare's days, and that it is this very strain that in the final analysis led to the closing of the theaters. Somehow, the new sense of selfhood developed by modern man is not immediately compatible with theatricality. (I wish to clarify the stress here: I am not saying that there is no compatibility, but that there is no *immediate* compatibility.) One could in fact suggest that the reason why English drama never really recovered from the closing of the theaters, the reason why drama never fully returned to its former cultural and aesthetic stature, is this very incompatibility. The new self (belonging to the modern individual) will turn to different art forms, notably the novel—simply because the private self of the modern individual stages itself differently, more immediately and metaphysically. Successful drama of the modern era will have learned to exploit this very contradiction and difficulty, instead of circumnavigating it.

One way of apprehending this problematic, crucial as it is for the deconstruction of presence in *Macbeth*, is to consider the nature of the antitheatrical trend in Western culture. In St. Augustine's attack on the theater, the first sophisticated one ever launched, it is equivocation that is the enemy. In order to be true to our nature, Augustine writes, we should seek truth that is not self-contradictory and two-faced.[93] The austere Puritan fundamentalists of the seventeenth century followed this cue, fanatically emphasizing a dichotomous universe: *either* God *or* the

Devil, *either* truth *or* deception.[94] The zealots of the Reformation viewed the player as a person in a state of demonic possession; for the duration of a theatrical performance, there was a loss of true selfhood.[95] Thus the theater, by dramatizing equivocation, was a standing threat to the rule and primacy of the one-dimensional reality that was often propounded from pulpit and lectern.[96] The parading of men in women's clothes epitomizes this subversion, being a threat to God's proper division between the sexes.[97] (Modern critics reading *Macbeth* exclusively in terms of rigid opposites—such as "good" versus "evil"—would appear to be unconsciously perpetuating this antitheatrical tradition in modern culture.) The sterner Puritan Fathers viewed players as evil, since actors tried to replace the self given them by God with a self of their own contriving.[98] Uncontrolled imagination wronged the frame of God's creation by violating "sincerity."[99] The distrust of the puritan is characteristically roused by shifty mimicry and smart impersonation.[100]

This information becomes relevant once we recognize first of all that the play *Macbeth* is highly centered on the question of equivocation, and second that the hero displays what several critics have identified as a distinctly antitheatrical drive. (I return to discuss this issue more elaborately when I comment upon John Bayley's interesting reading of *Macbeth*.) In fighting the equivocation promoted by the Weird Sisters, Macbeth comes to slip progressively into the condition I recently called "metaphysical servitude"—an obsessive quest for self-certitude in the name of truth; but as Sidney Homan perceptively argues, this "stand against paradox" is "almost atheatrical, unplayful."[101] (The fact that Homan speaks of a Shakespearean theater of "presence" does not spoil the poignancy of this observation.) The "mania for certainty" leads Macbeth into a reality that is metaphysical rather than theatrical. As Homan also recognizes, this tension between the theatrical and the metaphysical (between equivocation and "truth") gets *written* into the play as a conflict between two main types of language that it sports. I would perhaps call one of these languages a language of presence; Homan calls it a flatly "sincere" language, "language as commerce among humans."[102]

This metaphysical, antitheatrical drive in Macbeth—which I feel is something close to wanting to *read* the play instead of acting in it, to want to turn it into a novel, preferably autobiographical—gradually comes over as the feeling that the hero wants to end the drama prematurely. Macbeth wants to stop the performance. In a sense, he wants to close the theater(s). Chance has placed him in the situation of a leading actor, hero—and Macbeth progressively recognizes this state of affairs by referring to prologues, acts, and themes. But once he begins to get used to his "borrowed robes" and unfamiliar speeches, he slowly develops a desire to take over the show, this drama directed by female directors. As Thomas van Laan puts it, Macbeth soon wants "to make it his play rather than merely one in which he must act."[103] "He wants to know how the play will turn out, to possess it by that means since he does not seem able to take an active, collaborative part in the plotting."[104] This desire to appropriate (the) play is part of Macbeth's "mania for certainty," part of what I am calling his "metaphysical servitude"—and therefore it is only relevant that van Laan speaks of this desire in terms of knowledge. To *know absolutely* is one way of arresting play and risk, one way of getting out of the theater of existence. It would be comforting to hold this theater in one's hand (like a book, like a globe, like a crystal ball containing truth past, present, and to come)—to review it as "object." It would be reassuring, in short, to stabilize the theater as presence and knowledge, as known presence and self-present knowledge.[105]

The "antitheatrical" bias thus amounts to a strange process of *unstaging* in *Macbeth*. The hero is shown as yearning for some vast exit, and this exit is not simply a matter of escaping from an empirical predicament, but a matter of wanting to abandon the radical equivocations that are internal to theater as play and risk. Two important things are evident in this process. First, Macbeth does not fear risk as such (witness 1.3), but only the risk of losing metaphysical certitude. Second, the fight against risk and uncertainty takes upon itself the quality of a quest for meaning: Macbeth's mania for certainty is a mania for knowledge; and this mania for knowledge is a mania for meaning. This meaning is the absolute knowledge of oneself as presence, the certitude of oneself as the presence to oneself of one's ownmost truth. Macbeth is in quest of "Macbeth," is in quest of his "true" role in the drama opened up by the Weird Sisters.

"Unstaging," here (as I have called it), is from a deconstructionist viewpoint a desire to escape play and hoard meaning. It is the wish to *transform* play into meaning, meaning without play. "Meaning" for deconstruction is not simply any form of meaning, but meaning exactly in this sense: as the negation and closure of play. But if "unstaging" in *Macbeth* only amounted to this, to a narrowing down of play and equivocation into meaning and metaphysics, then the drama would be a poor thing indeed. Thus Shakespeare fights himself quickly out of this danger by exhibiting the unstaging as something that itself can be staged, opened up to radical play. The *process* of unstaging is staged, opened up to play; and it is precisely this difficult movement (most conspicuous perhaps in the "to-morrow" soliloquy) that gives us the strange sense that the hero is opening up in the very act of closing tight, that his transformation to metaphysician and "poor player" takes upon itself the formal properties of an opposite change: an awesome, exultant, and affirmative leap into the absolutely open and unknown. Hence the drive into (metaphysical) meaning that threatens to narrow down the scope of tragic suggestion to pointlike inertia is richly compensated by a process of poetic and linguistic discovery where language, to our relief, leaves mere "meaning" behind. Thus, although Macbeth gives way from the outset to a strange mood of nonparticipation or halfparticipation, he *participates* (linguistically, dramatically, poetically, even philosophically) in this very fall from participation. It is this paradoxical process, perhaps the most daring dramatic invention ever conceived, that permits Shakespeare to cast over his spectator the slightly unthinkable contours of an unprecedented spell.

2

2.1 The Questioning of Identity

Criticism of *Macbeth* usually has to start with a discussion of the Weird Sisters, and I will follow suit here not only because I think their role is pivotal, but also because I think this role is usually misrepresented and misunderstood. I take the silliest interpretation to be the claim that the witches represent "evil" and the best interpretation to be the idea that they monitor equivocation and Truth. From the viewpoint of the play as a whole, they distribute the economies of equivocation; from the viewpoint of the hero, they manipulate the question of Truth.

In saying that much, I am not disputing the fact that the witches presence evil and temptation; nor am I forgetting the topical context—the question of demonology centered on King James's pseudoscientific hobby, the dislike of Jesuits and their fraudulent exorcisms,[1] or even the cheap pyrotechnics of theatrical horror. I am simply saying that witchcraft in *Macbeth* is not reducible to these fairly harmless issues and that the main impact made by the Weird Sisters (linguistically, dramatically, and imaginatively) has very little to do with such superficial matters. Shakespeare used all kinds of quarries for his dramatic purposes, and his reckless and erratically disrespectful use of these sources in itself indicates the restricted implications of their mere presence.

One reason why it is futile to try to exactly *determine* the "function" of the witches (in the finite, verificationist, largely empirical sense) is that their status by no means was a stable and determinate thing in popular, monarchial, or scientific consciousness. Dover Wilson calls attention to this uncertainty: "The nature of the Three Weird Sisters has been much discussed by critics; yet it seems to have occurred to none of them that it was in all probability much discussed also by Shakespeare's public."[2] I return to consider some historical circumstances attending that discussion in a moment, but first I would like to give an outline of the witches as agents of indeterminacy.

To begin with, I think it is misleading to immediately want to compare the Weird Sisters with something *else*: with humans or spirits outside the play. This type of maneuver quickly establishes a shift of attention in order to neutralize the unsettling impact of the witches as they appear in the play. Sooner or later they have to be compared with themselves, have to be taken for what they are worth *in the play*. From this viewpoint, it is clear, the Weird Sisters are unique just like the play that they introduce; like Ariel and Caliban, it has sometimes been remarked, they are quintessentially Shakespearean and therefore not reducible to extra-Shakespearean entities. This fact makes it difficult to *get at* the witches, and discovering this difficulty the critic is much like the hero himself—one who is frustrated by the elusiveness of the sisters. These females cannot immediately be ravaged for information by too-confident males used to extracting meaning from every object they choose to query. Logocentric questions of the predictably dialectical type cease to be meaningful once the sisters have announced the (non)identity of their takeover: questions like "Is Macbeth a voluntary agent or merely a passive pawn?" "Is the source of evil inside or outside the hero?" "Are the witches independent entities outside Macbeth or personifications of his darker consciousness?" "Are the witches only humans (Bradley) or are they supernatural spirits?" Such questions, dialectically organized as they are, are not only unanswerable, but *structurally* unanswerable. The arrival of the sisters, which is always an arrival that already has taken place in *Macbeth*, turns dialectical unanswerability into a major condition of possibility for the drama. This unanswerability affects the hero much as it affects the spectator, affects the spectator much as it affects the critic. As soon as any one of these tries to force a mechanical "either/or-ness" out of the dramatic predicament, the weird hits back—and it hits back, in a sense, always through the Weird Sisters.

We have seen (section 1.2 above) how Stephen Booth catalogued types of radical and irreducible indefinition in *Macbeth*; he showed that entities and categories constantly slip away from clear-cut finality and determinate contour. And it can surely be argued that the Weird Sisters in an important sense govern this economy of the undecidable. James Bulman: "The Weird Sisters are the source of linguistic uncertainty in the play."[3] Sidney Homan: "[T]he witches . . . embody the principle of equivocation."[4] This fact that linguistic weirdness links up with theatrical weirdness affects the whole issue of meaning in *Macbeth*. It is not only that the sisters govern weird time (dismantling the opposition past-versus-future) and weird space (the non-euclidean space where the "quarters" of the map de-struct themselves, 1.3.11–16); it is not only that their linguistic weirdness "infects" empirical space and empirical time; it is also that this voiding of (normal) space and (normal) time hits back at language too, voiding it. There is two-way traffic, here, between linguistic oddness and empirical oddness.

As Robin Grove argues, then, "identity itself is under siege in Macbeth,"[5] and indeed so in the play as a whole:

> [W]hat the murder comes from, so the drama seems to show, is some equivocation or irresponsibility; not just in Macbeth himself, but (worse still) glimpsed at the heart of things. This takes us beyond the old considerations of the hero's fatal flaw, and in any case the tragedy of a great man greatly tempted would be easier to cope with than what we actually find, which is a conscience caught into self-destruction: suddenly and without warning caught into a state of disbelief or self-undoing, where previous certainties are lost and nothing holds as it used to at some sticking-place. More than Macbeth's private affliction, the possibility is at large in the world itself, an equivocation in it.[6]

It should have become clear from this type of commentary that the critical task of identifying equivocation as a foremost depth-formula in the play does not amount to saying that the hero in any way is forgivable. His murder of meek Duncan is a dreadful and distasteful act, and his subsequent political goriness, full of ruthless butcheries, is a crime that fetches its proper penalty. Yet, again, the point is that Shakespearean drama is not reducible to the moral issues that structure its empirical realities or its idealist truths. To avoid the interpretative closure provided by such merely banal aspects of dramatic suggestion, the critic must thus engage with the obvious questioning of identity in Macbeth. This struggle with identity, apparent in the frequency of the pressure on the common verb "to be," cannot be discussed without an analysis of the role of the witches—for they monitor, as witches inside witchcraft, a quasi-demonic arena where the loss of identity was ritualized and exorcised.

For the Elizabethan, the witch unbalances identity immediately. As Henry N. Paul observed long ago, the witch was often in a state of hysteria; she was in a chronic fit, a state of possession. To be in a fit is to be outside oneself, outside identity.[7] This situation was complicated by the fact that there was an epidemic of sham demoniacs. These females were not genuinely in a state of nervous displacement, but pretended to be so. Scholars could separate the two types fairly easily: long pins inserted into the body of a "genuine" witch would cause no pain, for the trance, as a medically real case of self-hypnosis and nervous derangement, would cancel the registration of pain in the brain. In some cases, however, there would be difficulty in drawing a firm line between a real trance and a fraudulent one,[8] a real loss of identity and a faked loss of identity. In any case, the testing procedure—as supervised by King James and other "experts"—is ontologically poignant: for here one is seeking to establish the "true identity" of one (the witch) who precisely *acquires* "her" identity by not having it. When one applied lighted candles and cruel pins to the body of a notorious witch like Mary Glover,[9] the purpose was to establish the authenticity of inauthenticity, the identity of the witch as one who has permanently lost her (normal, human) identity.

The interesting thing, of course, is that these fits associated with witches are related to the "fits" experienced—in a sense affirmed—by Macbeth. These fits of Macbeth, which should not be treated too lightly as being uniformly of the same constant quality, are crucial aspects of his stage presence, indeed of the development of this presence (the fits too "develop")—and I shall discuss them in their contexts later on. They are clearly related to the Weird Sisters, for Macbeth tends to embark into such fits when the sisters presence themselves to him or when they stage something for him. In a sense, as I just remarked, Macbeth affirms these fits and this affirmation suggests that he in some manner controls his loss of control. This too is an important notion, not only because it rehearses the type of controlled loss of control exhibited by the "possessed" women of Shakespeare's times, but also because it suggests to us that the unbalancing of identity in the hero is not an entirely passive process, not one that is entirely without traces of enjoyment, (un)self-discovery, and engineered questioning of identity as self-presence. Paul discusses the Elizabethan "fit" in terms of ecstasy.

> Persons with this sort of imagination are at times beside themselves. The mind leaves the body and watches it. "Ecstasy," the Greeks called it. The Latins called it "rapture." Macbeth after first seeing the witches "seems rapt" (1.3.57). The fit lasts for some time, until Banquo exclaims, "Look how our partner's rapt" [1.3.143].

Macbeth, too, knows about these fits. He writes to his wife that he "stood rapt" [1.5.6] at the wonder of the witches. But this rapture is not involuntary. He can control the fit if he wants to do so.[10]

Even more suggestive than the link between witch and hero is perhaps the possible link between both of these (insofar as they get "possessed") and the professional men of the Elizabethan stage: the actors, but also the playwright. It is not likely that the best Shakespearean actors have been untouched by states similar to "possession," and it is not likely that Shakespeare himself (an experienced actor), in the act of writing, was entirely unfamiliar with a feeling of (un)self-discovery that was "ecstatic"—that in a sense was a "fit." Indeed it is precisely this likely cross-fertilization between Shakespeare as player and Shakespeare as writer that dismantles the strict stage-versus-text fallacy recently discussed. Because Shakespeare, before he sat down to write, was familiar with the special "fit" of the hypnotic player (the hypnosis that permits the casting of a lasting spell over the audience), the actual *act* of writing was almost certainly for him sometimes very much the experience, already, of being on stage. The two "feelings," or types of ex-stasis, would no doubt approximate one another at times. But this type of rapprochement between writing and acting works both ways: just as writing opens itself up to the possibility of the player's "fit," so that fit gets charged with those potentials for intellectual discovery that are normally associated with the introspective act of writing. In fact players, once questioned, tend to acknowledge this very process. In *Macbeth and the Players*, Dennis Bartholomeusz presents evidence to the effect "that players achieve special insights into a text, insights not normally available to critics and scholars, in rehearsal and during performance, as musicians perceive the richness of the music they play in the very act of playing."[11]

What is being suggested, here, is of course not that good actors throw themselves into an epileptic fit or a state of demonic possession or any other kind of temporary madness; it is being suggested, instead, that actors unaffected by the peculiar "fit" outlined in the play misrepresent it, simply fail to be fully in touch with it. In a sense the player playing Macbeth must—not only as Macbeth but also as player—submit to the spell/equivocation cast by the Weird Sisters. Many actors experience a state of "extra-lucidity" as they let the rhythm of dramatic poetry guide their theatrical reflexes,[12] and stage history seems to suggest that the most prominent players have discovered a special "Macbeth" through the process of exposing themselves to the extraordinary poetry that Shakespeare has unleashed. Such a Macbeth does not terrify us because he is a butcher and stage-villain (an unlikely source of terror in today's world of video horror, and perhaps also in the brutal world of Elizabethan realities), but because he becomes coextensive with the uncanny.

The interpretations performed by the historically great players are important in the context of the current study, since the Macbeth they appear to favor is exactly the figure being delineated in these pages as a victim of metaphysical servitude. Garrick, perhaps the greatest of all actors, was so taken back by the sight of his murderous hands that his physical complexion actually changed, the skin whitening.[13] It is a well-known fact that his player's trance was intense enough to cause fainting among the spectators. Macready was trance-like and glassy-eyed after meeting the sisters. With uncertain movements and dramatic lapses of thought, he drifted in reverie through a vast visionary region, goaded by an unknown power.[14] Olivier pushed the butcher to the background and concentrated on the philosopher, a man of action paralyzed by reflection. Haunted by equivocations Macbeth became immobilized by an immense spiritual fatigue.[15] Paul Scofield gave to Shakespeare's language what G. L. Evans calls a "worried intimacy"; there was a constant weighing of meanings, so that each performance shaped itself as new discovery inside soliloquies that never settled down to finality. As he listened to his own rhetoric, the hero deepened interpretation, yearning for yet-closer engagement with ultimate meaning, a more thorough mastery of significance.[16] Nicol Williamson deepened this "introvertive" reading.[17] He spearheads a line of modern actors who seem almost to ignore the copresence of fellow players: the actor "recites" to his colleagues instead of engaging with them in social dialogue. What I have called "metaphysical servitude" becomes acute. Williamson's Macbeth stands isolated and secretive; as he becomes increasingly unreachable, all events appear to happen only inside his head.[18] Ian McKellen follows this tradition of acting, giving the hero an intensely "dual characteristic": he is alert and watchful, but somehow this watchful surveillance of everything seems to include the self—he looks "doubly alert."[19]

The idea of metaphysical servitude promoted by these players is the starting point for John Bayley's discussion of absent self-presence:

The tragedy itself may be bounded in a nutshell, but the minds of Hamlet, of Macbeth and Othello, make them kings of infinite space. F. R. Leavis writes that the world of action is where Othello has his "true part." But there is no such thing as a true part for any hero of Shakespearean tragedy, and certainly not in action. It is his consciousness that fills the play. . . . The usurpation by the mind of both practical action and purposeful idea in tragedy . . . is the most important feature of Shakespeare's relations with the tragic form.[20]

On Bayley's view, the tragedies as such, as well as the figures dramatized in them, fail to live up to the criterion of self-presence: fail, in other words, to live up to themselves. Bayley first observes the deviation from ideal self-presence in the dramas as such: Shakespeare's tragedies, "showing that they are tragedies, seem also to avoid being themselves."[21] But this complex notion—which becomes more intelligible once read in the context of Bayley's entire exposition—carries over into the tragic characters. As the play somehow moves out of the neat formula of its own ideality, or predictable self-presence, so also the tragic hero moves out of the role he seems destined to play. The likely logic of it all is "interrupted."[22] "Hamlet is a man dispossessed of himself, or rather one who has no chance to become himself."[23] Similar things may be said about Macbeth. "Macbeth and Lady Macbeth . . . are quite unfitted for their drama."[24] "Macbeth turns the norm of tragedy . . . outside in. The psyche is shown to be unfitted for the role that tragedy requires of it."[25]

Here, by way of comment, one might perhaps dare to radicalize a notion forwarded by Margaret W. Ferguson: that with Shakespeare we often feel that "the drama itself is the product of certain choices which *might have been different*. Like many students of Shakespeare, I have often felt that certain of his plays strongly invite the audience to imagine how the play would go if it were written according to a different set of generic rules."[26] As applied to *Macbeth* this line of thinking might be extended: here the feeling, to follow Bayley's cue, is that the *whole* play might have been different—and the feeling, curiously, can in some obscure way be experienced as coming from the hero. "Certain turns of plot," writes Ferguson, "are made to seem somehow *arbitrary*, and the effect of such moments is to shift our attention from the story-line to the invisible hand manipulating it."[27] But in *Macbeth* it is not only we who feel a "strange sense of potentiality"[28] as a result of such an intuition, but also the hero. This is no doubt so because the Weird Sisters from the outset manifest their power as a rather authorial one. Macbeth, feeling himself inferior to the drama as a whole, in a sense inferior to the writing of it, will seek to appropriate the writing and stabilize it into reassuring meaning without play.

2.2 Vanishings

If the introduction of the Weird Sisters and their field of special suggestion is one prominent feature in act 1, the tension between vanishing and presence is another. It is this tension that I shall now discuss.

I define "vanishing" as presencing that presences without presence and without presences. I give an example at once:

> For brave Macbeth (well he deserves that name),
> Disdaining Fortune, with his brandish'd steel,
> Which smok'd with bloody execution,
> Like Valour's minion, carv'd out his passage,
> Till he fac'd the slave;
> Which ne'er shook hands, nor bade farewell to him,
> Till he unseam'd him from the nave to th'chops,
> And fix'd his head upon our battlements.
> (1.2.16–23)

What interests me now is not the empirical truths of the storyline as they are being narrated here, but Shakespeare's rhetorical powers of suggestion and the way they create ontologically or hyperontologically poignant sensations.[29] Such crucial sensation is most intense in the line: "Which ne'er shook hands, nor bade farewell to him." The line promotes vanishing. Therefore, also, it negates presence and self-presence. This sensation is made possible by the problematization of appearance and appearing. Presence, in order to presence its presence and be momentarily self-present, must complete an act of appearing; but this act is precisely what keeps being withheld in *Macbeth*. Appearing is interrupted and prematurely erased, giving presences no time to perform their presencings, to *be* present. I identify this patterning in *Macbeth* as that of "broken appearance." Broken appearance opens up the possibilities of vanishing, is the first condition of possibility for vanishing. (Vanishing is a vanishing from presence, vanishing of presence, or vanishing presence.)

A thing that is fully present as (a) presence has a beginning and an end. In spatial and optical terms, this means that it has a clear, visible outline—a clear-cut shape and profile. In temporal terms, it means having a clearly defined moment of first appearing and a clearly defined moment of final disappearing. But Shakespeare, here as in so many other places, erases the contours at the front and at the back of what would like to make an appearance: "ne'er shook hands, nor bade farewell." From the banal viewpoint of "human intercourse," obviously, nothing remarkable is at stake: there is simply a cruel comment on the fact that the defeated enemy was done away with in a flash of lightning, a fell swoop so rapid that there was no time for polite exchanges before or after the fight. But since this type of patterning (broken appearance) is a prominent feature of numerous similar units in the play, the powers of linguistic suggestion are by no means exhausted by the empirical reading; on the contrary, the linguistic powers only become forcefully operative on a level of suggestion that leaves empirical meaning behind. What we are made to feel is that the appearing of "the slave" was his disappearing: all that truly appeared (or had time to appear) was the act of disappearing (of being cut up and annihilated by nihilating Macbeth). Theoretically, handshaking is the slave's manner of announcing his presence, of *presenting* his presence; bidding farewell is ideally his manner of announcing the departure of his presence, of clarifying the ending of a presence that has marked a stable duration of being-present. But in the vanishing speed of this military action, no true presencing has strictly speaking been possible. Or, put differently: to have been with Macbeth in that fight would have been to have this peculiar sensation that things were moving with a speed and intensity that cancelled the possibility of the normal presencing of presences.

I linger over this special dramatic sensation with considerable care, for not only is it poorly recognized in criticism; it is also the most important sensation that Shakespeare creates in his opening act. We are made to experience vanishing as a dramatic sensation, and we are made to feel that Macbeth, insofar as he is a fighter, is the center of this affirmative vanishing. This intuition is peculiarly important, since it is the very quality in and around Macbeth that immediately brings him into alignment with the mode of presencing favored by the Weird Sisters. They too affirm vanishing.

A further reason for emphasizing the paramount importance of this Macbethian vanishing is that it is necessary as a structural contrast to his later conditions: to the two main moods triggered by his fall into metaphysical servitude. In that introspective state of permanently inward reverie and swoon, he will on the one hand yearn desperately for a world of absolute (metaphysical) self-presence, on the other hand be thrown into vertigo by the failure of this self-presence ever to fully materialize. These two servile moods are characterized by a negation of vanishing and by a deepening of it. Later, as we shall see, these opposed "sensations" felt around Macbeth during his period of servitude are negotiated by the contacts with the sisters: "When I burn'd in desire to question them further, they made themselves into air, into which they vanish'd" (1.5.3–5). What is interesting here is not the banal and empirical fact that the witches actually can vanish, but that they come to represent a sphere where vanishing has replaced self-presence. Once in his servile state (of metaphysical anguish), Macbeth is not just one who fears the vanishing of the sisters, but one who fears that this vanishing is becoming emblematic of a situation where presence is eternally deferred. He does not burn in desire to have; he burns in desire to "question," to know. For he realizes that knowledge would arrest vanishing. The military and heroic vanishing that Macbeth initially *affirms* is thus crucially related to the metaphysical and servile vanishing that he later *fears*: solicited by the sisters, he swings round from an absolutely fearless man to an absolutely fearing man—and vanishing organizes this entire inversion by transferring itself, as sensation, from the outside to the inside, from athletic movement to inward quiver.

Vanishing, in the two worlds (that of fighting and that of metaphysical anguish), is not unrelated to the idea of knowledge. As I just remarked, Macbeth burns in desire to know, not to have. He does not want power; he wants inner certitude. Knowledge would arrest vanishing, would stop the acceleration of metaphysical panic. But in the heroic and military world of act 1 there is also this conflict and rupture between knowledge and vanishing. The bleeding Captain is enjoined to give a correct account: "Say to the King the knowledge of the broil, / As thou didst leave it" (1.2.6–7). But "it" here seems inadvertently to refer to "knowledge" as well as to "broil." The Captain has not only left the broil; he has also, in leaving that broil, left the knowledge of it. In fact Shakespeare rather scrupulously outlines a situation of military and political instability where events change their appearance so rapidly that knowledge somehow always is something secondhand. Knowledge (and implicitly also Truth) is not a pointlike and stable datum, but instead a provisional term mediating something else—probably another mediating term. To keep up with the pace of the battle and its dramatic shifts of fortune, a system of relays is thrown into extravagant activity, each new messenger telling a new story. But the mediating terms seem to crowd and get in the way of one another—"As *thick* as hail, / Came post with post" (1.3.97–98)—just as the King's feelings and words smother one another into choked silence: "His wonders and his praises do contend, / Which should be thine" (1.3.92–93). This overcrowding, or general thickening of things wanting to appear, may also be felt in its military form in the account of Rosse's appearance as he arrives from the battleground: "What a haste looks through his eyes!" (1.2.46). This is a marvelous phrase, Shakespearean in its almost stunning economy. Here the confusion of the battle is traced in the gaze of the beholder—who is one that is not only unbalanced because of the haste of his journey but also one who reflects the "haste" of the battle itself. This haste (of the battle) *itself* "looks through his eyes": so that we feel that the battle is the active part, the man and his gazing the passive. The newcomer is slightly distracted, but this is partly so because the battle itself is distracted: something hyper-ontologically pulled away from its own phenomenality, something full of disjointedness and unseaming rather than stabilized presences.

Before moving on, then, let me recapitulate my definitions of "vanishing" and "broken appearance." Vanishing is a negation of presence (though not in the mere sense of an empirical unpresencing of the presence). Shakespeare from the outset *situates* his hero in a sphere of action (and later thought) where the world, as in the "haste" of the battle, structures itself in terms of a loosening of fixedness, an unseaming of structurality. The mobile advance of Birnam Wood is the dramatic finalization of this general unfixing. Its overall force and impact are not neutralized by the ability of the empirical action of the drama to restore "order." Macbeth "belongs" to vanishing, because what is supersonic and infinitely up-speeded (whether in the physical or mental world) is an element in which he operates spontaneously. What sensation does Macbeth give us? We do not *first* sense a presence called Macbeth and *then* discover that this figure has vanishing/speed/action attached to it; rather, we feel that Macbeth *is* action: *is* speed, *is* vanishing. Why do we get this sensation? Because Shakespeare wants us to have it. Because Shakespeare's language never enables us not to intuit Macbeth in this special manner. With a character like Duncan things are quite different: there we certainly can take one thing at a time, first feel the presence of the man as a presence, and then attend to "what" this presence does. But in the case of Macbeth (as a fighter) being and doing are seamlessly unified. And vanishing here is not simply a passive attribute, some "quality" appertaining to a man; it is also something that the hero implements, radiates into his environment. The very relation of the self to its other is "vanishing." Again:

> For brave Macbeth (well he deserves that name),
> Disdaining Fortune, with his brandish'd steel,
> Which smok'd with bloody execution,
> Like Valour's minion, carv'd out his passage,
> Till he fac'd the slave;
> Which ne'er shook hands, nor bade farewell to him,
> Till he unseam'd him from the nave to th'chops,
> And fix'd his head upon our battlements.
>
> (1.2.16–23)

"Disdaining" Macbeth is one who disdains presence, one, we are made to feel, who unflinchingly runs right through and across presence by cutting it up. A number of units stress this sensation: "Disdaining," "brandish'd steel," "smok'd," "bloody execution," "carv'd out," "passage," "unseam'd." The conclusive "fix'd" ironically increases the stress on the unfixing of presence, for what gets firmly stuck in its proper place is precisely something that has for ever lost its proper place.

To return to "broken appearance," what the "slave" exemplified by failing to begin or conclude an act of normal appearing: this can be understood by considering our way of experiencing a "falling star" (meteorite). The fragment travels inconspicuously in outer space and only becomes visible during a process of illumination triggered by a violent passage through the earth's atmosphere. Since the meteorite usually gets completely annihilated in this atmospheric descent, the event is, quite literally and empirically, a vanishing and a disappearing. Thus, objectively speaking, the moment of the meteor's disappearance is its moment of appearance, indeed the condition of possibility for its full appearance (luminosity). The meteor has to disappear in order to appear. In a sense its disappearing *is* its appearing. But this situation is also subjectively operative. When we see a "falling star" (an event lasting for a fraction of a second), the recognition of the fact that the star is being seen *immediately* is also the recognition of the fact that the object is already disappearing from the seen (from the field of vision). Strictly speaking, all the observer really apprehends is this disappearing-from-sight. There is no *present* "star" prior to this moment of perceiving it as retreat from perception. Very much, in this manner, "vanishing" will come to signify a realm of Shakespearean suggestion where all presencing, already, is a vanishing-from-presence. The vanishing is, as it were, more important than "what" vanishes. As I have tried to indicate by giving a few examples (including "What a haste looks through his eyes"), this impression of vanishing is not only a feature of the first Macbeth-world but the very sensual nucleus that gives it constitutional atmosphere for all that follows. In addition, as I hope to suggest, the idea and sensation of vanishing is an important forestructure of the presencing of the idea of murder in *Macbeth*.

The notion of vanishing helps us identify the crucial tension between two "zones" of Shakespearean signification: the ontological zone and the hyperontological zone. The former promotes the sense of being and self-presence; the latter reveals an unbalancing and questioning of self-presence. I will be referring to both of these zones, indeed all ontologically poignant areas, as "ontodramatic" zones. The "ontodramatic," for me, will simply be anything in Shakespearean drama that is ontologically or hyperontologically crucial—either positively or negatively. "Ontodramatic criticism" will be criticism that discovers a hyperontologically organized distribution of dramatic tensions to be more important for signification than intuitive givens like "character," "imagery," "conventions," and so forth. I privilege the ontodramatic perspective because Shakespeare works with no differential system that is more important for him or for the work.

In *Macbeth*, as we have seen, the hyperontological zone is the one deployed by the Weird Sisters. It is a zone *of* the weird, a weird zone. It gradually expands until it in a sense covers the entire play. We might, somewhat playfully, call this a "radioactive" zone: radioactive because it is somehow rather dangerous to dwell in it and because the invisible "fallout" descending everywhere within its precincts is harmful according to undecided principles whose effects cannot be properly foreseen. Emotionally speaking, "radioactivity" is an experience or endurance of the uncanny; structurally speaking, "radioactivity" is the spontaneous emission of harmful "rays" signifying the disintegration of nuclei. As, literally, *fallout*, language is in the context of this provisional imagery a falling-out: where the locus of linguistic staging is at once the nuclear site of "meaning" and the "polluted" margins where fallen meaning recognizes the loss of meaning.

It may be helpful, at this point, to learn to identify some traits of the ontological zone that Shakespeare deploys to counterbalance his "radioactive," hyperontological zone (as governed by the sisters and by fighting Macbeth in the name of vanishing). For Shakespeare does not only create vanishing in his opening scenes; he also creates presence. This presence, however, which is a heroic presence, is quite different from the metaphysical presence that Shakespeare soon creates for a hero slipping into the anguished vertigo of metaphysical servitude. Such heroic self-presence can be directly intuited by gauging the worth of units such as: "good and hearty soldier," "brave friend," "brave Macbeth," "Valour's minion," "O valiant cousin! worthy gentleman!", "Mark, King of Scotland, mark," "The worthy Thane of Rosse," "God save the King!", "worthy Thane," "great King," "Norway himself," "Bellona's bridegroom." These units are not particularly interesting and in fact seem rather strained to us today in our unheroic times. Nevertheless, such units are ontodramatically significant, and to have them withdrawn from the play would amount to losing an important ontodramatic tension: that between heroic vanishing (Macbeth as athletic instantaneity) and heroic presence (heroic man as social exemplum). The units listed above together create a sense of stable selfsameness. All these beings are presented as being not only socially dependable but ontologically dependable: each being is part of Being, and this beingness in Being, or self-presence in it, comes over as the fact that each existent exists in an overwhelming concordance with his identity. Curiously—but significantly—this fact holds true also for enemies:

> The merciless Macdonwald
> (Worthy to be a rebel, for to that
> The multiplying villainies of nature
> Do swarm upon him) from the western isles
> Of Kernes and Gallowglasses is supplied;
> And Fortune, on his damned quarrel smiling,
> Show'd like a rebel's whore
>
> (1.2.9–15)

All rebels are strictly speaking unworthy (since they are no longer worthy from the viewpoint of the target of the rebellion). But through the unit "Worthy to be a rebel," the rebel is not, entirely, an unworthy one. He is worth his salt, *qua* rebel. The rebel links himself to himself as the worthiness of himself: he fits the mould of the platonic category "rebel" perfectly. The "worthiness" achieved (as a linguistic and dramatic sensation) is not strictly speaking a moral quality here, but instead an ontological one. It is the achievement of identity and presence that is foregrounded: not personal or social identity, but identity in the sense of internal congruence. (This inward congruence, as we shall see, is a significant feature in the dramatic deployment of several totalizations in the play: Lady Macbeth demonizing her own spirit into utter blackness, Macbeth totalizing his murderous projections, and so forth.)

Inconspicuous as it might seem, the unit "Worthy to be a rebel" engages with the ontodramatic shifts of the play as a whole—for Macbeth, precisely, is one who in an important sense is *not* worthy of being a rebel. Not only is Macbeth unworthy (morally speaking) as one subverting the state; also he is unworthy from the viewpiont of rebellion. Macbeth's real unworthiness is always ontological. He is ontologically unworthy. As we noticed in John Bayley's commentary, Macbeth cannot really live up to the role he is to play—is not really worthy of this role. Much of his behavior throughout the play could be interpreted in the light of this remark. He is unworthy of being a rebel because, as his wife keeps remarking, he is not quite up to the task of playing the part.

A further feature must be identified in the ontological zone. Heroic presence is not only promoted by soldiers mutually recognizing their partners and enemies as stable self-presences, but also by the foregrounding of dialectic through a primordial and primitive "struggle to death."

> Dun. Whence cam'st thou, worthy Thane?
> Rosse.   From Fife, great King,
>   Where the Norweyan banners flout the sky,
>   And fan our people cold. Norway himself,
>   With terrible numbers,
>   Assisted by that most disloyal traitor,
>   The Thane of Cawdor, began a dismal conflict;
>   Till that Bellona's bridegroom, lapp'd in proof,
>   Confronted him with self-comparisons,
>   *Point against point, rebellious arm 'gainst arm,*
>   Curbing his lavish spirit: and, to conclude,
>   The victory fell on us;—
>   (1.2.49–59)

Heroic power is here a controlled dialectic, a mastery in which A directly faces B in a symmetrical display of idealized balances. The emphasis on mastery is conveyed by the idea that Macbeth held back ("Curbing") the excess ("lavish spirit") of the enemy: hence excess as such (in this particular passage) is neutralized, captured in a system of dialectical balances. This dialectical platform of heroic recognition and heroic self-presence is important for the play as a whole, for Shakespeare later on lets us understand that *this* type of primitive self-presence (unlike metaphysical presence) is fundamentally accessible as a last reservoir of meaning for the cornered hero. Heroic and dialectical meaning is always a possibility that in some way is reassuring. Macbeth's reappearance in act 5 in the capacity of a heroic master is partly engineered by this fragile possibility, and so are his traces of self-presence in the Ghost scene. The ghost of Banquo, produced neurotically by the deepening of metaphysical servitude, cannot be coped with in terms of that servitude, and hence the dialectical world of meaning produced by the "struggle to death" looms as an ultimate exit. A duel in an aboriginal world, a desert still uninhabited by civilization (ontologically speaking), is a place where the (dialectical) production of meaning is absolutely certain:

> What man dare, I dare:
> Approach thou like the rugged Russian bear,
> The Arm'd rhinoceros, or th'Hyrcan tiger;
> Take any shape but that, and my firm nerves
> Shall never tremble: or, be alive again,
> And dare me to the desert with thy sword;
> If trembling I inhabit then, protest me
> The baby of a girl.
>
> (3.4.98–105)

Without the preparatory work performed by Shakespeare in act 1, this passage is partly meaningless. What is being said here is not simply that Macbeth, because of "guilt," is afraid of a resurrected cadaver and that he would prefer to face some more concrete opponent; it is being suggested instead that Macbeth somehow is aware of the fact that his heroic courage (as displayed in 1.2 and 1.3) is quite intact. (Parts of act 5 support this notion.) It is not that fear has replaced courage in him, but that the *world* where heroic courage was possible has vanished (as possible ground for the whole self) during the course of the tragic development. To resurrect the primitive and heroic "struggle to death" (for dialectical recognition and man-to-man prestige) would not simply be to return to a physical level of animalistic bravery; it would be to resurrect the world where dialectical meaning is produced by dialectical fighting—precisely the world Shakespeare carefully delineates in act 1.

Generally speaking, this notion that Macbeth always conceives dialectically established truth as a source of possible reassurance is useful for the understanding of some of his complex soliloquies. Since the Weird Sisters radiate an equivocation that unbalances dialectical truth, Macbeth will tend to resuscitate dialectic in the very speeches and reveries where he is also reluctantly exploring the weird suggestion that dialectic is being withdrawn as a logical possibility. Michael Goldman discusses this complex wavering between dialectic ("polar opposites") and nondialectic with considerable subtlety of phrasing. Notice the sensual quality of the analysis:

> The murkier soliloquies suggest that the action here is an effortful keeping apart of polar opposites. They collapse and contaminate each other when Macbeth is alone. Thus the characteristic combination of movements in the more private passages: quick, forward, out of the murk; slow, mesmerized, sinking deeper into it.[30]

In summary, then, there is presence and vanishing in the heroic world of masters fighting for ideals, and there is also presence and vanishing in the servile world of metaphysical quest (for Truth). This gives four basic positions: heroic presence (the *meaning* of the "struggle to death"), heroic vanishing (the *sensation* of reckless struggle as athletic instantaneity), servile presence (the reassuring *notion* of Truth as foundation), and servile vanishing (the anguish and *vertigo* caused by the endless deferral of metaphysical Truth as self-presence).

2.3 Cuttings

I am now about to discuss a peculiarly important thing in *Macbeth*: the cut. To begin with, one might situate the *problematic of the cut* in a literary-critical context by mentioning the fact that one of the prominent Shakespeare critics, John Dover Wilson, theorized *Macbeth* as a mutilated play, one full of cuts. Wilson could not make the play fit his logocentric expectations, so he posited some ideally "original" text and said that all we now have left is a vastly "abridged" play, one cut to pieces. Most critics refute this theory, some of them no doubt agreeing with Kenneth Muir when he claims that Wilson finds cuts because that is what he is looking for (KM, 10).[31] But Dover Wilson's quest for "cuts" is more poignant and ontologically absurd than we might first realize, for in a sense the play *Macbeth* does structure itself in terms of cuts. The cut, in other words, is a productive and constitutive feature *of* the play—not merely something external that may (or may not) happen to the text after the time of its completion. It is as if Shakespeare, like certain painters, had worked with a sharp knife instead of a brush, or with both at once. There are slits, slashes, and forced openings, all of them hastily created in a fury of artistic nihilation.

This cutting/slashing/nihilating, we saw a while ago, was what defined Macbeth's action in act 1: he "carv'd out his passage" and "unseam'd" the slave in a twinkling (1.2.19–22). In this way, I argued, Macbeth approximated the hyperontological sphere of "vanishing" monitored by the Weird Sisters, a sphere where presence has no time to stabilize itself into self-presence. Before the enemy slave is truly present, he is already gone, wiped out by Macbeth's slashing onwardness. Macbeth too is "gone," has vanished, already, into the next rank of enemy resistance. It is this immense swiftness that makes fear, as a form of presence, impossible in the sphere of military vanishing: "Nothing afeard of what thyself didst make, / Strange images of death" (1.3.96–97). In a world where each new horror is gone, immediately, because it is replaced by a further one, fear gets *cut* out altogether: it is cut out and away from its phenomenological presence in a world of empirical presences, but it is also cut out and away from its possibility and nascent will to appear. Shakespeare makes us feel that Macbeth obliterates the very horrors that he is making. He cuts a horrible wound, but then he cuts out that cut/wound. He not only cuts, but cuts cutting.

"Nothing afeard of what thyself didst make, / Strange images of death." Again Shakespeare's economy is alarmingly effective. We feel that Macbeth cuts out the horrors of his cutting/wounding; but we also feel, through "what *thyself* didst make," that horrors are bearable for Macbeth if their production somehow is organized round his own efforts and active desires. Horror is bearable—indeed it is in a sense not even horror—if it is mastered, if it is controlled by the "I" surveying its economy; hence it is the shift of horror to a sphere outside the self and its mastery that will truly horrify.

My main purpose, however, is not to discuss the relation between horror and self here, but to call attention to the connection between the cutting associated with Macbeth and the cutting associated with the Weird Sisters (the topic of this subsection). I discuss this connection in order to clarify the way in which both types of cutting promote the sensation of vanishing, thus consolidating the general feeling that Macbeth and the sisters share a common zone of hyperontological suggestion.

The world of military conflict in act 1 is one of blood, wounds, gashes, an excess of terrible openings everywhere. But the torn apertures and open wounds engage directly with discourse, as we see at the end of the passage below, by being associated with linguistic expenditure:

> But the Norweyan Lord, surveying vantage,
> With furbish'd arms, and new supplies of men,
> Began a fresh assault.
> *Dun.*   Dismay'd not this
> Our captains, Macbeth and Banquo?
> *Cap.*   Yes;
> As sparrows eagles, or the hare the lion.
> If I say sooth, I must report they were
> As cannons overcharg'd with double cracks;
> So they
> Doubly redoubled strokes upon the foe:
> Except they meant to bathe in reeking wounds,
> Or memorize another Golgatha,
> I cannot tell—
> But I am faint, my gashes cry for help.
> *Dun.* So well thy words become thee, as thy wounds:
> They smack of honour both.—Go, get him surgeons.
>
> (1.2.31–45)

Here, linguistic expenditure, as the cut/wound, causes us to feel that the *power* of human articulation is something structurally close to cutting/wounding/nihilation. But as we listen to language as the Weird Sisters celebrate it at the beginning of act 4, we see that this same association between linguistic affirmation and *the cut* is at the forefront of Shakespeare's attention. I say that the sisters "celebrate" language, because when they chant the recipe for the demonic broth to be stirred in the cauldron, Shakespeare makes us feel that language itself, *its* formulaic procedure, is structurally equivalent to the demonic recipe. The weird quality in the broth is as it were not only a function of the recipe as material substance (what empirically gets thrown into the cauldron) but equally so a function of the recipe as language. You cannot simply make the broth without chanting its formula, and conversely you cannot chant the formula without making the broth: the two operations, that of language and that of weird doing, are coimplicative. This reciprocation between speaking and doing (exemplified by the bleeding Captain above and now by the sisters) can be taken literally when it comes from witchcraft, for it is clear that Shakespeare often gives us the impression that the Weird Sisters only have to think something to create it (1.3.11–14). I suspect indeed that Shakespeare would not have been hostile to the idea of letting the witches perform the "making" of the brew in terms of mimicry, without any empirical kitchen-work at all. In this sense what I said above could be taken literally: you cannot chant the formula *without* (automatically) making the broth.

If it can be understood, then, that language and action coimplicate one another immediately in certain parts of *Macbeth*, it can perhaps also be understood that the negative version of this coimplication amounts to the recognition of a common factor shared by linguistic nihilation and physical nihilation. Language and physical action tend to be "dangerous" in the same way: they move forward, hyperontologically speaking, as *cutting*. From this viewpoint, it is interesting to observe that what gets thrown into the demonic cauldron is not simply a set of fragments, but cuts (a notion I shall clarify presently). This situation is absolutely crucial in that it conclusively brings military vanishing and occult vanishing into a common field of ontodramatic suggestion. What vanishes in the horrors of heroic fighting is the cut/horror—because further cuts/horrors (we saw) cut out the possibility of (apprehending) the cut/horror. Similarly, what gets boiled (away) into demonic liquids and weird vapors in act 4 is a heap of cuts/wounds/horrors whose massive self-despoliation is the very action of the weird cooking. In this process the cuts multiply in a multiplication that causes their vanishing and liquefaction. Doctor Johnson once called attention to this sense of multiplication: Shakespeare "multiplies all the circumstances of horror. The babe, whose finger is used, must be strangled in birth; the grease must not only be human, but must have dropped from a gibbet, the gibbet of a murderer; and even the sow, whose blood is used, must have offended nature by devouring her farrow."[32] But this multiplication in demonic "vanishing" is already visible in the "multiplying villainies" that "swarm" in the world of military vanishing outlined in the opening scenes (1.2.11–12).

The result, in both cases, is inevitably that presence is punctured and disrupted—that presence, quite simply, is cut. This general cutting, whether in heroic fighting or weird cookery, displaces the center, presence as self-presence and centeredness. As act 4 opens, the modern stage direction opens a center, a "middle:" "A house in Forres. In the middle, a boiling cauldron." The middle is round, but it is boiling. The central boiling is a weird middle. Indeed the purpose now is not to center the center, but to decenter it. The purpose now is not to center the center, but to boil it.

True, the boiling is said to take place *in* the center; and perhaps this is strictly the very case, empirically speaking. But empirical speaking is not really the kind of speaking that weird discourse now speaks. It speaks instead in terms of the cut, in terms of a general cutting-up that appears to put centricity at risk:

> SCENE 1.—*A house in Forres. In the middle, a boiling cauldron.*
> *Thunder. Enter the three Witches.*
> 1 Witch. Thrice the brinded cat hath mew'd.
> 2 Witch. Thrice, and once the hedge-pig whin'd.
> 3 Witch. Harpier cries:—'Tis time, 'tis time.
> 1 Witch. Round about the cauldron go;
>   In the poison'd entrails throw.—
>   Toad, that under cold stone
>   Days and nights has thirty-one
>   Swelter'd venom, sleeping got,
>   Boil thou first i'th'charmed pot.
> All. Double, double toil and trouble:
>   Fire, burn; and, cauldron, bubble.
> 2 Witch. Fillet of a fenny snake,
>   In the cauldron boil and bake;
>   Eye of newt, and toe of frog,
>   Wool of bat, and tongue of dog,
>   Adder's fork, and blind-worm's sting,
>   Lizard's leg, and howlet's wing,
>   For a charm of powerful trouble,
>   Like a hell-broth boil and bubble.
> All. Double, double toil and trouble:
>   Fire, burn; and, cauldron, bubble.
> 3 Witch. Scale of dragon, tooth of wolf;
>   Witches' mummy; maw, and gulf,
>   Of the ravin'd salt-sea shark;
>   Root of hemlock, digg'd i'th'dark;

> Liver of blaspheming Jew;
> Gall of goat, and slips of yew,
> Sliver'd in the moon's eclipse;
> Nose of Turk, and Tartar's lips;
> Finger of birth-strangled babe,
> Ditch-deliver'd by a drab,
> Make the gruel thick and slab:
> Add thereto a tiger's chaudron,
> For th'ingredience of our cauldron.
> *All.* Double, double toil and trouble:
> Fire, burn; and, cauldron, bubble.
> *2 Witch.* Cool it with a baboon's blood:
> Then the charm is firm and good.
>
> (4.1.1–38)

The affirmation here of the *cut* as linguistic and physical nihilation can quickly be appreciated by looking at the spurious sequel that Muir has included in his edition, well knowing that it in all probability is a non-Shakespearean interpolation. Here, the center/cauldron, instead of disrupting its middle, becomes a pot where meaning reassuringly accumulates into "gains" that all and sundry come to "share":

> *Enter Hecate, and the other three Witches.*
> *Hec.* O, well done! I commend your pains,
> And every one shall share i'th'gains.
> And now about the cauldron sing,
> Like elves and fairies in a ring,
> Enchanting all that you put in.
>
> (4.1.39–43)[33]

One of the typically Shakespearean things missing here is sensuality in its combination with nihilation: the sense that negativity is used not merely to gain necromantic suggestion but in order to give sensually aggressive outline to the linguistic nihilation of the world's passive furniture. The things that get thrown into the cauldron are not random objects cut off from their parents in an arbitrary fashion; on the contrary, Shakespeare carefully outlines the likely contour of each sensuous incision, like a craftsman taking pride in the most obscure and messy parts of his work. Eloquence and craftsmanship (in the sense of cutting/carving/sculpting) are here impossible to distinguish from one another—a fact brought out first by the bleeding Captain whose words and wounds were equally articulate of heroic passion. There is artistry here, right in the middle of negativity (here "evil"); but this sense of the unification of negativity and artistry was conspicuous right from the outset when Macbeth was felt not only to be a killer, a professional butcher, but also a military artist of the first rank: an artisan who "carv'd out" his line of attack (1.2.19). Here in act 4 the quality of being "unseam'd" forced upon the enemy by Macbeth in the early fighting (1.2.22) returns in the controlling symbolic images of bloody ripping (Second Apparition), severed head (First Apparition), and severed tree (Third Apparition); and the nihilating curvature and cutting arc in things being "carv'd out" reappear in the minute details that depict the actual cuttings thrown into the cauldron:

> Gall of goat, and slips of yew,
> Sliver'd in the moon's eclipse;
> Nose of Turk, and Tartar's lips;
> Finger of birth-strangled babe,
> Ditch-deliver'd by a drab
>
> (4.1.27–31)

The cut, as nihilating curvature, is here prominent in the slicingly sensual unit "Sliver'd," in the crescent formed by the progressively eclipsed moon (gradually cut out, through a widening bite, by the round edge of intruding earth), in the aquiline orientalism of the Turk's nose, in the undulating symmetry of the Tartar's lips, in the finger (gently curved, like all infant fingers) removed from the baby—and even in the double curvature of the prostitute's grasp round the neck as she strangles her newborn child. Most of these images are thoroughly horrible, yet so are implicitly (and to the same infinite degree) the "[s]trange images of death" (1.3.97) that Shakespeare, as we have seen, shows as being integral to Macbeth's sphere of original performance.

Johnson, we may remember, spoke a moment ago of Shakespeare in 4.1 as one who "multiplies all the circumstances of horror." It is this auto-multiplication, the Doctor suggests, that reflects the "touches of judgment and genius."[34] It is clear, however, that the multiplication in itself in no way produces genius and in no way betokens genius. Any writer can pile horror on horror, graft horror on horror; the cheapest story on the pulp market will reveal the most extraordinary "multiplication" of horrors multiplied with horrors. In point of fact, Johnson is unable to identify what it exactly is that allows Shakespeare to move us so strangely even through this banal abracadabra.

The clue is surely to be found by attending, once more, to

Shakespeare's tendency to dismantle binary opposites: this time multiplication and division. It is not the ingredients (in the brew) that are multiplied, but their division. Division itself is multiplied. Which is to say that we are in a world where multiplication *is* division, where division *is* multiplication. It is the cutting and division that produce the excess, not the cumulative and multiplying augmentation itself. There is not a joining of thing to thing, but a joining of cut to cut, of unjoining to unjoining.

Since unjoining evokes the notion of wounding, the tension between joining and unjoining is peculiarly fragile in *Macbeth*, a play where the hero in a sense is eternally trying to heal some terrible opening thrown open by weird solicitation. Macbeth seems always to want to smooth over some original wound in reality: a wound that splits his mind from side to side but which also splits his apprehension of an externally uniform world. Just as the fighter Macbeth appears to be engaged in an activity one might call original wounding, so the introspective and servile Macbeth appears to be engaged in a process one might call original healing. As the categories "joining" and "disjoining" come to cross one another in the hero's increasingly tangled system of nervous reflexes, a *chiasmos* is created so that each term folds its signifying norm over into its opposite. This crossing can be sensually experienced by attending to the units emphasized below, all of them suggestive of opening-versus-closing (wounding-versus-healing).

>   *Macb.* We have *scorch'd* [i.e. slashed] the snake, not kill'd it:
>   　She'll *close*, and be herself; whilst our poor malice
>   　Remains in danger of her former tooth.
>   　But let the frame of things *disjoint* . . .
>   　　　　　　　　　　　　　　　　　　　(3.2.13–16)

>   　There's comfort yet; they are assailable:
>   　Then be thou jocund. Ere the bat hath flown
>   　His *cloister'd* flight; ere to black Hecate's summons
>   　The shard-born beetle, with his drowsy hums,
>   　Hath rung Night's yawning peal, there shall be done
>   　　A deed of dreadful note.
>   *Lady M.*　　　　　　　　　　　　　What's to be done?
>   *Macb.* Be innocent of the knowledge, dearest chuck,
>   　Till thou applaud the deed. Come, *seeling* Night,
>   　*Scarf up* the tender eye of pitiful Day,
>   　And, with thy bloody and invisible hand,
>   　Cancel, and *tear to pieces*, that great bond

> Which keeps me pale!—Light thickens; and the crow
> Makes wing to th'rooky wood;
>
> (3.2.39–51)

Generally speaking, the basic polar tension here (as marked by the emphasized units) is the one between closing/blinding, which signifies the desire to look away from horror, and tearing/opening, which signifies the horrible violation itself. But these polar opposites (protective blinding and violent cutting-up) are in the final analysis folded into one another—or, literally, *sewn* into one another: "Come, seeling Night, / Scarf up the tender eye of pitiful Day" (3.2.46–47). As suggestive of Macbeth's paradoxical and precarious situation, this unit folds over wounding into healing and healing into wounding. The image, taken from falconry ("seeling"),[35] of someone running a fine thread through the eyelid of a hawk *joins* the notion of slashing (cutting a slit) to the notion of healing (closing an aperture, the eye). For whereas the "seeling" is visibly the closing of a gap, the seaming of an aperture—and thus something visually close to the healing of divided skin into firmly restored uniformity—the fine cruelty of the actual clinical operation is precisely suggestive of the reverse: of that acute piercing of skin ("scorch'd") which triggered the entire sequence of images. On the one hand we get a visual experience: the sewing of the hawk's eyelids. On the other hand, more or less unconsciously, we get a hyperontological experience. The joining of the eyelids *joins* joining and unjoining: healing and wounding, violation and repair.

3

3.1 The Assassination of Intentionality

As I now approach the dramatic crisis of murder itself, my criticism will situate itself inside what is loosely known as the "noble-murderer interpretation." This is the reading favored by actors like Garrick and Olivier and discussed by quite a number of significant critics. The basic idea, here, is that Shakespeare's genius does not bother to stage the banal notion of a bad man entering evil but of a very good man entering evil. However, and this is a crucial dimension of the current enterprise, I do not myself read this transition (in the noble-murderer reading) from good to evil as a "fall" from good, as a common type of tragic "tainting." I do not think that Macbeth at any point "becomes evil" in order to become a murderer (although murder in itself obviously is evil). I think, with John Bayley, that it "is essential to the hypnotic tension of the play that Macbeth should not seem in any ordinary way 'responsible' for his actions."[1] (The stress here is on "ordinary"; one is not freeing Macbeth from responsibility.) In short, my position is this: anyone arguing that Macbeth "turns evil" and that this inner darkening is the crucial trigger device for the murder and the tragic action is not only misconceiving Shakespeare's dramatic design but also disfiguring the imaginative and aesthetic potentials of the play.

In fact, that type of secondary-school reading also disfigures most of the enormous psychological potentials of *Macbeth*. Several critics are generously willing to acknowledge the greatness of the play, while at the same time voicing the curious prejudice that Shakespeare is a poor psychologist who sacrifices psychological truth for the sake of dramatic effect. One is willing to recognize the feeling of tragic greatness, but finding that this greatness does not fit any logocentric model of psychological causation, one decides that the play is successful in *spite* of its psychology. I hold precisely the opposite view. I think there is a very special psychology in this play, and I think that critics *replacing* this psychology (which is beyond their ken) with their own "temptation-and-fall" theories (taken from popular logic) are simply transforming the play into something that is more immediately manageable for them than it really is. E. E. Stoll has argued that the tragic thrill comes from seeing the good man falling into horror, but that Macbeth's deeds would be more in keeping with psychological realism had the hero had some real cause to dislike Duncan.[2] This, to me, is the silliest possible notion. If Macbeth really has had a grievance, then the whole play called *Macbeth*, far from being one of the most brilliant dramas ever devised, would sink into mediocrity and indifference. In this same vein and fashion, Gustav Rümelin tells us that Shakespeare "exaggerates" at the expense of real "psychological truth" but still somehow creates a play that is his most powerful and mighty tragedy.[3] In his review of these two positions, J. I. M. Stewart limply follows suit (with respect to this particular issue) by stating that Shakespeare was always prepared to use a "non-realistic" move[4] and that tragic fall might be related to the fact that "everybody" is subject to weak moments of exposure in which some "lurking" evil runs through us.[5]

The idea that Macbeth is "treacherous" (in the ordinary sense) is no doubt promoted by his tendency, shown from the outset, to speak in asides. The "Cumberland" aside (1.4.48–53) is a case in point here: "Stars, hide your fires! / Let not light see my black and deep desires." But two things need to be said about the incriminating asides. First, the "Cumberland" aside, as the only really "evil" one, is almost certainly an interpolation—as Granville-Barker, Fleay, and others have observed (KM, 25).[6] I suspect that this interpolation was introduced by someone with precisely the kind of attitude exemplified by Stoll and Rümelin above: that Shakespearean psychology had to be "improved" (indeed introduced!) so that tragic intentionality could be "made clear." Second, the hero's tendency to speak in asides is not necessarily a social event, denoting undercover action and withdrawal, but a technical necessity: Shakespeare wants to display a transition toward introversion, and the only way of giving the audience access to this introversion is to use asides and soliloquies.

My own view is this: that Macbeth never has had the intention to murder Duncan, and that *throughout the play he never has any such intention*. His intention is not only absent, it is structurally absent.

Absence, generally, is structural in *Macbeth*; and absent intentionality is the specific form that tragic crisis gives to this general absence. I cannot really see how the play as a whole can function

The Assassination of Intentionality

in its specifically Shakespearean form of suggestion without there being a (conscious or unconscious) recognition of this peculiar organization.

In a sense—and this is what is truly terrifying in *Macbeth*—there is simply nothing of the murderer in the hero. Partly, this murderous emptiness inside the murderer can be explained in terms of constitutional weakness; one can posit a failure of nerve, of proper disposition, or even (as we have seen in Bayley's criticism) of dramatic suitability: the hero's mind is "unfitted for the role that tragedy requires of it."[7] But things can be taken much further—in a sense logically have to be taken much further. The murderous emptiness is not only the function of "weakness" but a function of strength—of an intensity of mind that is unprecedented. Tragic paralysis, in *Macbeth*, is not a merely passive event; on the contrary, it is highly active. Tragic action, while being interiorized so as to mostly take place inside the mind, does not dissipate its energies there, become mere misty sluggishness. Macbeth wrestles with a spell, and in a sense with a paralyzing one; but the paralysis affects his bodily actions and military readiness, not his mind. The spell, far from being something that drugs his intellect, is something that keenly awakens it to unprecedented acuteness and sensitivity. What this extra-lucid intellection now comes to engage with (as I shall argue in a moment) is the activity of an unthinkable watchfulness: Macbeth begins the weird process of *watching* the absence of his own intention (to murder).

Because of this Shakespearean move, the scene presencing the hallucinated dagger cannot (as Olivier and others recognized) be turned into a conventional horror scene, full of mere knee-knocking and guilt. In Olivier's performance, there was no melodramatic recoiling from the air-drawn dagger, and the soliloquy was spoken as if in dreaming. Delivering his speech as drugged whisper, Olivier managed to create a sense of total unreality. Although Macbeth appeared as a man of immense sensibility, this sensibility did not sensitize him to the murder itself but made him rather indifferent to it (indifferent to its *presence*). Sensibility was now directed toward something else. His comments after returning from the king's chamber were delivered in a strangely flat tone, signifying a lack of real self-involvement.[8] It might be argued here that Macbeth is not actually interested in murder but in the aura of absences around it, that he is not hypnotized by murder as action but by the ever-receding (non)supports in which it is embedded. Macbeth's intellect is from this viewpoint a deepening of a process identified by Margaret Ferguson in *Hamlet*: the hero's tendency to be attentive to the passive rather than the active: "Hamlet does not inquire very deeply . . . into the meaning of his action [when killing Rosencrantz and Guildenstern, etc.]. This seems odd, since he has shown himself so remarkably capable of interrogating the meaning of his *inaction*."[9] In spite of the larger inclination toward action of Macbeth, the remark remains relevant for him too—for as I will be continuing to argue, action for him tends to presence itself in terms of inaction. This fact applies to all the temporal phases: past action, present action, and future action. Thus the "dialectic" between action and inaction as it surfaces in *Hamlet* is here taken down into a deeper state of reciprocation, for here one side of the dialectic is often sensed to actually amount to its polar opposite.

The idea of Macbeth as one immersed in "ambition" seems to me to be a red herring in this general context. We are told that he is exceedingly ambitious—so ambitious, in fact, that he is prepared to commit a terrible crime against a sovereign who is politically innocent and not even an ordinary "political enemy." But while Lady Macbeth is the ambitious one, and the one trying to persuade her husband that he is her equal in this respect, Macbeth hardly ever displays political behavior that betokens ambitious thoughts. The end of the "If it were done" soliloquy is interesting from this viewpoint:

>   I have no spur
> To prick the sides of my intent, but only
> Vaulting ambition, which o'erleaps itself
> And falls on th'other—
>
> (1.7.25–29)

From the orthodox perspective the meaning is that ambition is pure cause, the only cause. There is a circle of ambition, so that ambition itself causes ambition. But if ambition is circular and solipsistic in this sense, the circularity ("Vaulting") surely refers to effect rather than cause. Ambition is circular as effect. In *Macbeth* there are in a sense *only* effects (as I shall presently argue). The ambition is "vaulting" and circular because it has no punctual source or origin; it does not originate from any empirical fact, whether of treacherous mind or political actuality. The "ambition" is ultimately empty of substance, of empirical content; and for this very reason it is nonambition. Macbeth does not say that he has "only ambition"—or only an ambition that,

The Assassination of Intentionality

sadly, happens to be vaulting. He says that he only has *vaulting* ambition. It does not overleap its target (since it has none), it "o'erleaps *itself*." It traces only the formal presence of its formal possibility. It "falls on th'other—" . . . what? Side? In any case it falls on something else, on something beyond itself, on something that has nothing to do with ambition.

I would now like to forward the first of the three main critical notions in this subsection. This is the notion that the idea of the murder is stronger for Macbeth than the murder, and that he therefore in a strange way has to perform the murder in order to murder the idea of it.

This line of reasoning presupposes certain assumptions similar to those made by John Bayley. "*Macbeth* may seem simple enough, but it is also in fact the play with the clearest and most terrifying discrepancy between inner consciousness and action."[10] This fracturing of the spirit, leading to extreme inwardization, is what I have been identifying as "metaphysical servitude". In fact Bayley at one point happens to use this very word ("servitude") in a similar fashion: Shakespeare shows us social chaos but he also shows us chaos in the mind, "its nightmare servitude to an irrevocable act."[11] My commentary would only add this single qualification: that it is not to the act that Macbeth ultimately is the slave, but to the idea of it. This difference may seem slender, "academic." But in fact the whole drama pivots on it—and it is by ignoring this very difference that criticisms tend to prematurely wreck their logic. It is clear that if the "servitude" of the tragic hero is a servitude to the idea rather than to the actual act as such, the servitude can precede the act and thus in a sense come to be viewed as causal.

There are two main ways of explaining the crucial difference between a murder/idea nexus where murder is dominant and a murder/idea nexus where idea is dominant, and I begin with a procedure that discusses this particular notion in relation to the cardinal concept of the entire play: Truth.

Those favoring the theory of ambition will no doubt point to units such as: "Glamis, and Thane of Cawdor: / The greatest is behind" (1.3.116–17) and "Two truths are told, / As happy prologues to the swelling act / Of the imperial theme" (1.3.127–29). The first of these units appears to indicate that Macbeth is now ambitiously looking forward to the remaining third of his monarchial career; but while I can agree with the fact that he certainly is looking forward, I cannot agree with the idea that he is looking forward mainly in terms of ambition. The forward-looking is engineered logically, not emotionally. If a gypsy looks in a crystal ball and tells me I win eight hundred dollars next Wednesday at seven o'clock, and that I win eight *million* dollars the following Wednesday at seven o'clock, then it is not particularly surprising that I will be looking forward with a thumping heart to that second Wednesday evening if the first Wednesday evening to my surprise brings me in exactly eight hundred dollars and exactly at seven o'clock. But what does this new thrill depend on? It depends exclusively on my quite normal ability to perform cognitive acts of simple induction. This is precisely the mechanism that Shakespeare is working with in *Macbeth:* and the brilliant point about it all is that subjectivity as causal agent in an important way can be bracketed. My hopes, just like those of Macbeth for the crown, are in a sense *not* monitored by a subjective act of will. Although we have come to desire the promised thing, the "approach" of that thing, its coming into the horizon of our ownmost view, its closeness, is not a function of desire. Instead a rather abstract and lofty mechanism of logic out there *in the world* has presenced these bewildering hopes; they are, as such, beyond my control and influence. Indeed, there can only come into action the sense of a really self-determined subjective mastery through a negation of the hopes: only by *resisting* them can I gain back the initiative that right now has slipped away into chance, weird predestination, or whatever you want to call it. "Glamis, and Thane of Cawdor: / The greatest is behind." If the lines are spoken with the gluttony of poorly concealed expectation, then Macbeth, I admit, is already implicitly a murderer and a villain, a new Richard III. But I do not think the lines should be spoken with the dark glow of intense ambition radiating from the eyes, and I do not think that *Macbeth* in any significant way recapitulates *Richard III*. The words might better be spoken in stunned, mechanical, incredulous reverie.

The idea of the "happy prologues" does not really endanger this reading, for "happy" does not necessarily at all refer to an emotion (a growing happiness inside the cogito "Macbeth") but, indeed, to "prologues." It is not happiness (as a subjective state of mind) that is at stake here, but the idea of happiness; and this idea is an ideal: happiness as the completion of the perfectly drawn metaphysical circle Glamis–Cawdor–King. The happiness lies most of all in the completion of the circle, in the happy presence to itself of the circle's possible realization. The "prologues" are happy because their identities *as* prologues are quickly being enhanced by the general turn of events.

The second way of discussing the ascendency of "idea of murder" over "murder" is to call attention to certain psychological states involving delinealized temporality and reversed causation. Macbeth, we know, suffers right from the first encounter with the sisters from a "fit"—call it a "murder fit." But this fit is not an emotion or passion in which he suddenly, like Mr. Hyde, realizes that he wants to murder; instead the fit is a state where he realizes that his identity-as-murderer is already formed "out there" in logical space. The entity Macbeth-as-murderer "exists," immediately, as a ready-made thing out there. It is premature and trivial to call this thing an "idea" or a "thought"—because Shakespeare is perhaps in the final analysis shaking our confidence in being able to state what an idea or a thought is. What is a thought? What is an idea? These questions do not simply follow the Macbeth-problematic as "interesting points" to be made about a finished dramatic experience; rather, these questions are internal to the dramatic experience as such—not as questions, but as movements charged with questioning possibility.

The "fit" that seizes Macbeth can be compared with the one that seizes many people who come to a precipice. What is interesting here is the mechanism of "original reaction" or "originary fear." It is related to what I discussed a while ago as "originary healing." The psychological mechanism only appears in humans, though certain higher apes have similar tendencies. In this type of experience, there is not *first* a perception of the abyss, *then* a fear of it, and *then* a readiness to jump off—in order, as it were, to cancel the horrible swelling of the fear. Instead there is from the outset a sense of vertigo: the very first perception of the abyss *is* the perception of one's horrible fate at its bottom. That, precisely, is what the abyss is all about: that all along it has been waiting for you there; or, to make things more gruesome and Shakespearean: that all along *you* have been waiting down there. "You." A corpse. The fallen you waits for you, just as in our play the fallen Macbeth (who already has murdered Duncan) "waits" for the not-fallen Macbeth. In a sense greets him, quite solemnly. "Hail Macbeth!" The existence of specters in such a world does not at all surprise one from this viewpoint: corpses, rising from the abyss; an absolute beyond speaking from inside the bosom of one's tightest self-presence.

This mechanism can be theorized in minute detail with reference to the hero's system of reflexes. Macbeth does not *first* feel that he might eventually want to murder Duncan and *then* see the bloody scenario in front of him and *then* finally find himself in full flight from the feeling/thought/image. This reassuring sequentiality is what afflicts Mr. Smith in the common horror story; but Macbeth is not Mr. Smith and Shakespeare is not "into" horror stories. What happens to Macbeth, instead, is that he begins with the horror/flight. He begins not with the flight from something, but just with "from": the flight-from. He does not begin with the horror of something, but just with "of": horror-of. Gradually he has to "fill in" the missing object, make it present and self-present.

> My thought, whose murther yet is but fantastical,
> Shakes so my single state of man,
> That function is smother'd in surmise,
> And nothing is, but what is not.
>
> (1.3.139–43)

Here, it is not only that the consequences of murder have not yet been fully grasped; murder is not "fantastical" merely because it is unreal and unfamiliar *as* a fully developed notion. The unit "fantastical" instead indicates that murder at this point refuses to be, precisely, "a fully developed notion." Thought, still, has not formed the idea "murder," and conversely "murder" is not yet part of thought but part of what is "fantastical." "Murder," from this viewpiont is weird ("fantastical"), and the important word sequence "thought, whose murther" (which hits the spectator as word sequence, not idea) indicates that thought itself is drawn into the dangers, risks, and unrealities of "murder," that "thought" and "murder" are coimplicative—but in a way that cannot yet (or perhaps ever) be understood.

The idea I am trying to promote, here, is that repulsion in a difficult sense is primal and originary in Macbeth; repulsion is "causal" as it is in cases of deathward anguish near the precipice. *Because* one is so frightfully repelled by the horrible abyss, one is sucked down into it. Analogously: *because* noble Macbeth is so frightfully repelled by the idea of murder, he is drawn relentlessly into it.

The important soliloquies of the opening act are all structured by this primacy of repulsion. Thus Shakespeare does not make us feel that Macbeth is a pulsional man, full of the blood-hot passion of murderous desire, and that metaphysical deliberation is some kind of hesitant latecomer, some mere process of deferral.

Instead Shakespeare makes us feel that repulsion "organizes" pulsion, that the repulsive reflex is so dominant and intense that whatever eventually gets done in the name of its opposite (in the name of murder) really in a fundamental way is structured, determined, and *limited* by that original and irremovable repulsionism.

This queer organization can be felt in the important "If it were done" soliloquy. Here, already, and under the influence of Lady Macbeth's manipulations, the hero is beginning to try to *think out his revulsion in terms of its opposite:* "real" desire to murder. But precisely because revulsion still plays the leading part—the part it remains playing for the duration of the tragedy—the soliloquy does not take Macbeth where "he"/murder would have liked it to go.

3.2 Soliloquy

> If it were done, when 'tis done, then 'twere well
> It were done quickly: if th'assassination
> Could trammel up the consequence . . .
>
> (1.7.1–3)

There is pragmatic calculation here, a man prepared to overlook transcendental issues ("jump the life to come," 1.7.7) in order to carefully consider the worldly consequences of a mean deed. So goes the common reading. And it will be supported by critics like Bertrand Evans, theorists who argue that Macbeth has no moral awareness at all, and that this soliloquy reveals the shallowness of his moral capacities.[12] We are told that Macbeth in no true way is raising moral objections to murder in this soliloquy, that his moral logic is lame and insufficient.[13] I agree entirely. But for the opposite reasons. Why is this pro-and-con soliloquy empty of moral substance? Evans says it is because Macbeth lacks moral sensibility; I say that it is because Macbeth *has* moral sensibility. The moral debate is superfluous (and thus structurally empty for Macbeth as "dialectic" or inner tug-of-war) precisely because he has absolute insight into the immorality of the deed. If Evans's notion of Macbeth as a moral idiot were true, we would have no tragedy at all. In Shakespeare's complex organization of the tragic mechanism, the very murder requires an absolute recoil as a first trigger for its later effectuation. For Evans the hero's rhetoric only indicates that the murder is assessed as being "particularly risky,"[14] and the unit "We'd jump the life to come" is identified as a "casual" pronouncement.[15] Macbeth's feeling that the murder will be blown in every eye is said to refer to the villain's fear of punishment as a consequence of universal protest.[16]

> If it were done, when 'tis done, then 'twere well
> It were done quickly: if th'assassination
> Could trammel up the consequence, and catch
> With his surcease success; that but this blow
> Might be the be-all and the end-all—here,
> But here, upon this bank and shoal of time,
> We'd jump the life to come.—But in these cases,
> We still have judgment here; that we but teach
> Bloody instructions, which, being taught, return
> To plague th'inventor: this even-handed Justice
> Commends th'ingredience of our poison'd chalice
> To our own lips.
>
> (1.7.1–12)

The trouble with distortions and simplifications of Macbeth's tragic mind is not only that the hero's subtle character gets ruined but also that we end up with a falsification and sentimentalization of the relationship between Macbeth and Lady Macbeth. Because Bertrand Evans thinks that Macbeth is a moral idiot, he also thinks that Lady Macbeth knows Macbeth in a very deep manner. Indeed, in their conjoint "understanding" of Macbeth as a moral idiot (and therefore also a pathetic coward) Evans and Lady Macbeth form a perfect pair. Their readings of the man Macbeth and of the particular nature of his inner predicament are equally acute. This "superlative wife," we are informed, reads Macbeth like a "primer."[17] His expressed reluctance to proceed with the evil plan is the function of "lame" rationalization, a pathetically "whining" set of excuses.[18] She only has to tell him the "plain truth"[19] and show him how to avoid getting caught in order to demolish his dams of resistance.[20]

Shakespeare, of course, is really doing something utterly different in this soliloquy. Murder is a completely monstrous thing for Macbeth, and the soliloquy ends up in the constatation that murder is out of the question. It may seem that this decision is a function of the foregrounding of all the nasty "consequences" of murder; yet as the end of the speech indicates, the final *sensation* has nothing to do with "consequences" but with the apprehension of a vast visionary nothingness in which the nullity of motivation and the nullity of desire are beginning to be indistinguishable.

> his virtues
> Will plead like angels, trumpet-tongu'd, against
> The deep damnation of his taking-off;
> And Pity, like a naked new-born babe,
> Striding the blast, or heaven's Cherubins, hors'd
> Upon the sightless couriers of the air,
> Shall blow the horrid deed in every eye,
> That tears shall drown the wind. —I have no spur
> To prick the sides of my intent, but only
> Vaulting ambition, which o'erleaps itself
> And falls on th'other—
> (1.7.18–28)

Although murder (and not merely its "consequences") is prominently horrible for Macbeth in the soliloquy, he permits some distant part of his mind to mechanically go through what amounts to an elaborate *hypothesis of murder*: quite simply to clarify the absurdity of the deed's possibility. The academic silliness of taking various linguistic units at their surface value quickly emerges from a consideration of "We'd jump the life to come" as it appears at the beginning of the speech (1.7.7). Far from indicating a callous readiness to obliterate the transcendental horizon, this unit merely indicates the highly provisional suppression of that idealist notion. It is obvious that instead of being a worldly pragmatist caring only for mundane consequences the hero is in deep levels of his being profoundly conscious of the transcendental dilemma. *Macbeth remains a transcendentally oriented figure throughout the play.* And, what is more, all his moments of crisis are in the final analysis monitored and organized by his intense transcendentalism—the very transcendentalism that Shakespeare troubled to clarify in his opening scenes. Indeed, none of the hero's moments of tragic crisis are adequately grasped if they are not viewed in relation to the hero's sustained idealism. Although he starts, in this soliloquy, with a lower-than-divine sphere of reference ("here, / But here"), it is eminently clear that the latter parts of the speech reveal a very strong sense of divine infringement: "The *deep damnation* of his taking-off" (1.7.20). In his misreading, Evans fails to see that rhetoric overpowers "meaning." If you look at the end of the soliloquy, with all its images of "heaven's Cherubins" and nakedly new-born Pity, it is easy to see that the generally moral and religious frame of reference is precisely what is most vivid and important in Macbeth's state of mind. Who, in this speech, is not in "deep damnation" if not Macbeth?

But if part of the soliloquy can be viewed as a function of the very moral inclination in Macbeth that certain critics refuse to acknowledge, another part is a function of a vaster mechanism that is still not fully developed but which can nevertheless be intuited at this early stage. This mechanism is perhaps best described as a form of staging. Macbeth begins a highly imaginative process of self-projection where the extravagance of image and sentiment at once flattens and deepens the sense of personal involvement. This involvement, now at one and the same time growing more shallow and more troubled, is an engagement with a "new" Macbeth, or a Macbeth on the "other side"—a person somehow possible at the farther side of "murder," behind and beyond its reality. In this staging—theatrical in an almost melodramatic manner that will not fade in subsequent scenes—it is not merely the question of nonmurderous Macbeth learning how to project himself into the cold-bloodedness of murder; rather, it is the question of quite stable Macbeth learning how to become the absence-from-Macbeth that he already to some extent is on account of prophecy and on account of the weird "original guilt" promoted in the what-is-not soliloquy.[21] The more absent Macbeth learns to become, the more does he become *present* to the self-absence that already is his odd destiny and tragedy. This process of increasingly melodramatic and forced staging can be related to Bayley's notion (discussed recently) that the hero is unfit to play his part in tragedy. Michael Goldman thinks along similar lines when he speaks of Macbeth "learning to perform" the murder, "as an actor might."[22] In psychoanalytic terms: the more one "plays" being "the murderer" (whether positively or negatively, whether "sincerely" or hypothetically), the less does one have to answer for murder personally. But the play's mechanism does not exactly parallel the Freudian notion that revulsion from murder secretly indicates murderous desire; here, rather, it is the other way around: desire, curiously enough, betokens revulsion, betokens what I have referred to as "originary revulsion" or "originary repulsion."

Two main "levels" can thus be identified in the "If it were done" soliloquy—and both of them unbalance the "stage-villain" reading forwarding this great speech as a discourse on worldly obstacles. First there is the clear view of Macbeth as a morally conscious man—a view deliberately and elaborately staged by

Shakespeare. Macbeth, searching his heart, finds that murder is *not* tolerable as a political deed or human act. But precisely because Macbeth is so obviously moral, precisely because he himself is so profoundly conscious of his own ingrained idealism, the "moral dimension" of his thought is almost automatized: he does not have to carefully think out the reasons for not murdering Duncan but instead merely has to call them into view. Indeed, we feel that part of his mind is absent from this cataloguing of moral considerations. As we have seen, there are critics who prematurely rationalize this slight absence in Macbeth from the moral issues as a "moral lack." But the lack is not a moral lack but a lack. Just that, a vacuity and minus. Macbeth listens to himself go through a routine act of logical argumentation, but what interests him is the astonishing fact that he can at all deliberate such matters in a reasoning manner. As the sense of dreamy unreality intensifies, he can fuel the absence-oriented process by permitting his sense of slipping foothold to merge with the "deep damnation" in Duncan's "taking-off." Macbeth actually himself takes off, joining those equally unreal creatures in the aerial corridors of sightless couriers and heavenly cherubim.

It is clear by now that the "If it were done" soliloquy simultaneously forwards the sense of two opposite movements—and that discourse, deconstructing the oppositionality of this (dialectical) opposition, unifies *and* separates the "two" motions in one and the "same" operation. *On the one hand* the act in which Macbeth makes "murder" more present as an imaginatively developed structure of mind is indistinguishable from his desire to explode that structure and ride recklessly away on the fantastical *improbability* of its reality. *On the other hand*, and conversely, the very negation of murder has a striking suggestion of being an imaginative effort to dig into its possible reality, to discover its possibility *as* real. The real equivocation, in summary, is not produced by the pros and cons of murder, by advantages and disadvantages, but by the fact that the collapse of dialectical oppositionality opens a "unified" sphere of precarious suggestion in which the *entire* corpus of the soliloquy can work at once for and against murder. Macbeth desires the absence of his presence to murder, but he also desires the presence of his absence from murder. From the deconstructionist viewpoint these "two" movements are (1) the same thing, and (2) not the same thing. The space "between" these two last alternatives is unthinkable, or is to be thought only in terms of unthinkability. The space "between" these two last alternatives is not a space. It cannot be intellectually "visualized"—but exists "in" (or through) discourse as a non-spatio-logical "instance."

"Present fears / Are less than horrible imaginings" (1.3.137–38). Yes. But the presence of the horrible imaginings themselves is at once a move in the reassuring direction of "present fears" *and* a move away from what can be present. It is this "double" (and yet not double) movement that I shall consistently track throughout *Macbeth*: that Macbeth in servile fashion frantically presses all entities into their reassuring presence; but that this presencing in a sense is a mock-presencing of mock-presences, since "what" is made present is somehow always already intuited as empty of (full) presence. Thus Macbeth in a sense walks into a trap (the trap of "presence"); but since he has darkly foreseen the abyssal absence in the bosom of all presence, we may be entitled to feel that his self-entrapment is partly self-organized. Macbeth rids himself of "Macbeth," paradoxically, by setting out to find him: he vaguely realizes that the prey, once caught, will vanish and thus cease to bother him.

3.3 The Daggers of Absence

"Present fears / Are less than horrible imaginings" (1.3.137–38); "It is the bloody business which informs / Thus to mine eyes" (2.1.48–49); "My strange and self-abuse / Is the initiate fear, that wants hard use" (3.4.141–42). Vainly, Macbeth will attempt to rationalize the unbalancing of presence by trying to explain it (to himself and to others) in terms of lower-order mechanisms: inexperience, guilt, and so forth. As I have pointed out, Macbeth often follows the cue of Lady Macbeth in attempting such rationalizations—and, as I also have pointed out, the critics who themselves have a vested interest in bringing down the entire play to lower-order logic inadvertently come to share the sterile "either/or-ness" of the logical Lady. Macbeth's submission to Lady Macbeth's general initiative is at its most conspicuous degree of dishonesty in the Ghost scene of act 3:

> *Lady M.* Sit, worthy friends. My Lord is often thus,
>   And hath been from his youth: pray you, keep seat;
>   The fit is momentary; upon a thought
>   He will again be well. If much you note him,

The Daggers of Absence

> You shall offend him, and extend his passion;
> Feed, and regard him not. Are you a man?
> *Macb.* Ay, and a bold one, that dare look on that
> Which might appal the Devil.
> *Lady M.*   O proper stuff!
> This is the very painting of your fear:
> This is the air-drawn dagger, which, you said,
> Led you to Duncan. O! these flaws and starts
> (Impostors to true fear), would well become
> A woman's story at a winter's fire,
> Authoris'd by her grandam. Shame itself!
> Why do you make such faces? When all's done,
> You look but on a stool.
>
> (3.4.52–67)

A moment later:

> [*Macb.*] Do not muse at me, my most worthy friends,
> I have a strange infirmity, which is nothing
> To those that know me.
>
> (3.4.84–86)

The infirmity "is nothing." That is an interesting unit. Indeed the word "in-firmity" is itself of interest, strategically placed as it is.[23] But primarily, here, the infirmity is nothing to the "worthy friends," to "those that know me." One implication of this statement is that the Macbethian "fit," as unthinkable "infirmity," is a meaningless "nothing" once translated into the world of Lady Macbeth and the "worthy friends." The fit simply does not exist there, for it is not even possible there. But the stress on the unit "know" is also significant. The fit is meaningless once translated into the world of those that "know me." This unit is related to a previous one, appearing right after the assassination:

> [*Lady M.*]   —Be not lost
> So poorly in your thoughts.
> *Macb.* To know my deed, 'twere best not know myself.
>
> (2.2.70–72)

Self-knowledge (and by implication also self-presence) is not compatible with the Macbethian condition. To *know* Macbeth is to be excluded from the dimension in which the in-firmity reigns. This situation cannot be reduced to a mere question of guilt, that he does not want to "know" about his naughty misbehavior; nor can it be reduced to a question of insanity, that the fit is loss of self-presence in the medical sense. Although both of these "explanations" are moderately relevant and operative, they do not at all cover the main thrust of the dislocation that Shakespeare is working with: Macbeth's encounter with the unthinkable, with the absolutely weird and uncanny.

Lady Macbeth's "diagnosis" of Macbeth's ailment is clearly reductive. But while she (with certain critics) is blind to the naiveté in this mechanically organized pseudodiagnosis, the hero is not. Indeed, a striking feature in his entire tragic comportment is that he is "convinced" while still remaining unconvinced. He is "convinced" that he wants to murder Duncan, "convinced" (by Lady Macbeth) that the deed will come off well, "convinced" that *present* fears will be less than horrible imaginings, "convinced" that his nerves will steady as political treachery becomes habitual, "convinced" that guilt is the cause of the hallucinated air-drawn dagger—but throughout all this conviction he remains secretly unconvinced. There is no conviction in Macbeth: and this, exactly, is what defines his metaphysical servitude. In metaphysics one is not convinced about anything; one doubts. And most of all one doubts oneself.

By being excluded, structurally, from the Macbethian fit and from the "radioactive" zone governing it through the Weird Sisters, Lady Macbeth is blind to the deconstruction of binary opposites that now unbalances presence and the possibility of presence. She thinks Macbeth ought to decide to be either sane or mad, either courageous or cowardly. Macbeth protests right in the middle of his fit that he is "a bold one" (3.4.58), and he is absolutely right—since Shakespeare, obviously, is forcing us to grasp an absolute quaking that is *not* a function of mere "fear." Her intellect remains at the level of empirical positivism: "When all's done, / You look but on a stool" (3.4.66–67).

Through the curious sex-anthropology in this play, with its inversion of sexual distributions and of patterns of gender domination, Lady Macbeth comes to assume all the obnoxious aspects of patriarchal thinking. She patronizes Macbeth, seeks to bring him back into the logical system of masculine dialectic, male dominance in the name of order: "Are you a man?" (3.4.57). But this cheap trick of trying to coax Macbeth back into dialectical heroism founders on the fact that Macbeth's masculinity is not reducible to logical masculinity, to dialectic as mastery. There is a type of masculine affirmation, or affirmative masculinity, in Macbeth that outruns Lady Macbeth, "vanishes" from her presence and possible imagination. *This* masculinity, always already in touch with the weirdly androgynous (as monitored by the sisters), is only moved by her appeals to logical common sense in the most superficial way. Lady Macbeth's tragedy is that she thinks her cheap appropriation of Macbeth in the name of "male" logic prior to the murder ("you would / Be so much more the man," 1.7.50–51) actually has a profound effect on him—actually could match the completely different influence exerted by the sisters. Again it is relevant to consider how Macbeth's tendency to be "convinced" reflects its opposite. But Lady Macbeth, dull to the *play* of opposites inside the soul of her husband, mechanically goes on dispatching her favorite medicine: the crude appeal to "maleness:" "What! quite unmann'd in folly?" (3.4.72).

Having assumed the pseudoheroic qualities of the dialectical male ("unsex me here," 1.5.41), and having turned this maleness into the *presence* of what is "masculine" ("*fill* me, from the crown to the toe, top-*full* / Of direst cruelty!", 1.5.42–43) Lady Macbeth organizes her own presence as that which must necessarily be absent from the depth-formula of the play: equivocation. As one negotiating sexual difference as a dialectical difference, she cannot in any vital sense engage with the sexual play of the drama; she can only play that play melodramatically, by means of overacting: "Great Glamis! worthy Cawdor! / Greater than both, by the all-hail hereafter! / Thy letters have transported me" (1.5.54–56).[24] There is a tonal difference between this discourse and that similar one used by the Weird Sisters to greet the hero (1.3.48–69), and while the latter greeting casts a spell over him, the former almost has the effect of putting him off. Lady Macbeth speaks univocally, pointing to the target of what will need to be present, pointing to self-presence in ideal presence; but Macbeth is already attuned to a quite different appeal—so that his wife's effusions are slightly boring, almost embarrassing. When he finally agrees to move along with her empirical project (which she wants to make present *immediately*), he is much like a husband who agrees to go on a holiday with his wife while secretly realizing that he is not going to enjoy himself and that he has not really swallowed the "convincing" arguments for the enterprise. Ironically, by having prematurely abandoned her femininity in a simplistic fashion, Lady Macbeth removes herself from participation in the "woman's story" that she derides: "O! these flaws and starts . . . would well become / A woman's story" (3.4.62–64). The play *Macbeth*, as equivocal discourse promoted by the sisters, as undialectical action evading patriarchal logocentricity, is in a certain sense exactly that: "A woman's story." Lady Macbeth not only fails to be able to actively participate in this story/play, not only becomes more and more disconnected from its principles and possibilities; she also is shown to be permanently falling away from a dialogue with its protagonist, from any vital proximity to him.

"O proper stuff! / This is the very painting of your fear: / This is the air-drawn dagger, which, you said, / Led you to Duncan" (3.4.59–62). The connection that Lady Macbeth establishes here is important: not only does Shakespeare make us feel that the fit in the banquet scene (3.4) is related to the dagger-fit (2.1); he also makes us feel that Lady Macbeth's radical uncomprehension of the entity "fit" antecedes the murder as such: she is not only out of touch with a tormented post-murder Macbeth full of "remorse," but also out of touch with the very Macbeth who saw murder as such presence itself in terms of its opposite (repulsion-from-murder) and absence (absurdity).

Significantly, it is Lady Macbeth who interrupts Macbeth (at the end of his "If it were done" soliloquy) at the very moment when he has realized that his attraction to murder is in an originary way organized by its unattractiveness, that he *thinks* about murder (more and more obsessively) because his purity of mind utterly forbids such thinking. But when Macbeth has come to the consolidation of the idea that "murder" is a cognitive circuit in his mind, no more than a self-determined nothingness, Lady Macbeth interrupts this line of thought and immediately turns things down into the lower-order levels of relevance: getting the business done, moving along the path of ambition without further inhibitions. The "surrender" of Macbeth to her acts of "persuasion" is less interesting here—on account of the emptiness of the surrender, its quality of theatrical staging—than the mind of the hero as, *quite unaffected by the token-commitment to "murder,"* it goes on exploring the future in terms of the absence of murder/future/commitment.

The soliloquy on the air-drawn dagger is now obviously a speech of great importance. The dagger makes its entry as an utter stranger ("Is this a dagger, which I see before me, / The handle toward my hand?" 2.1.33–34)—and, most strange of all, as an absolute stranger also to the business of murder!

So absent indeed is Macbeth from murder as volitional enterprise that he requires that pointing dagger as an indispensable connective link that is to attach him to the possibility of murder.

The Daggers of Absence

He needs the dagger to connect him with the dagger; he needs the *pointing* of the dagger to feel its point. I am saying, in other words, that the hallucinated (and therefore "absent") dagger presents Macbeth with the intention that he should have had.

The dagger is a dagger of intentionality. It points to the chamber; it signals the direction of an intention. But the intention is not in the subject, not in Macbeth. It is in the dagger, in the not-Macbeth. *The dagger becomes present to Macbeth as Macbeth's absence from it.*

> Is this a dagger, which I see before me,
> The handle toward my hand? Come, let me clutch thee:—
> *I have thee not,* and yet I see thee still.
> Art thou not, fatal vision, sensible
> To feeling, as to sight? or art thou but
> A dagger of the mind, a false creation,
> Proceeding from the heat-oppressed brain?
> I see thee yet, in form as palpable
> As this which now I draw.
> Thou marshall'st me the way that I *was* going;
> And such an instrument I *was to* use.—
> Mine eyes are made the fools o'th'other senses,
> Or else worth all the rest: I see thee still;
> And on thy blade, and dudgeon, gouts of blood,
> Which was not so before.
>
> (2.1.33–47)

The contradictory structure is obvious. On the one hand, Macbeth already knew the way he was to go ("the way that I was going"); on the other hand, the dagger has to point out this way. The dagger is a supplement. The marshalling is at once a supplementary necessity and an absurd surplus, it is at once purely dispensable and purely indispensable.[25] On the one hand, the supplementary dagger (in hallucination) gives Macbeth the murder weapon he requires for murder's possible presence; on the other hand, he already has at his immediate disposal this very dagger that is to bridge the gap between nonmurder and murder—indeed he draws it and places it beside its visionary partner.

Curiously, but not insignificantly, we are made to feel that the absent dagger is more present than the present one. The one that Macbeth draws for comparative contemplation is a kind of inert equivalent that nevertheless is no equivalent: it lacks the power of its visible/invisible copy. The secondary (hallucinated) dagger acquires a hyperontological primacy, and the prime weapon itself—the one to be used in the butchery—remains behind in a world of uninteresting secondariness, drained of drama, equivocation, and tragic vision.

It seems to me, however, that the absent dagger (of hallucination) slides *into* the finite, real, and material dagger that Macbeth is ready to use. In this way, the *absence of the dagger* is carried over into the gesture of murdering itself: so that in an important sense that murder is never truly actual, never truly present. The air-drawn dagger fills with alien intention a Macbethian intentionality that is at bottom structurally empty; but conversely, the very unreality of that hallucinated weapon *preserves* murder as something nonempirical and "distant" in Macbeth's inner drama. It is interesting from this viewpoint that Macbeth "forgets" to leave the daggers he uses near the corpse (much to the surprise and frustration of his wife, 2.2.47). It is indeed as if the act of being hypnotized by "the dagger" continues to be operative even when "real" weapons have replaced "air-drawn" ones. Macbeth trembles at the sight of his bloody hands and bloody daggers (a fact suggesting mere retreat and repulsion); but as I shall argue later, there is a process of attraction beneath the fear—which is precisely why there is more than "fear" in motion here. Macbeth *sticks* to blood/hands/daggers, and he does so, I suggest, because these things maintain the work of absence (from murder) that the air-drawn dagger (as something absent) has inaugurated.

From an orthodox viewpoint, the sudden appearance of "gouts of blood" on the dagger (2.1.46) seems to call forth the horrible future of the impending deed: the knife's transformation from spotless innocence to gory sacrilege. But in my view a more suggestive movement is also being dramatized: the further filling of empty and absent intention with the "stuff" of its required order. Just as the hallucinated dagger provided Macbeth's absence-from-murder with a modicum of suggestive presence-to-murder, so the reddening of the abstractly dangling blade signals a deepening of a presentation of intentionality as such. Macbeth *sees* his intention gather into intention—into sanguine reality of purpose—but this very hardening, coloring, and materializing takes place outside him, in a sphere not quite inhabited by any self-present presence.

In summary, then, the dagger shows Macbeth the way, but it is of course Macbeth who is showing Macbeth the way. The "first" Macbeth, as heroic master committed to idealistic "struggle to death" for transcendental recognition, has an absence of intent to murder Duncan; the "second" Macbeth, the metaphysically servile cogito, has a full and self-present intent to murder. But this second, servile Macbeth, *who is self-present and fully intentional,* is quite absent, has to be "created": has, indeed, to be dramatized and staged. Hence the dream of that self-presence and full intentionality will remain punctured by the spacings of dramaturgy and creative nonpresence. Macbeth seeking to clutch the dagger is Macbeth seeking to clutch Macbeth, desiring the palpable presence of his own self-present thought, some creature who could be the absolute monarch of his own intentionality. Yet as I have tried to show in this analysis, this act of wanting to presence a self-present cogito carries with it *traces* of the originary resistance to this process. I see the "air-drawn dagger" as such a "trace."[26] By pointing, it traces into the future what full presence has lacked from the outset.

4

4.1 Horror and Pseudohorror

It is commonly said that Macbeth's sensibility declines during the course of the tragic action. The demoralizing consequences of murder amount to a brutalization of his formerly "poetic" hypersensibility. This mechanical schematization of what happens in the play seems to me to be reductive. The hypersensibility and the brutality do not form a binary opposition, and the hero does not slip from the one to the other. On the contrary, these two things are "sides" of a single force, and there is no point or place in *Macbeth* where the dramatic space ceases to be negotiated by the interaction of these two sides. At any moment, Macbeth can switch from one to the other—and this rule holds for the entire duration of the play. Subjectively speaking this means that absolute numbness and absolute pain are at once "opposite" and "identical" things for the hero. The actor, intuiting this strange reciprocation, can move freely from one extreme (brutality) to the other (sensitivity), because each extreme is always immediately at hand in the presence of its polar antagonist; yet this crossing of the superfine dividing line can never become uncontrolled or careless—it must itself demand of the actor all the resources of his creative nervousness, the complete straining of his life-nerve. Following accurately the subtle modulations of Shakespeare's ever-changing language, he will come to sense the spectral demarcation lines where the presence of absence suddenly turns into the absence of presence, those tracelines of stretched thought where zero-distinctions fold the world over into its frightening opposite.

I have said earlier that Macbeth in a sense comes to perform the murder in order to murder the idea of murder: the act, as something that in theory can be *present*, is less haunting than the idea of murder. Or so it seems. An absurd deed looms as a possible way of arresting a strange type of anguish. And anguish, as Sartre argued in *Being and Nothingness*, is not simply a deepening of fear, but a fear *of* fear. Fear is fear. But anguish is fear-of-fear.

> Vertigo is anguish to the extent that I am afraid not of falling over the precipice, but of throwing myself over. A situation provokes *fear* if there is a possibility of my life being changed from without; my being provokes *anguish* to the extent that I distrust myself and my own reactions in that situation. The artillery preparation which precedes the attack can provoke *fear* in the soldier who undergoes the bombardment, but *anguish* is born in him when he tries to foresee the conduct with which he will face the bombardment, when he asks himself if he is going to be able to "hold up." Similarly the recruit who reports for active duty at the beginning of the war can in some instances be afraid of death, but more often he is "afraid of being afraid."[1]

The Weird Sisters, I have been arguing, affirm equivocation—and they "strike" Macbeth, producing his characteristic fit, by presencing an equivocation which he cannot master but which he immediately wants to master. Equivocation is not only something that the promise of (imperial) Truth brings along, but also something that from the outset comes to define the "shape" of (the idea of) murder. This idea is charged with indefinition, since it is promoted—rather than restricted—by the act of resisting it. The more Macbeth fights against murder/horror, the more he increases it. This mechanism is structurally internal to "murder" (and therefore a permanent aspect of it), since murder/horror "originated" in an act of flight from it: however far we move backward into the causal past of Macbeth's intellect, we still fail to discover a point where murder is not, already, the resistance to it, the panic and flight that hurries away from "it." This situation, it may be objected, is extravagantly queer; indeed the very mechanism is quite odd, almost unthinkable. But this is precisely the problem: this is what produces the remarkable "fit" in the hero, the absolute upheaval in his mind. In order to free himself from this unsettling oddness, Macbeth eventually decides to commit a terrible deed. This deed, in itself full of horror and indeterminacy, promises to bring a finite form of horror to replace a more general, almost universal, one. In short, the murder is done in order to achieve release: release from equivocation. This project, of course, fails. But the absolute horror that arrives after the completion of the murder is not so much produced by the ethical monstrosity of the act as by the much more frightening fact that

Macbeth intuits the endlessness of the quest for the arresting of indecision. Equivocation/horror/anguish returns. He can never kill *it*. The more he seeks to end indeterminacy by a determinate act, a furious affirmation of the determinate, the more indeterminacy hits back. In today's terms: Macbeth becomes increasingly aware of the futility of the quest for full presence.

In this chapter I will be examining the growth of servile anguish in the middle portions of *Macbeth*; but I will also be reviewing a quite different ontodramatic movement: the hero's tendency to affirm horror. This secondary process is a mechanism that is triggered by the peculiar "logic" of weird presencing (already discussed): fighting horror increases it. If this mechanism is valid, affirming horror, conversely, must decrease it. This notion can be thought in terms of the Sartrean model discussed a moment ago: fear of fear. If anguish is fear-of-fear, then the affirmation of pure fear (rather than fear-of-fear, rather than "double" fear) ought to diminish anguish. One can move from anguish to mere fear by trying to find something that univocally is a question of fear. This sliding can be reformulated in terms of presence. Anguish is a fear of something *not* present; it is a fear of something that is distant, and which, in that distance, is present to "another" fear. The soldier anguished by the possibility of bombardment is shifted from anguish to (mere) fear, when he himself moves from a place where bombardment is imaginary and nonpresent to a place where it is real and present.

Now I would like to argue that Macbeth on several important occasions is shown to be someone deliberately trying to make horror *present:* in a sense following the notion that "[p]resent fears / Are less than horrible imaginings" (1.3.137–38). In this desire to *presence* the horrible, to make horror *a* presence, Macbeth comes to promote something that is quite different from the horror imposed on him by the Weird Sisters and by equivocation—something I will call "pseudohorror." Absolute horror in *Macbeth* shapes itself as some disturbing displacement, deferral, or disfiguration of presence; pseudohorror, by contrast, is a present horror that is reassuring on account of its presence: it does not equivocate but is *there,* straight in front of you, complete in all its visible fulness. Whereas Macbeth fights weird horror, running away from it, he affirms pseudohorror. As he stages this lesser type of horror, he creates a "theatrical horror," a horror orgy that is close to an entertainment, a "show" where horror, as that which can now be made present, is the *showing* of the horrific. The Murther/Tarquin scene is a case in point:

> Now o'er the one half-world
> Nature seems dead, and wicked dreams abuse
> The curtain'd sleep: Witchcraft celebrates
> Pale Hecate's off'rings; and wither'd Murther,
> Alarum'd by his sentinel, the wolf,
> Whose howl's his watch, thus with his stealthy pace,
> With Tarquin's ravishing strides, towards his design
> Moves like a ghost—Thou sure and firm-set earth,
> Hear not my steps, which way they walk, for fear
> Thy very stones prate of my where-about,
> And take the *present* horror from the time,
> Which now suits with it.
>
> (2.1.49–60)

It may be argued and felt, of course, that Macbeth is affirming absence here: indeed he almost designates himself as the "ghost" (2.1.56) that moves through the fantastical unrealities of the visionary landscape. Yet I would argue that the movement toward presence is even stronger; for while the vision is one of absence, self-absence, and unreality, the self is still appropriating that dreamy nothingness in the name of itself, in the name of a cogito desiring to presence otherness: all of it. His fear that the "very stones" may prate betokens no mere fear of waking others, of waking the world, of waking God himself—but rather the fear of waking himself. If Macbeth woke from his trance, *he would be horrified by the lack of horror.* He needs horror to lack it: nothing must "take the present horror from the time, / Which now suits with it." Because horror suits horror, fits the mould of its best possibility, is fully present to itself as the identity of itself, it is masterable. Thus, as pseudohorror, it is not horror. In fact, as horror, it is almost an ecstatic enjoyment of the lack of horror.

This relation between horror and mastery can also be studied in Macbeth's encounter with the various apparitions staged by the sisters. In the quasi-social atmosphere that is ironically established, Macbeth acquires a neurotically undecided master-versus-servant position. Each occult figure represents the illusion of perfected Truth that Macbeth is aiming at, and hence Macbeth can command it in his own name (which by now is "identical" with Truth); but since he has intuited the evasive doubleness of "Truth," the masterful commanding is never free from its implicit opposite, an absolutely servile dread. Macbeth is now (act 4) furiously arrogant as well as pathetically submissive, contemptuously impetuous as well as respectfully humble, commandingly straightforward as well as ceremoniously cautious.

We feel that Macbeth, momentarily director as well as spectator, is directing the showing of his human futility—in itself the worst of horrors. We feel that he is hastening the speed of a showing and that he intuits the tragic "plot" behind the theater of his imperial eagerness in the very stage productions that forward the hopes of eluding that tragic plot.

> *A show of eight Kings, the last with a glass in his hand; Banquo following.*
> Macb. Thou are too like the spirit of Banquo: down!
>   Thy crown does sear mine eye-balls: —and thy hair,
>   Thou other gold-bound brow, is like the first:—
>   A third is like the former: —filthy hags!
>   Why do you show me this?—A fourth?—Start, eyes!
>   What! will the line stretch out to th'crack of doom?
>   Another yet?—A seventh?—I'll see no more:—
>   And yet the eighth appears, who bears a glass,
>   Which shows me many more;
>
> (4.1.112–20)

The question that now should be asked is this: What *is* the entity "horrified Macbeth?" I think this question has to be asked, since the tension between horror and pseudohorror appears to create at least *two* types of "horrified Macbeth." This ability of horror to divide Macbeth, or in fact of Macbeth to divide horror, may be intuited by considering some expressions of horror here in act 4: "filthy hags!", "Start, eyes!", "Horrible sight!" (4.1.115–22). These moments certainly cannot be called moments of faked horror; yet they are surely not of the same quality as those evident in the original moments of the terrible "fit." There seems to me to be a touch of gloating in Macbeth's horrible "surprises"—so that he vaguely is thrilled by the quiver of his own terror, as children are in the dreadful moments at the amusement park. It may be meaningful, in other words, to think of a distinction between agony and pseudo-agony. This latter agony is not an empty agony but one that falls away from the worst agony by being vaguely accessible through the mastery of (its) presence.

If weird horror is "deep" and if theatrical horror is "shallow," we might say that Macbeth encounters deeper waters when he moves into absence through reverie and that he slips into more shallow waters when he concentrates on some manifestly visible horror that is within the actual reach of his perceptions. It is his reveries that his wife really dreads: "A foolish thought to say a sorry sight" (2.2.21); "Consider it not so deeply" (2.2.29); "These deeds must not be thought . . ." (2.2.32); "Be not lost / So poorly in your thoughts" (2.2.70–71). Thought as such is dangerous here, for by abandoning its moorings in what is (or could be) present, it reels off into the uncontrollable. Perception, by contrast, introduces *some* token of stabilizing presence. And when reckless thought begins to focus some such unit of perception, one can begin the process of steering thought back into the arena of what can be made present and self-present. It is here, as I have stated, that the movement from horror to pseudohorror takes its beginning. After the deed, the hero says he is "afraid to think what [he has] done" (2.2.50). But is he? Why the elaborate savoring of the details of the deed?

> What hands are here? Ha! they pluck out mine eyes.
> Will all great Neptune's ocean wash this blood
> Clean from my hand? No, this my hand will rather
> The multitudinous seas incarnadine,
> Making the green one red.
>
> (2.2.58–62)

Does a man who really fears the sight of his own murderous hands look at them at length in this manner? On one level of suggestion, there is obviously a negation of the possibility of purification, of cleansing through great Neptune's ocean; yet the very act of picturing that liquid infinity of the oceanic expanse somehow manages to lift the hero to a level of poeticized intellection where some purification of the mind actually takes place. One feels, almost, that he takes a sensual delight in the elongated ideality of "multitudinous" and "incarnadine," just as a hypochondriac enjoys describing the exquisite details of his particular ailment. The metamorphosis that turns the green sea into a red sea comes upon the scene with a kind of platonic finality—with the precision and necessity of ideal metaphysical forms finding one another in beautifully symmetrical patterns of reciprocating destiny. The aesthetics of presence is here the full presence of what is aesthetic.

It might be objected, predictably, that we are overlooking the mighty question of "conventions." Shakespeare is an "Elizabethan," a man of "the theater," and one working with "dramatic conventions": Macbeth's self-commentary is not in all its space a subjective act of self-analysis, for it belongs to the conditions of premodern theater that dramatic figures speak in huge digressions about their peculiar ongoing predicaments. But while this in a sense is true, it is also important to recognize that Shakespearean speech acts are not reducible to the conventions that they may be activating. In Shakespearean discourse, precisely, no firm line can be drawn between "convention" and "subjectivity." Moreover, the *development* of dramatic techniques effectuated by Shakespeare entails (among other things) a gradual "subjectivization" of theatrical discourse: so that what subjectivity does not appropriate becomes more and more marginal.[2]

It is fairly pointless, in this type of context, to try to clarify anything significant by vaguely referring to Macbeth's "imagination." What is imagination in Macbeth? What is imagination in *Macbeth*? And most important of all: What is imagination? All of Macbeth's soliloquies can be discussed and rationalized in terms of the empty formula "imagination," and the problem is not only that it is impossible to distinguish Shakespeare's imagination from Macbeth's, but that Macbeth is overimaginative in two entirely opposite ways. Depth-horror, as originally promoted through the Weird Sisters, is a function of "imagination"; but so is pseudohorror. Because of this opposition between imagination and imagination (paralleling the opposition between horror and horror), it is sometimes possible to trace acts of elaborate imaginative projection where the hero can be said to be negating imagination: where he is using an imaginative force that he can control and master (in the name of its *presence*) to oust an imaginative force that he cannot control and master—but that instead keeps striking him from the deadly "outside" of uncanny equivocation and deferred Truth. Imitating the self-infinitizing momentum of horror and its image-ination, Macbeth places himself in the nuclear site where the weird now can be monitored from its center. This is an act of fraudulence (and therefore doomed to failure in the long run) since the weird, precisely, is what lacks a center. But as Macbeth now seeks to appropriate the weird, limiting and finitizing its reach, he not only centers it, not only gives it a center—he also makes himself into this center, centers horror on himself. In this way horror becomes self-centered in two ways: self-centered because it is centered on a self (on Macbeth), and self-centered because it is centered on itself (on its own being as possible self-presence). Horror, however, cannot have center, being, presence, or self-presence.

We can observe this attempt to center and centralize horror in the speeches where the centrifugal force of the horrific is mastered by the feeling of a nuclear eye placed inside a system of circles. Here the self is a pointlike unit that *possesses* the outward-bound motion of horror toward dispossession and loss. This sensation is foreshadowed at the end of the "If it were done" speech, where we felt the explosion toward the celestial horizon of angelic images. Similarly, in the Murther/Tarquin speech, we could feel how Macbeth gradually extended the mastered sensation of *his* horror by progressively moving out into the concentric circles of his imagination: from Murther, to his wolf, to the wolf's howl, and so forth. The ululation spreads like rings of imaginative thought, reverberating, as the resounding *plenitude* of fully self-present horror, in the being of "murder." As the concentric circles widen, we feel that Macbeth is part and parcel of that widening, that he "counts" the receding horizons of fright, thus making it internal to the economy of his ownmost willingness to become horrified. Similarly, in the speech on great Neptune's ocean (just reviewed), the expansion implemented by the sense of dilution ("multitudinous seas incarnadine," 2.2.61) creates a sense of absolute loss, but Macbeth's appropriation of this loss through theatrical gloating turns it into a loss that is momentarily experienced as "inside" him, as part of his "poetic" and theatrical egocentricity. A finite amount of blood (on his hands) spreads like a magic solution throughout the entire realm of the aqueous; yet this aqueous expanse, already, is Macbeth's own imperial spirit. *His* imagination, momentarily, keeps pace with that of the equivocating forces attacking him.

I am saying, at this stage, that the act of centering horror and turning it into a presence is soothing. Imaginative horror, then, is the source of pain but also of the cancellation of pain. This ability of imaginative horror to become an anesthetic can be observed in another speech where horror is centered. The anesthesia is here literally a question of putting to sleep:

> *Macb.* Methought, I heard a voice cry, "Sleep no more!
>   Macbeth does murther Sleep," —the innocent Sleep;
>   Sleep, that knits up the ravell'd sleave of care,
>   The death of each day's life, sore labour's bath,
>   Balm of hurt minds, great Nature's second course,
>   Chief nourisher in life's feast:—
> *Lady M.*   What do you mean?
> *Macb.* Still it cried, "Sleep no more!" to all the house:
>   "Glamis hath murther'd Sleep, and therefore Cawdor
>   Shall sleep no more, Macbeth shall sleep no more!"
> *Lady M.* Who was it that thus cried?
>   (2.2.34–43)

The narcotic drive is quite obvious, climaxing in "Balm of hurt minds." Macbeth is certainly in pain here, and I grant that he also allows this agony to magnify into cosmic torment; yet, and at the same time, there is an even more important movement away from pain, so that discourse itself is balm for the hurt mind. There is something hypnotically soporific and somnambulistic about the entire speech. Its rhythm marks the growth of an imaginative territory that comes to encompass and master the very pain that seems to shatter it. Through "Sleep," which in itself almost becomes a metaphysical conceit, Macbeth quickly comes to *possess* the void left by murder—filling it now with imaginative substance. Sleep suggests the innocence of sleep, the recurrence of sleep, the sanity and healthiness of sleep, the mock-finality of sleep, the indispensability of sleep. In the end we have come for a moment to feel—with the hero—that sleep is the most essential thing in the entire world. This notion is in itself a palliative. A moment ago sleep was a blissful interlude, or happy blank; but then it became a pleasure, a delight; now it is the very center of life, "great Nature's second course, / Chief nourisher in life's feast." Macbeth himself feeds from this feast, himself is nourished by the "chief nourisher."

This type of pseudohorror may be compared with the real depth-horror that strikes Macbeth in the encounter with Banquo's ghost in act 3. I will be discussing the ontodramatic context for this Ghost scene in the next subsection, but by way of anticipation a few remarks may be forwarded at this point.

A while ago I offered two main alternatives: (1) fighting horror increases it; (2) affirming horror decreases it. (1) Weird horror is produced by the act of trying to resist its suggestion; (2) pseudohorror amounts to a reversal of this movement: instead of resisting horrid suggestion and getting drawn further into its hellishness, one dives straight into the suggestiveness, engaging immediately with it as if it were or could be (a) presence. In the Ghost scene Macbeth definitely behaves according to the first model. In fact he faces the Ghost as he first faced the unthinkability of murder: in terms of what I have called "originary reduction." The reduction, as I have said, is "originary," for we cannot ever find a thing-in-itself (murder, weird apparition) which precedes—or *could* precede—the reduction of "it." Resistance is originary, or co-originary. The thing and its reduction are co-originary, are "equally" original. In fact "they" cannot be separated. From the outset, the "thing" and the "resistance-of-thing" are the same: the same thing but also the same resistance.

It is this circumstance, often overlooked nowadays on the stage, that causes fury to be a *necessary* aspect of the presencing of the Ghost:[3] for the fury, in the spectral encounter, is precisely the originary resistance to it.

Macbeth calls the Ghost "horrible shadow" and "unreal mock'ry" (3.4.105–6), and these units reveal some consciousness of illusion or illusory being: the spectral figure mocks reality by appearing as its shadow. The hero is in other words conscious of a merely "phenomenal" presence and its lack of objective substance. This notion at first looks comforting. The only problem, though, is that the reality of a ghost *is* its unreality. Calling it "unreal" thus in fact is a reductive gesture that ultimately is productive. The reduction of the Ghost is internal to its production, *and this process may be backtracked to a moment that precedes the actual first appearing of the Ghost*. The "origin" of the Ghost *is* its reduction. The Ghost emanates from "originary reduction"—*its* originary reduction.

Generally speaking, it is difficult to see how the play *Macbeth* can at all be grasped as a work of genius without some intuition of this Shakespearean breakdown of the binary opposition production-versus-reduction. What the (non)structure of the play paradoxically states is that these opposites, while remaining opposites, *are* one another—and immediately.

Farnham has remarked that the accusation flung at the Ghost ("Thou hast no speculation in those eyes," 3.4.94) is a one-way gesture that uniformly serves to restore self-presence.[4] But whereas Lady Macbeth—as after the murder—clearly is promoting such self-restoration, Macbeth is engaged in a more complex activity. The very emphasis on the nonspeculative quality of those spectral eyes, far from diminishing the ghostliness of the Ghost, only increases it. Absencing the Ghost presences the Ghost. On the one hand it is soothing to know that those eyes are incapable of sight and human intellection; on the other hand that very nonsight-in-sight is what makes the Ghost a Ghost.

> Avaunt! and quit my sight! let the earth hide thee!
> Thy bones are marrowless, thy blood is cold;
> Thou hast no speculation in those eyes,
> Which thou dost glare with.
>
> (3.4.92–95)

This remark, it may be added, is also poignant in the sense that Macbeth's eyes are the victims of the very inadequacy and lack that they are identifying: Macbeth, in observing the observatory activity of the Ghost as pseudo-observation, is himself the very paragon of pseudo-observation. He is seeing something that has faulty vision; but the faulty vision that he sees ("Thou has no speculation") is the faulty vision that is seeing (Macbethian "vision" as hallucination rather than perception).

4.2   The Active Phase of Servitude

In order to understand the Ghost scene of 3.4 it is necessary to grasp the hero's passage from passive servitude to active servitude. I begin a review of that transition—which is Shakespeare's main concern in the middle portions of *Macbeth*—by defining what I have for a long while been tentatively referring to as the question of "Truth."

It will be remembered that I supported John Bayley's view that the cataclysmic transformation engineered in the hero involves an inwardization of all his faculties: Macbeth becomes all mind. This interiorization is conspicuous in other Shakespearean heroes, notably Hamlet, but nowhere is it as pivotal as in *Macbeth*. Act 1 shows us an "external" Macbeth, the rest of the play an "internal" one. Also, it will be recalled, I supported Bayley's view that Macbeth is not guided by desire for power: "He has no appetite for mastery or for evil."[5] This lack of genuine involvement with power can be sensed also in the dealings with Lady Macbeth: he is prepared to let her have her way quite often—not because he could not dominate her if he wished, but because he simply is not centered in the mainly empirical sphere of presence where she acts and thinks.[6]

I suggest again, then, that the imperial Crown does not chiefly promise power; it promises Truth. And by Truth here I do not mean some abstract thesis, but truth as something that anchors man to his own image of an absolutely ownmost essence: truth as presence in self-presence. As absolute self-presence, the presence of truth (i.e., Truth) comes to oppose play—and insofar as he comes to yearn for truth as pure self-presence, Macbeth indeed comes to oppose play, oppose play according to the antitheatrical formula that we have already discussed at some length. Man, Derrida once famously stated, is the being who "has dreamed of full presence, the reassuring foundation, the origin and the end of play" (*WD*, 292).[7] This formula could sum up Macbeth's entire status in the middle portions of the drama.

When servile, Macbeth is willing to play a part in the play, if the play comes full circle according to the logic of Truth as self-presence (Glamis/Cawdor/King); but Macbeth is not willing to play a part that involves play as playing: as risking the truth-totality that has been promised. On the contrary, he will be playing against that risk. Put differently: he will not be playing. He will now be watching the play, keeping an eye on its plot: and he will always be ready to butcher the script in order to ensure a proper and satisfying outcome.

"All hail, Macbeth! that *shalt* be King hereafter" (1.3.50). It looks like a promise but in a cunning way is a threat. The Weird Sisters force Macbeth to *want to be*. There is a touch of sadism in this solicitation of the hero, for while the sisters forward presence as a promised ideal, they themselves represent equivocation and "know" that equivocation in the long run will wreck presence. They presence Meaning/Truth/Self/Presence as a possible ideal that could be free from the contingent vicissitudes and violent equivocations of man's temporal predicament as a creature torn by irreducible contradiction. Although (in an act of cunning reserve) they presence Truth in the *form* of contradiction and enigma, the meaning of its promise is posited as that which runs free from risk, contradiction, and uncertainty. Macbeth gets the feeling that the absolute presencing of his name/being/presence amounts to the achievement of invulnerability. Yet the secret vulnerability imbedded in this absolute self-certitude is slyly adumbrated from the outset through the orphic quality of weird discourse. The true tragic strain on Macbeth, then, is not simply the political and moral one imposed by the notion of assassination but the one imposed by the originary tension between a world of cosmic contradiction and a world of cosmic noncontradiction: between play and Truth. The world of noncontradiction, the more "true" one, by absorbing into its essence the name and presence of "Macbeth," becomes also a world of non*self*-contradiction. Because Macbeth's ideal world in this way becomes a logically idealized entity rather than a mere projection of subjective desire his ideal balance becomes metaphysical rather than empirical. Its operative reality and horizon of meaning become a function of certainty: certainty of truth and certainty of self. In fact the certainty now *is* the coinciding of these things, truth and self—just as truth now *is* the perfect coinciding of certainty and self, just as self now *is* the perfect identity of truth and certainty.

As I have remarked, following a host of critics, the Shakespearean focus on the self as self-defining entity, referring itself exclusively to truth rather than to social order and divine hierarchy, is a historically poignant gesture. The monadic cogito that Descartes soon was to postulate was already "in the air" in Shakespeare's times, preparing the way for the modern sense of atomic privacy and social individualism. The monarch, and especially the absolute monarch, by centering many of the strains and pressures that were accumulating around the new concept of selfhood, was at one and the same time the pure negation of the possibility of free individualism and a curiously elevated prototype for its egocentric realization. The dramatic relevance of this monarchial egotism is not diminished by the fact that the mind of Renaissance man very much was a public theater, just as the monarch's mind was a court theater: James is caught in a world of all-pervasive theatricality, a world where everybody is onstage[8]—but now post-Renaissance man, defiant of all quasi-medieval inhibitions, is already obscurely staged in that theater.

In the epoch of high-metaphysics, fully released by Cartesianism, the subject becomes a center around which all other entities in the world revolve as "objects." Man becomes in Heidegger's words "the representer of all representing, and therewith the realm of all representedness, and hence of all certainty, and truth."[9] Man begins to assess himself not according to his achievements, but simply because he is of consequence as an individual. Charles Guignon summarizes the cataclysmic transformation of "man":

> With the rise of this subjective individualism, a transformed understanding of what is at stake in being human appears on the scene. The true self is to be found by a kind of inner concentration which draws together the different strands of the subjective life. There is a growing concern with being "integrated," "centered," "fulfilled" . . . Since I am self-defining and autonomous . . . religion, occupation, and national origins are appendages or decorations that may be cast off ["Golden opinions . . . Not cast aside so soon," 1.7.33–35] in my search for integration. My ethical and social relations are contrived, conventional devices superimposed over me through the demands of expedience. . . . When the [new, servile, metaphysical] subject is interpreted as the ground of all beings, Being comes to be understood ["be the be-all and the end-all—here, / But here," 1.7.5–6] as something merely at man's disposal. . . . We become quiescent and complacent in our assurance that with [technical manipulation of the external world] we will achieve full mastery and dominance ["sovereign sway and masterdom," 1.5.70] over all beings. . . . [W]e

can gain final control over Being by making it fully explicit and intelligible ["burn'd in desire to question . . ."].[10]

In the opening scenes, dread comes as a stranger to Macbeth. This is the passive phase of servitude, a time when the "object" of dread is unknown, a time when dread is not endangering anything that so far has been self-consciously posited as its opposite. In the active phase of servitude, by contrast, the self seeks actively to avoid the dread and the "objects" that trigger it. When dread now comes, as for instance in the form of Banquo's ghost, it no longer comes as a stranger but precisely as that which Macbeth *knows* as his incurable ailment, precisely as that which Macbeth *recognizes* as the sign of his fundamental vulnerability and irreducible absence from full self-presence.

Act 3 shows how the epochal regime of servitude deepens into a metaphysical quest for "being" that is anguish and into an anguish that is a metaphysical quest for "being." "Being" here is tantamount to perfect self-presence; and perfect self-presence is tantamount to perfect safety. Truth thus becomes no mere general certitude, but self-certitude. Truth is the truth of the cogito, and the cogito only *is* Truth if it knows its own presence and being to be perfect. A flaw in the self is a flaw in the cogito, and hence a flaw in the self is a flaw in "being"—or worse, in Truth. If "man" is not perfectly self-present as his own self-certainty, then "being" itself is not perfectly self-present in the truth it should be. Macbeth, we see, has now as his chief concern the question of safety: "To be thus is nothing, but to be safely thus" (3.1.47). It is a mistake, as I shall argue in a minute, to think that this Macbethian concern for safety is reducible to a political or empirical feeling.

As Macbeth moves into his servile and extremely inwardized phase, he will not cease to do deeds; but all the deeds will uniformly be directed at forwarding a single thing: Truth ("King hereafter"). Deeds do not simply perform certain actions, effectuate certain motions, take care of certain requirements: they now, all of them, are there to ensure the crowning of Truth. "To *crown* my thoughts with acts, be it thought and done" (4.1.149). The crowning of thought is not simply a question of mundane self-realization and fulfillment in general; it is a question of bringing thought up to an idealized elevation/elation where *its* a priori self-completion gets verified. As R. G. White points out, Macbeth's quest for the "round / And top of sovereignty" (4.1.88–89) is the quest for the circular summit of absolute plenitude in self-presence: "The crown not only completes ... and rounds, *as with the perfection of a circle,* the claim to sovereignty, but it is figuratively the top, the summit, of ambitious hopes."[11] The crowning circle, the circle of the crown, is in fact no mere roundness in a royal emblem but the circularity (and therefore completeness) of Truth itself. In the process of crowning in the play, it is not merely Macbeth that gets crowned but "Macbeth"—not merely the ego who carries the name Macbeth but the idea/ truth of that ego as it is elevated to the idealized status of a metaphysical absolute. Conversely, the threat of uncrowning is not simply the matter of a crowned ego losing its political position as the pinnacle of power, but a question of the uncrowning of Truth itself—*its* horrendous demise. For Macbeth—and there is little in the tragedy that does not come over toward the spectator as being "for Macbeth"—it is perfection itself that is at stake in the circularity of the crown, the perfect circle that it forms. Unsafety, here, is the rupture of the circle, the questioning of its circularity. "Unsafe" (3.2.32) is the key word now as Macbeth seeks to eliminate the tiniest risk of uncrowning. Politically speaking, the risks he faces look pretty slender; but because the question of the crown now is a truth-question, a snowballing obsession that leaves no peace of mind, "obstacles" are not only blown out of all proportions but also "created" in paranoid fashion. In fact, the process of "uncrowning" is always already in aggressive motion toward Macbeth even when tangible political threats are absent: the opposition does not have to materialize for him to tremble and have another "fit"; indeed the opposition does not have to take material form at all, as the Ghost scene shows. It is enough, in this logical world of metaphysical obsession, that there are traces of the *idea* of the other, of what Truth so far has not managed to appropriate.

If, as I just said, "uncrowning" is always already in motion in Macbeth, "crowning," conversely, is never really completed—is always deferred. The completion of murder is by no means completed for Macbeth in its completion; for the murdering amounts to the finalization of "crowning," and this "crowning," by being an act of absolute metaphysical accession, can never materialize as such. "I have done the deed" (2.2.14). But has he? It is commonly thought that Macbeth pronounces these words with shock and horror, with stunned emphasis on the factual completedness of what is empirically achieved and definitized. Yet as Olivier and other actors have shown, Macbeth lives in a world where "doing" is somehow impossible—and this "impossibility" of doing climaxes in this very pronouncement. Macbeth immediately senses that the completion/crowning/murdering is dramatically deferred; indeed everything in the play that follows this pronouncement (that follows 2.2) could be defined as the dramatization *of that deferral*. It is against this kind of background that one should assess other comments on "doing": "If it were done, when 'tis done, then 'twere well / It were done quickly" (1.7.1–2). It is of course possible, necessary, and natural to read this statement in literal fashion: "It would be nice to get this over quickly"; "It would be nice if murder ended at that—if one could perform it and then escape from the nasty consequences in its trail." But again Shakespeare's language-power is not reducible to the elementary level of empirical reference. This unit forms part of a constellation of Shakespearean comments on the problematic of "doing," and this Shakespearean commentary draws attention to the crux I have just identified: the structural inability of "doing" to make full presence and full "crowning" perfectly available.

Against the background he has prepared, Shakespeare now elegantly presences a crowning paradox: that Macbeth is willing to take greater and greater risks in order to close the epoch of risk. In each phase of anguished servitude, he focuses a particular obstacle, feeling that only *this* hindrance spoils truth. Gradually growing more conscious of the enslavement to fear, the subject comes to identify the truth-deferring object as the single and privileged source of his fear. The delineation of Macbeth's fear of Banquo typifies this mechanism: "There is none but he / Whose being I do fear" (3.1.53–54). Banquo looms as one who will gain from Truth the absoluteness of metaphysical self-extension that seems to be withheld from Macbeth through the absence of heirs in his lineage. Because Banquo now appears to occupy the fulness of Truth that Macbeth would like to reach, and because any absence from this absolute fulness of Truth sets up an unlimited servile quaking in metaphysical man, Shakespeare can employ Banquo as the governing center for an entire nexus of fear imprisoning Macbeth.

If the ontodramatic perspective is missed, all that remains of Shakespeare's complex design is the commonplace notion that Macbeth succumbs to Banquo's ghost simply because of guilt following the act of having him assassinated. But in itself such guilt is as inadequate an "explanation" as it is for the task of accounting for Macbeth's strange behavior after the murder of Duncan. It is only when we recognize Banquo's truth-role (as Macbeth's partner in the orphic quest for transcendental Truth) that we can fully appreciate the hero's special relation to him. Speaking to the murderers on the subject of Banquo, Macbeth discusses the royal self-presence as something that "in his death were *perfect*" (3.1.107). Banquo is in other words viewed as the exact and unique thing that keeps Macbeth away from the idealized perfection that prophecy originally promised. Is it therefore strange that Macbeth should find the Ghost of Banquo *absolutely* terrifying?—the Ghost of Banquo being of course the presence of Banquo when Macbeth has made him absent (from Truth/"Macbeth"/Crown), the continued presence/absence of that which by now should clinically be only absence.

The presence of Banquo (real or spectral) now equals the absence of Macbeth. Conversely, the absence of Banquo equals the presence (and self-presence in Truth) of Macbeth. This balancing is no mere political either/or but of course an equation where the very question of Truth hangs in the balance. The absence of Banquo *is* the presence of Macbeth, indeed the self-presence of Macbeth in *terms* of Truth. For this reason Banquo's presence to Macbeth can become an absolute threat even when it is nonempirical and nonpolitical: Macbeth can fear a Banquo who appears as a politically defunct reality (in the Ghost scene) but who nevertheless remains a metaphysically real presence (a continued unit of Truth/Thought/transcendental self-crowning). The threat constituted by Banquo, then, derives from the fact that Banquo embodies all that obstructs the absolute *presence* of Truth as the self's own self-perfection. Banquo *is* less-than-perfect Macbeth, not just a mere political "problem" that Macbeth has to manage in order to complete his monarchial campaign. Hence we see that the news that Banquo's presence survives in the shape of his escaping son Fleance hits Macbeth not as a political setback but as a metaphysical catastrophe.

> *Macb.*   Thou art the best o'th'cut-throats;
> Yet he's good that did the like for Fleance:
> If thou didst it, thou art the nonpareil.
> *Mur.* Most royal Sir . . . Fleance is scap'd.
> *Macb.* Then comes my fit again: I had else been *perfect*;
> *Whole* as the marble, *founded* as the rock,
> As broad and general as the *casing* air:

The Botcher 115

> But now, I am cabin'd, cribb'd, confin'd, bound in
> To saucy doubts and fears.
>
> (3.4.16–24)

How different this world is from the world of heroic fighting in act 1. Macbeth is still a reckless fighter, still one ready to champion the enemy to the uttermost; but all that fighting is now a struggle that takes place under the huge cupola of metaphysical fear and self-incertitude. As we perceive in units like "best" and "nonpareil," Macbeth's entire language is by now obsessed by the idea of perfection and self-perfection—a feeling that is finalized in "I had else been perfect." The units that then consolidate the Macbethian sense of his ideal self-materialization under the rubric of Truth—"Whole," "founded," "casing," "rock," "marble"—announce a conception of reality that ontologizes thought, removing all traces of the "vanishing" that characterized the affirmative escapades of the opening scenes of the play. Vanishing and metaphysical presence now oppose one another extravagantly, and the well-known words burst out once more: "[T]he name of man [is] the name of that being who, throughout the history of metaphysics ... has dreamed of full presence, the reassuring foundation, the origin and the end of play" (WD, 292).

4.3 The Botcher

The quest for metaphysical presence is not only internal to tragic suggestion in the play *Macbeth* but also internal to certain critical attitudes to that play. In the present subsection I shall discuss a logocentric move that blurs the line between hero and critic—and therefore also the line between the inside of the work and its outside. I will be centering my discussion on the unit "leave no rubs nor botches"; but to facilitate a comprehension of the forthcoming analysis of that unit, I would first like to clarify the context in which it occurs. Macbeth turns to the murderers:

> Within this hour, at most,
> I will advise you where to plant yourselves,
> Acquaint you with the *perfect* spy o'th'time,
> The moment on't; for't must be done to-night,
> And something from the palace; always thought,
> That *I require a clearness:* and with him
> (*To leave no rubs nor botches* in the work),
> Fleance his son, that keeps him company,

>Whose absence is no less material to me
>Than is his father's, must embrace the fate
>Of that dark hour.
>
>(3.1.127–37)

The unit "material" suggests presence, for it signals the actuality of something as the realization of its felt structure, its available texture. But what Macbeth wants as material presence is the *absence* of someone else. The phrasing, "Whose absence is no less material to me," is in fact a crucial clue to Macbeth's fit in the Ghost scene—for there it is the absence of Banquo that becomes material to Macbeth in the form of his specter. The absence of Banquo, because it so materially engages with the completion of the project for Truth, is something that in Macbeth's thought is not simply the passive disappearance of Banquo but the truth of his nonbeing, the tangible reality of his nothingness. As I have argued, absent Banquo is not simply a Banquo who is absent but a Banquo whose absence promises the absence of all the things that might be thought of as endangering transcendental presence in self-presence. Fleance, similarly, is just as much a Banquo as Banquo himself: for what is important in Banquo is (still for Macbeth) not his empirical humanity but his occupation of the locus that Truth has reserved for the one who is transcendentally elect. Thus Macbeth is just as afraid of Fleance as he is of Banquo, just as afraid of the shadow/ghost/copy of Banquo as of the original. Something *remains* of Banquo after Banquo, for Banquo is merely a minor form of "Banquo": the truth/name/being of Banquo as that which extends endlessly in promised time through the work of Truth and transcendental meaning.

First, two important things should be noticed about Macbeth's fit at the banquet. He foresees the fit before the moment of its actual arrival as a nervous collapse ("Then comes my fit again," 3.4.20); and he realizes that it is a function of the withdrawal or deferral of full presence ("I had else been perfect; / Whole as the marble," 3.4.20–21).

As we just saw in the line quoted above, the notion of perfection and perfectibility is conspicuous also in "the perfect spy o'th'time" (3.1.129). Critics have argued at length over this phrasing, some, like Johnson, claiming that there is a reference to the third murderer of 3.3.[12] But this reductive reading spoils the beauty and volatile complexity of Shakespeare's thinking. The "perfect spy o'th'time" is no simple reference to the third murderer but a typically unstable Shakespearean unit, opalescent in its rich indeterminacy and pregnant with multiple registers of suggestion. The magnetic core of this unit is the concept of temporal precision. What is in fact being played out here is a tension between definitude and indefinition. On the one hand, space and time must be definitized in order to secure the proper effectuation of the assassination of Banquo and Fleance; on the other hand, this necessary self-identity of the murder must be acted out at a certain indefinite distance from Macbeth ("something from the palace," 3.1.131) in order to leave him out of its shadow. Given this overall polarization, we can easily see that Macbeth's introductory remarks definitize first space, then time:

> I will advise you where to plant yourselves,
> Acquaint you with the perfect spy o'th'time
>
> (3.1. 128–29)

The "espyal" of the time is the knowledge of the perfect time to act (Chambers),[13] or the exact intimation of the right time (Heath);[14] and this notion is no doubt blended with "the exact time most favourable to your purposes" (Steevens).[15] In this unit, then, "spy" suggests at one and the same time (1) Macbeth perceiving/discovering the right time and (2) time itself fatally perceiving/discovering the victims at a certain moment when they are optimally exposed. In context the units reviewed will be seen to show how Shakespeare is creating an elusive tension within the spatial as well as within the temporal:

> Within this hour, at most,
> I will advise you where to plant yourselves,
> Acquaint you with the perfect spy o'th'time,
> The moment on't; for't must be done to-night,
> And something from the palace; always thought,
> That I require a clearness
>
> (3.1.127–32)

Time, like space, is definitized as well as indefinitized. Just as "something from the palace" suggests a will to flee the precise, visible horror of the deed in the very act and moment of giving it local specificity, so "Within this hour, *at most*" reflects at once the certainty of a short duration and the lack of firm contour given to that duration. The pauses, marked by commas, are significant. Macbeth wants to control events, to master time and calculate temporally. Yet, as Bradley puts it, he is exposed to a radical "incalculability."[16] There is a certain hesitation, or deferral, even in his most ruthless and onward-moving commands. Although, in a sense, he wants to get directly *at* Banquo, this directness—because it is servile rather than masterful, metaphysical rather than heroic—is not to be effectuated directly, freely, and spontaneously. Macbeth wishes to be direct indirectly. Or: the type of directness that he now favors (servile directness) has to rely on indirectness in order to achieve its purposes, its directness. Ontodramatically, this new world opposes the world of "vanishing" in Act 1—where directness was directly directness (the enemy slave getting slashed to pieces in a twinkling, and so forth). Macbeth has accepted the mediacy of the murderers (and is not willing to do the deed himself); yet he is now desperately trying to make this mediacy immediate, to give mediacy the sensation and texture of its opposite. The mediacy must not be mediacy. There must be no *traces* of mediacy as such, no *writing* suggesting its work. There must be "no rubs nor botches."

The unit "require a clearness" (at the end of the passage quoted above) presents a ticklish dilemma, here, and I shall presently renew an engagement with it on a metacritical level. First and foremost, to "require a clearness" (3.1.132) means to clear a space for oneself, to make a clearing for the self, to space out self-presence and make room for it. This also means that the *other* (any alien entity threatening self-presence) must be kept at a distance. But here, this other that keeps a distance is precisely that which must be *got at*. The text, therefore, dramatizes a peculiar dilemma, an uncanny to-and-fro in which "distance" is both presence and spacing, that which offers protection as well as that which opens up the protective enclosure to the invasion of incalculable alterity.

> *Macb.*   Both of you
>   Know, Banquo was your enemy.
> *2 Mur.*   True, my Lord.
> *Macb.* So is he mine; and in such a bloody *distance*,
>   That every minute of his being thrusts
>   Against my *near'st* of life: and though I could
>   With bare-fac'd power sweep him from my sight,
>   And bid my will avouch it, yet I must not,
>   For certain friends that are both his and mine,
>   Whose loves I may not drop, but wail his fall
>   Who I myself struck down: and thence it is
>   That I to your assistance do make love,

Masking the business from the common eye,
For sundry weighty reasons.

(3.1.113–25)

Macbeth rationalizes as a social dilemma (open versus secret authority) a difficulty that is hyperontological. His references to the psychosocial sphere are hazy and indefinite: "*certain friends*," "*sundry weighty reasons*"—counterparts of "*something from the palace.*" The vagueness is politic, but the politic does not exhaust the signifying potential of the vagueness. An irresolvable conflict shimmers just below the surface. Self-presence, as pure interiority, must guard itself against the hostile outside (Banquo). Yet the erasure of the hostile outside, the setting-aside of menacing exteriority, inevitably involves some kind of contact with it. The ability of the outside to make contact *through* the very rupture-of-contact (desired by the metaphysically active inside) can be registered in the shudder that runs through "distance." This shudder is not a nervous shudder but a weakness and strain in the ontological terrain. The "bloody distance" that Banquo keeps is not only a distance-from but also a distance-to. This spacing-out (of the fighters)[17] is ironically precisely what ensures their intimately deadly engagement. Here "distance" is the very thing that permits Banquo to reach (into) Macbeth: "in such bloody distance, / That every minute of his being thrusts / Against my near'st of life." Hunter, accordingly, gives "distance" two distinct meanings: (1) dissension; (2) space between combatants in fencing.[18] But because Shakespeare also uses the notion of spacing to mark self-presence ("I require a clearness," 3.1.132), the linguistic drama fascinates by dramatizing an entire intrigue between fusion and separation, self-proximity and self-removal, self-defending and self-offending. The space between the two conceptual forms of "distance" itself becomes a spacing: something that examines its own possible dynamic. The unit "distance" comes to feel a distance in and from itself.

Space, now, is at one and the same time the passive clearness/clearing that the self measures out round itself to provide a safety margin for its center *and* the active distance/spacing that the selfsame self requires as a corridor through which to aggressively run out and make violent contact with the foe.

It is a well-known fact, as we have already seen, that the name of the critic deploring numerous "cuts" in *Macbeth* is John Dover Wilson. Absent meaning is for Wilson regularly meaning that once was fully present in the "original"—in some hypothetically uncut play that Shakespeare once wrote. Access to this originary source, now fallen from the beatitude of its perfect self-presence, amounts to access to full meaning—or *would* amount to such access (in the best of possible worlds). What is absent in the play is present in the original. What is missing in play is not missing in its originary truth. I wish to suggest, here, that Wilson's obsessive quest for "flaws" in the play (marks of its descent from transcendental perfection) in the final analysis is a function of the type of servile quest for self-certitude (in the name of Truth) exemplified by the tragic hero. In this context, I am for a moment breathless when I stumble on two minute explanatory phrasings in Wilson's criticism—phrasings "outside" *Macbeth* (since they belong to criticism rather than drama) yet somehow also strangely inside *Macbeth*. These phrasings are indirectly and directly related to a passage we have interested ourselves in:

>   always thought,
> That I require a *clearness:* and with him
> (To leave no rubs nor *botches* in the work),
> Fleance . . .
>
>   (3.1.131–34)

First some lexical clarification. Muir points out that "clearness" implies "completeness," and it is related to the notion of avoiding "rubs" and "botches." As he also observes, editors wrongly assume that "rubs" in this case refers to "impediments" on the bowling green—as in *Hamlet* 3.1.65 and *King John* 3.4.128. In *Macbeth*, however, "rubs," like "botches," suggests "roughness; an unevenness or inequality"—in a piece of work, or generally (KM, 80). The rubs and botches are in other words quite simply the possible flaws that might disfigure the perfect countenance of perfect Truth ("clearness" was "completeness").

These crucial units reflect the distribution of the entire tragic tension of act 3: the conflict between presence and supplementarity, metaphysics and play, perfection and time. The logic of identity faces the logic of the supplement. On the one side we have a world of "clearness" (transparent meaning and artificially ideal self-presence) which is always on the verge of cracking up into rubs/botches; on the other side we have play and vanishing (linguistic as well as physical) where reality is nothing *but* a composite geography of running fractures and cutting dislocations, nothing *but* a complexly rich diffraction of rubs/botches/

marks. The rubs and marks and slashes that were affirmed in terms of vanishing and cutting in the opening scenes are now objects of systematic exclusion. In the clearing made by the metaphysically anguished self there is made to remain a cleared center for the cogito, a transparent and perfectly static arena prepared uniquely for the reception of transparent meaning.

> I require a clearness
> To leave no rubs nor botches in the work

It is precisely at this moment, with a kind of sideward dread, that the corner of our eye catches the critic—as metaphysician—slipping into the words that Macbeth speaks: that we see the critic himself, behind that anguished rhetoric, appealing to us in the name of truth. In this play where Shakespeare warns us about the tragic process of wanting to absence *all* rubs and botches, the critic appears to be succumbing to this very fallacy. Having explained certain "cuts" and "interpolations" by calling attention to the damage done by Thomas Middleton, John Dover Wilson proceeds to develop this idea in the cloak of Macbeth's own language: "I suggest that this *botcher* is Middleton."[19] There are, then, "botches in the work." And Wilson, looking for the fulness of meaning and for the presence of the text (the uncut "original"), abhors these botches in the work. But it is not only this unit botches/botcher that catches the eye, but also the unit "clearness." Wilson too requires his clearness, is determined to have it. Witness: "the perfect spy o'th'time [] Obscure. J. and others take it as referring to 3 Murd. in 3.3 . . . I agree with J. and suggest that a line or two, *making the reference clear*, has been cut after l.29."[20]

What do we need—to ascend to perfect meaning/Truth, to make the clearness we require? Nothing at all. Just "a line or two." Or a murder or two. (Preferably two.)

The critical commentary (provided by Wilson) is innocent enough. He means no harm. What, after all, is strange about a scholarship desiring clarity? But what makes the critic's linguistic units ("botcher," "make . . . clear") so ontotheologically suggestive—contingent as they are empirically speaking—is their closeness to Macbeth's own desire as his anguished gaze obsessively seeks cracks and unsettling fault lines in the building of truth. What we end up with, in a gesture of critical awareness that is at once phantasmic and sober, is a vision of the two men (Macbeth and Wilson) passively miming with their synchronized lips an utterly deafening formula, one drowning their individual voices. This quite overbearing formula, whose logical weight covers a whole culture like a gigantic overturned megaphone become turret-roof, speaks the sonorous measure of Western philosophy itself:

"I require a clearness
To leave no rubs nor botches in the work."

5

5.1 Ontological Relief

For some time now we have been considering the middle portion of Macbeth's tragic career, his period of metaphysical servitude. Dominated by his mania for certitude, the hero experiences servile vanishing. Various "fits" shake Macbeth as his quest for metaphysical presence inside monarchial perfection becomes a fear of fear. He wants presence but gets its vanishing; he wants the "reassuring foundation" but gets play; he wants self-certitude but gets doubt and anguish. As I pointed out at an early stage, this servile self-vanishing (into the nothingness of "fits") is *ontodramatically* related to heroic vanishing and witchcraft. In the military world of the opening scenes, Macbeth "vanished" into the enemy ranks; and he also caused a "vanishing" in the enemy slave. By thundering through his mere empiricalness, treating his body and that of the enemy as worthless nonentities, Macbeth from the outset created the sensation of pure affirmation as pure speed: the athletic act of immediately being the forwardness of absolute military ecstasy. In addition, the Weird Sisters doubled this sensation of "vanishing" at the beginning of *Macbeth* by suggesting the power of what I called a "radioactive" zone. In this hyperontological zone, vanishing was felt to be structurally "stronger" than presence, since the sisters appeared to jeopardize presence in a number of ways. They presenced the possibility of Truth in terms of its impossibility: prophecy's promise seemed to vanish into nonsensicality and oracular mystification. Also, of course, the occult presence of the witches was itself a suggestion of nonpresence; at the height of their "presence" the witches simply vanished—leaving man to doubt that they at all could have been present in the full materiality of a full presence. I also showed how the privileged position of *the cut* in the discourse of the witches (and in the cauldron where they accumulated disrelationships) enhanced the sense of weird "vanishing."

Generally speaking, then, I have suggested that major portions of *Macbeth* are organized in terms of the hyperontological sensation of "vanishing." Put differently: "vanishing," by being a common property of various crucial discourses and scenes, organizes the most significant aspects of the play by bringing them into suggestive interrelation.

In this chapter I will be examining the other side of this question. What happens to those parts or aspects of the play that are *not* organized by "vanishing?" This issue can also be put differently: "vanishing" organizes certain dramatic dimensions positively, others negatively; through its structural absence in certain special places, "vanishing" also organizes the play in terms of its absence. In these special parts, presence, as that which is "weaker" than vanishing, will provisionally master and define the general profile of dramatic sensations. The things I will be discussing as structured by this "weaker" force (or as structured by the absence of the "stronger" force) are in turn of order: (1) the Porter and his "Hell," (2) Duncan, (3) Lady Macbeth, and (4) Malcolm.

Most of the important differences that I am calling attention to—as for instance between presence and vanishing—come across to us in terms of tone. Weird discourse has a certain tone, nonweird discourse another tone. The Weird Sisters organize one kind of tone, Duncan a completely different one. This presence of the dramatic figure in terms of his or her tone also organizes such important tensions as the one between Macbeth and Lady Macbeth. Lady Macbeth's presence very much comes over as a special tone that she masters, and her mastery is almost entirely a question of the dominant power of this tone. We might also like to consider the play as a whole in terms of tone. Consider for instance the difference of tone between the opening scenes, piloted by the sisters, and the concluding scenes, dominated by the victorious thanes. Why are the sisters absent from the end of the play? Why has Shakespeare chosen to omit some kind of final statement that they could have made? What happens to "tone" in the middle of the play? What happens to "tone" in act 4? What happens to the "tone" of Macbeth's soliloquies as they slide across the surface of the play from its beginning to its end? Do they all belong to the same tone, to a tonal selfsameness? Or does the tone actually change? Is there something called Macbeth that then adds tonal differences to its presence? Or is there a sliding of tone that we gradually come to be aware of as the slippage "Macbeth"? What is the tone of the Porter? Why is his dramatic role a tonal one? What does he *do* to tone?

Before beginning this inquiry into "tone" by discussing the Porter, we should perhaps recognize the fact that tone is precisely what metaphysics always wants to dispense with; philosophical discourse (including the branch called criticism) forwards its mastery by favoring an "atonal norm."[1] But since "tone" is what normative "scientific" discourse excludes in order to give itself the semblance of neutral truth-language, tone tends to become the very thing that eludes inquiry of the "logical" kind. One of the reasons why "scientific" discourse cannot manage the question of tone is that tone, according to a structural necessity, escapes from identity and definition. Tone is by nature indefinite, promoting indeterminacy. Tone is not "present" as other things in discourse may be, and therefore the quest for the identity (as self-presence) of tone is always strangely incomplete. In fact this ability of "tone" to always withdraw from fixedness and logical definition forces us to shape the inquiry into its operations as a negative task: we cannot determine what a particular tone *is*, but we can arrive at an approximate intuition of it by defining those things that the tone does *not* promote. Tone, by always already bursting (its) identity, traces the movement of what is ready to de-tonate,[2] to explode into tonal disorder. Exceeding denotation, the detonation of "tone" leaves us in a zone of tonal indecision—the very type of tonal indecision that I shall now review in the Porter's discourse. "Tone" does not refer. "It" has no directly empirical level of signifying relevance. It is "inside" the building of dialectical logic, just as the world of the Porter is "inside" the stronghold now mastered by Macbeth and his metaphysical mania; but this "insideness" in no way marks the essence of any belonging. "Tone," while being on the "inside," is not itself part of being as being-inside, inside as being being.

What is the "tone" organized by the Porter? It is an intimate tone; but is it a tone of intimacy? If there is intimacy here, then surely it is a pseudo-intimacy. The tone is superficially reassuring, for discourse now opens a world where the weird and unthinkable have been put aside and where language as "human intercourse" suggests speaking as commerce between "men": man is now an inert given, and "men" are the understandability of this given "man," its mode of being present to itself in a primordial fashion. We now encounter a universalized, levelled, homogenized humanity where all men come together under the common interests of generalized desire: drink, sex, sleep, and so forth. But this very "flattening" of the human spirit (into biological needs) draws attention to what has already been awesomely staged; we feel how tremendous is the gap between a world where the human soul is at stake through the conflictual nature of thought and a world where a porter drifts aimlessly about making whatever recovery he can make from his hours of dissipation. On the one hand we have a hyperontological world of "vanishing" where nothing is self-evident; on the other hand we have an ontological world of "being" where human experience is so narrow and overdetermined that utter strangers instantly form a knowing man-to-man understanding. This basic ontodramatic sensation determines our general apprehension of the Porter: we sense that he is so firmly planted in the soil of basic human needs that no risk is encountered in his grand theoretical excursions into areas of extreme conceptual indecision. If one for a moment doubted the (provisional) veracity of an empirical conception of reality as ontological presence, one would not be able to laugh with the Porter at his objects of derision.

The Porter shares with Lady Macbeth the suggestion of desire narrowed down to bodily enjoyment as well as a general tendency to be ontologically domesticating in outlook. (He is, after all, not only a liminal creature poised professionally on the threshold of things, but also a *housekeeper*: one who preserves the domestic enclosure by supervising its entrance.) Lady Macbeth's attitude to murder is a domesticating one favoring the "concrete" and practical: the instruments of assassination are things she presences: makes present as ready-to-hand. She lays them out, clarifies their absolute availability, organizes their material reality in terms of domestic display—like that of knives and forks *showing their presence* on an absolutely fresh tablecloth. "I laid their daggers ready; / He could not miss'em" (2.2.11–12). In this hyperontological drama where daggers and Macbeth are never quite "ready" for one another and where the tangential approach to murder always involves some "missing" of the mark of (its) full presence, Lady Macbeth clarifies the empirical simplicity of the murderous performance in terms of what cannot be ontologically missed, in terms of what is *too* ready to be missed. But the Porter's discourse also involves this macabre domestication of the horrendous other. The Hell that he playfully presences is itself a home and domicile. His references to napkins and roasting (2.3.6, 15) further the household sensation promoted by Lady Macbeth. In 2.1 and 2.2 we have encountered Hell as a place of enduring hyperontological agony and we have recognized a stretching of thought beyond itself so that unthinkable pain accompanied the experience of a belonging to absolute alterity; but here in the Porter's ontological discourse Hell is a home-Hell, a domestic Hell, a here-Hell, a present Hell: a place where "is" merely is as it always is. Nothing has happened to "is" in the Porter's Hell. His Hell *is*. And Macbeth's *is not*. Hell is structurally—in mythological, theological, and psycho-ontological respects—a place standing out of normalcy. But in the Porter's discourse, this standing-out, though described and alluded to, though indeed elaborately *referred* to, itself is described within a reassuring ontology that wishes to have nothing whatsoever to do with negative *ekstasis*. On the contrary, the Porter's standing-out, as a merely sexual event, is a profoundly stabilizing matter; it calls to mind the automaticity of arousal that centers man in biological recurrence and mechanical self-perpetuation. Being itself is ontologically centered in such harmless standing-out.

We today no longer think of the Porter's presence as "comic relief"; but I would like to suggest that relief is indeed a crucial notion here. This relief is neither comical nor emotional. Rather, it is ontological: ontological relief. The Porter's scene forwards an ontological sensation by cancelling the hyperontological tension that has dominated the play. But Shakespeare is technically brilliant here. He provisionally eliminates the hyperontological strain—which by now is almost as unbearable in the spectator as it is in the hero—but he preserves at the forefront of our attention all those notions and slidings that the dramatic hypnosis has utilized. He removes the inner plan but not the furniture that composes it.

Hell, like murder and death, has no being, organizes itself around no nuclear identity, cannot structurally belong to any knowable essence that, in all tranquility, it could call its own. It is absurd to speak of a proper Hell, just as it is absurd to speak of a proper murder or a proper death. These things are by definition the exceeding of the proper. But the Porter definitizes and ontologizes the unthinkable other in terms of such proper thought. He appropriates Hell, his good humor playfully turning it into a property he masters. "Who's there?" he cries, as one newcomer replaces another. His tone is one of surprised delight, undercut by knowing calculation, like that of a commercially successful innkeeper welcoming one stranger after another.

> Here's a knocking, indeed! If a man were Porter of Hell Gate, he should have old turning the key. [*Knocking*.] Knock, knock, knock.

128   DECONSTRUCTING *MACBETH*

> Who's there, i'th'name of Belzebub?—Here's a farmer, that hang'd himself on th'expectation of plenty: come in, time-pleaser; have napkins enow about you; here you'll sweat for't. [*Knocking.*] Knock, knock. Who's there, i'th'other devil's name?—Faith, here's an equivocator, that could swear in both the scales against either scale; who committed treason enough for God's sake, yet could not equivocate to heaven: O! come in, equivocator. [*Knocking.*] Knock, knock, knock. Who's there?—Faith, here's an English tailor come hither for stealing out of a French hose: come in, tailor; here you may roast your goose. [*Knocking.*]
>
> (2.3.1–15)

To be fully self-present in Hell one needs a certain appropriate amount of "napkins." These towels or handkerchiefs are to stop up a certain crucial excess in Hell—an excess of sweat produced by a surplus of heat ("here you'll sweat for't"). To "have napkins *enow* about you" suggests a certain being-present, a certain going on as you always have, a certain "Carry on chaps!" The notion of an *appropriate* supply of napkins appropriates the otherness of Hell, indicates the suitability of a certain adequate set of equipment. We feel we are in the presence of one who is wholly at home with himself in Hell, of one who, in entering the other, fails to do so. The Porter's ironic discourse obviously reverberates against a background of common understanding that we share with him: the surplus of heat in Hell ought to be structurally infinite; therefore no finite number of napkins will ever be able to soak up the forthcoming perspiration. In spite of this self-conscious irony, however, the "nonironic" surface level retains powers of signification that come to prevail. Careful attention to *this* tone in the tonal complexity of the Porter's discourse reveals that he is not quite present in his irony. Irony being a form of absence (a "secondary" signification absencing a primary one), the tonal absence of the Porter from irony is his tonal absence from absence: his *presence* in the domestic immediacy of his homely imagery. In his secular foregrounding of himself, he forwards a stark ontological naturalism and we sense that his jolly belief in Hell is as void of spiritual content as is his belief in the Jesuit's Heaven. We feel that the Porter is structurally absent from the quasi-moralistic and quasi-theological credo that he seems to affirm. Hence the ontology that he in the final analysis creates is perfectly flat: a kind of realistic nihilism promoting an ontological uniformity that fits perfectly into the temporal condition of his brief stage presence, a hangover.

Webster's dictionary gives "hangover" as: "a letdown following great excitement or excess." This sense quite accurately captures the ontodramatic shift monitored by the Porter. Things come down from an unthinkable altitude, or from the altitude of the unthinkable, and they hit a naked floor where ontological reality rids itself of all real strain, paradox, and lasting conflict.

In *Macbeth* such lasting paradoxicality comes over, as we have seen, through weird equivocation, the kind of indecision governed by the Weird Sisters. The Porter's relation to equivocation is curious in this context. He certainly equivocates, yet equivocation is above all something he appears to attack. "Dissimulation" and "equivocation" were vivid words in popular consciousness: as one who swears "in both the scales against either scale" (2.3.9–10) the equivocator is one who promotes a pseudo-balance, a balance that really amounts to a headlong plunge into the abyss of terrorism, treason, and prevarication. At first it might seem that the "equivocator" forwards indeterminacy, but in the final analysis he is dangerous in terms of overdetermination. It is true that he manipulates truth by submerging its contours in dangerous ideology; but what above all defines the presence of the Renaissance Jesuit is his ideological overdetermination: his adherence to the doctrine that the end justifies the means. In rejecting the equivocator—in the name of the popular opinion that is merrily damning him in the playhouse—the Porter is thus not primarily staged as a man of high principles, a man with rigorous faith in metaphysical absolutes. On the contrary, he is himself an equivocator, a man of sane indeterminacy and human resilience. But equivocation is here held inside the anthropocentric sensation that dominates the Porter's presence. Equivocation does not endanger or question the being or presence of the Porter. He is a healthy and secular sceptic who despises anyone who goes to extremes: the farmer who puts all eggs in one basket, the religious fanatic, the absurdly mean and calculating tailor.

But what about the Porter's own excess? How is his own hangover appropriated? I defer the inquiry into these matters, since the idea of *drink* is an ontodramatically poignant unit in *Macbeth*—deserving as we shall eventually see, its share of special attention.

5.2 Deconstructing Character

If the Porter's discourse provides "relief" from hyperontological pressure in *Macbeth*, it might be said that Duncan condenses such relief into "character." In both cases the sudden absence of the weird creates the sensation of something odd—creates a sensation that is itself weird, but this time by negating what so overwhelmingly is weird.

What I wish to deconstruct in this section is the opposition between two views of Duncan circulating in critical inquiry: the view of him as the epitome of good and the view of him as a duplicitous politician. The former view attributes no internal contradiction to Duncan's subjectivity, while the latter view does. According to this latter view there is a tension between surface and depth in Duncan, so that behind the smoothness of his meek social presence there is hidden obscure political cunning. Without suggesting any compromise between these two readings of Duncan, I shall be arguing that both are false. The solution I will be forwarding will be based on the refusal to acknowledge the basic assumptions internal to the two options listed above.

We might begin by looking at the schoolboy reading. From such a viewpoint very little movement exists in the scene where Macbeth encounters Duncan (1.4). There is a certain amount of inflated jubilation, a strengthening of the community sense following victory over the potentially disruptive enemy, and a royal portioning-out of certain verbal and social rewards—notably the Cumberland title on Malcolm. From this commonsensical perspective the ethical situation is dialectically pure. On the one side the good ones are verbally and heroically manifesting their perfect goodness; on the other side, as already a somewhat darkened intruder, Macbeth is a seed of evil inside the camp of virtue. Dover Wilson tells us that Duncan senses this seed of evil in Macbeth and that it makes the king uncomfortable. Duncan finds Macbeth's hearty greeting (1.4.22–27) "a little chilling."[3] The benevolently overflowing mood of courtly happiness and heroic presence is broken by Macbeth, whose arrival is "an unforeseen accident."[4] Although interesting and relevant, Wilson's reading is in fact quite conjectural; there is nothing in the text to warrant his assumption that the council meeting was planned in order to effectuate the "Cumberland" announcement.[5] Indeed many critics believe that the company in general are quite as surprised as Macbeth and that Macbeth's arrival caused no displeasure among the assembled thanes.

The reason why Dover Wilson's reading is inadequate is that it posits hostility between two hostile subjects, Macbeth and Duncan. The reason why Dover Wilson's reading is significant, on the other hand, is that it calls attention to an important and conspicuous tension between Macbeth and Duncan. But how can this

Deconstructing Character

tension operate dramatically—that is, *for the spectator*—if there is no hostility inside the subject Macbeth toward Duncan and no hostility inside the subject Duncan toward Macbeth? Because Shakespeare has already made sure that the spectator understands the ontodramatic conflict between the zone of "vanishing" and the zone of "presence," and because it is by now clear that Macbeth and Duncan organize these two zones as well as the tensions between them, their incompatibility. Because the zones are incompatible, Duncan and Macbeth are too. This situation is fatal, tragic—a modernized version of the tension in Greek tragedy between the two hemispheres of reality, family and state.[6] Such a basic conflict has moral consequences and implications: but neither the ontodrama nor the characters caught in it are reducible to this morality.

The spectator, I am saying, does not need to grope for any hidden self behind either Macbeth or Duncan to feel the tension between them. Indeed, the spectator does not even have to grasp them as characters in order to sense the tension of character between them. Without "entering" either Macbeth or Duncan (without placing himself inside their "personalities"), the spectator can already feel that one of them belongs to heroic vanishing, the other to heroic presence: that one of them cuts up presence, making it vanish, while the other conserves presence, making it a property of the state. The spectator who by now has visualized Macbeth as arrogantly vanishing fighter, with an entirely reckless attitude toward empirical selfhood, cannot help noticing that the world centered on Duncan is, comparatively speaking, a spatio-logical construct utterly devoid of the thrill of absolute negativity and affirmative vanishing. But no subjectivity "inside" the name "Duncan" organizes this absence of vanishing in him, this absence of athletic nihilation, this withdrawal from the defiance of presence. The characters can be dramatized as clashing without there having been effectuated any real drawing of character. We do not have to posit any "real" Duncan behind the Duncan rhetoric to acquire a sense of the tension between Duncan and Macbeth. All we need—all indeed that Shakespeare gives us—is a linguistic conflict. This tension (between language and language, rhetoric and rhetoric) itself permits—indeed forces—the characters who appear in it to engage in a conflict that they themselves hardly pilot in terms of volitional subjectivity and personality.

An interesting aspect of this situation, and one that has significant aesthetic implications, is that language is here really on the side of the "evil" character. Precisely because language only yields its most affirmative potentials by embracing the violence of negativity and the self-violence of absence, the recklessness of the violent man stirs language in a way that the nonviolent man does not. The violence of Macbeth—which is external as well as internal, athletic violence as well as imaginative violence—lashes language into those very tormented forms that, through Shakespeare, we have come to associate with the apotheosis of language, its own heroic splendor and poetic ecstasy. This is not to simply say, as Bradley did, that the hero is "poetic." What connects Shakespeare with his hero is not the fact that both of them were "imaginative men," rapturous personalities "given to poetry." What connects them, instead, is their readiness to become linguistically visible on a horizon of cosmic suggestion where the violence that the universe does to itself is indistinguishable from the violence that language *can* do itself: not destructively and thoughtlessly, but creatively, adventurously. In this context it must be recognized that the negativity that the imaginatively violent mind brings toward itself cannot be harnessed and mastered inside the reassuring notions of "meaning" and "authorial intentionality"; for what vanishes in the moment of linguistic and tragic *ekstasis* is also the "self" that could fully possess the direction and reach of its creative power. Shakespeare cannot be understood "in his own terms," for his linguistic and imaginative desire, by being infinite rather than finite, inexhaustible rather than exhaustible, is precisely what breaks and transgresses those very terms. In reviewing the common demand that we must understand the genius "in his own terms," Heidegger writes that such a task is impossible: "impossible, because no thinker—and no poet—understands himself."[7] We can take up a thinker's quest and pursue its line of imaginative suggestion, but we cannot "understand" the thinker himself, least of all "in his own terms."[8]

The difference between the "zones" we have been mapping, then, is not only important as a theatrical difference but also as a linguistic one. Put bluntly, and with special reference to the scene being discussed: Duncan's language is normally boring and Macbeth's language is usually not boring. Thus Macbeth's language is "closer" to Shakespeare—indeed, one might say, closer to language. Language is "closer" to language in Macbeth than it is in Duncan, if by closeness we mean the willingness of language to engage with itself: violate itself, attack itself, rend itself, find some new awesome opening in itself which will mark the emergence of that which is absolutely innovative and unprecedented. Thus, to cite Heidegger again, language is not a "mere system of signs, uniformly available to everybody,"[9] but a space of ongoing discovery and unconcealing. The great writer, by being sensitized to "the mystery of language,"[10] transgresses language as system and intercourse, abandons language as a network of "signs" facilitating commerce among personalities. Shakespeare facilitates nothing. In 1.4 ontological language for a moment withdraws from the hyperontological mystery of language, becomes this very facile commerce among humans. Rhetoric in this scene deliberately veers away from the weird, and it might possibly be said that Macbeth and Duncan deliberate or negotiate this deflection. Language is fine speaking: Duncan wrapping his polite and effete compliments in an ontological language that calculates its self-present centeredness, appropriating signification as it moves along. The real resources of language are held back and for a brief interlude there is nothing that gives to air quivering with attention the free dangers of an absolute expectation.

The situation that I am now discussing is not to be confused with the difference between speech as dramatic commentary and speech as personal statement. Minor characters often slip into poetic effusions that cannot be related to any "poetic" disposition in their personalities. Thus, as Nicholas Brooke points out, the sunset rapture of the first murderer (3.3.5–7) cannot possibly suggest a poetic kernel in this man's human essence.[11] In such cases a character simply speaks what has to be spoken in the play at a certain moment: it may be trivial, it may be poetic; it could be prosaic, but it could also be moving. But whereas the absence of the first murderer from his poetry is an abstract absence, one having no effect whatsoever on our apprehension of him as character, Duncan's absence from the full signifying potentials of his language helps to structure our awareness of his character. Macbeth's character works to constitute itself by pushing language to its most daring poetic limits, and Duncan's character works to constitute itself by not pushing language to such limits—by not, as it were, taking such conspicuous linguistic risks. As we see from the latter instance (Duncan's) the absence of full linguistic thrust in dramatic speech can itself help to constitute character: indeed the incompleteness of linguistic affirmation is *just* as much a constitutive factor of character as is complete linguistic affirmation. Language runs at full throttle in Shakespeare's hyperontological presencing of Macbeth, and language does not run at full throttle in Shakespeare's ontological presencing of Duncan; yet in both cases the creation of character is equally prominent. One type of character "needs" language more than another. And, more interestingly: one type of character needs "less" language than another.

What I am trying to stress here is the fairly familiar notion that the suggestive force or depth of a character is not necessarily a function of the kind of "psychological" realism that we are familiar with in the modern world and that critics tend to impose on Shakespearean drama. Shakespeare, at least linguistically, is not involved to the same degree with all his characters, and an expert craftsman in "character" is not the one who, like some Victorian and post-Victorian novelists, gives "character depth" to all and sundry. A dissertation on the "true nature" of Duncan's interior mind is faintly ridiculous, for one of the main features of his dramatic presence is that he lacks such a full interior, such an "inner self." Such a lack, however, is no lack caused by Duncan's own desire to promote surface appearances for political reasons, but a lack caused by Shakespeare's theatrical requirements. But the most interesting and paradoxical fact is perhaps that Duncan's lack of full character presence (technically speaking) is precisely what gives him character, what enables him to be a character. There is a character-shallowness in Duncan, and this very "flatness" of his character *is* its presence: human as well as dramatic. Furthermore, as my phrasings just happen to have suggested, it is curiously enough the very shallowness of Duncan's character-presence that enables him to represent presence (rather than "vanishing") in the play. By living through the torments of an infinitely complex mind (Macbeth's) and by experiencing its volatile thought in terms of vanishing, we come to experience the reaction discussed some minutes ago: that any nonvolatile human soul appears coarse and flat. The stable and fixed spirit seems to live in the ontological platitudes of boredom. But conversely, also, the "flat" and banal character seems to promote the opposite of vanishing and volatility: to merely be present in his presence. This is Duncan's fate as a character—to be so dull and flat that his monarchial equanimity comes to suggest the lethargy, self-sufficiency, and suffocating unimaginativeness of a world of full presence.

Given the total atmosphere of the play, its huge impact as intellectual and spiritual challenge, Duncan comes to emerge as a blind spot—an area unsensitized to reality as originary contra-

Deconstructing Character 135

diction and originary pain. He knows that men can be treacherous (as was the former Thane of Cawdor) but he is unable to intuit the radicalness of this treacherousness in humanity. We semiconsciously feel that something is "wrong" with Duncan because for the duration of 1.2 and 1.3 we have become accustomed to a hyperontological weirdness: "vanishing" and originary paradox as presenced by the Weird Sisters and their "radioactive" zone of influence. Duncan (and also the *signification* distributed through his verbal "wisdom") appears as an ontological center of meaning devoid of these cosmic displacements. Precisely because he looks so stable, real, dependable, and unself-contradictory we come to be slightly disturbed by his presence. Already—alarmingly enough—we have like the hero accustomed ourselves to the hyperontological spell cast by the sisters and by the play. Already, we are associating signification with the weird and contradictory. Now, because Duncan so easily signifies, we suspect that he does not.

My argument works toward the recognition of an essential doubleness in Shakespeare's scheme: on the one hand there is something "wrong" with Duncan, but on the other hand and at the same time he is a perfectly good and innocent man. Criticism not recognizing both of these sensations is spoiling the tragic pattern. Critics who think that the two sides of this problematic are mutually exclusive have to sacrifice one of them: the critics sensing some turbulence around Duncan rush in to inform us that he is slightly malevolent, while critics clinging to the virtuousness of the king are reluctant to admit the existence of any shadow or insufficiency cast by him.

It could be argued, following a cue given by Holinshed, that Duncan is a *Rex Inutilis,* a weak ruler who is ineffectual and senile. Such a king would compensate for his military impotence by being politically cunning, and we could in that case read the kindness shown in volunteering to visit Macbeth's castle as feeble fence-mending after the "Cumberland" move. But the problem with this entire line of interpretation is that it ruins the basic condition of possibility for the tragic action: that Macbeth should have no cause to murder Duncan *whatsoever.* Macbeth is clearly conscious of Duncan's impeccable character and record (1.7.16–20), and the idea that he was not only meek (1.7.17) but also "clear" (1.7.18) in his office indicates an absence of significant error in his royal comportment.

In sum, the critical act of soiling Duncan and marginalizing his monarchial perfection is triggered by the inability of positivist criticism to account for the unease and turmoil created around the presence of Duncan. Because this unease radiates from the presence of Duncan, such criticism draws the "logical" conclusion that it must emanate from Duncan himself, the real man. But the real man Duncan is primarily an archetype: the very image of goodness and the very image of ruling goodness (virtuousness in a ruler). It is only when Duncan is seen ontodramatically as an embodiment of presence and as a negation of hyperontological vanishing that his peculiar negativity can be recognized as such—without recourse to fantastical speculations about political ingenuity.

One way of understanding how Shakespeare structures tensions around Duncan ontodramatically rather than psychologically is to look at the king's ability to neutralize Macbethian excess. It is Duncan's language (not his mind) that organizes this appropriation of the hyperontological excess produced by military vanishing—suggesting that the appropriative maneuver is governed by a particular type of culturally conditioned discourse rather than by any particularly fascinating ego.

> O worthiest cousin!
> The sin of my ingratitude even now
> Was heavy on me. Thou art so far before,
> That swiftest wing of recompense is slow
> To overtake thee: would thou hadst less deserv'd,
> That the proportion both of thanks and payment
> Might have been mine! Only I have left to say,
> More is thy due than more than all can pay.
> *Macb.* The service and the loyalty I owe,
> In doing it, pays itself.
>
> (1.4.14–23)

There is no need, here, to construe some immensely subtle undertone in the dialogue: as if Duncan were full of dishonest praise, Macbeth of faked allegiance and dutiful servitude. Yet anyone familiar with the play as a whole recognizes the sensation that Duncan somehow seems to hold back Macbeth. Macbeth is "far before," says Duncan, and we sense that this excess (or exceeding) in Macbeth is one that might trouble Duncan: Duncan as presence rather than cogito. Shakespeare has just shown us the hero exceeding all empiricalness and empirical presence in order to preserve Duncan and Scotland; but at this moment the social situation seems to demand of him that he quickly "fit" into some niche, some proper place of honor where the monarch can overlook his best fighter as a fixed ornament of the state, one of the objects for its enduring pride. But something has to be curtailed in Macbeth in order for this "fitting" to be performed. We sense that Duncan (and indeed Macbeth) is slightly embarrassed by this process of necessary adjustment— and perhaps we are too. It is clear, in any case, that something has to be lopped off during the course of this ontological neutralization of Macbethian extraordinariness. (It should be emphasized that the ontologization of the extraordinariness is not a negation of it; on the contrary, as I am suggesting, the neutralization works most effectively when it gives itself the form of positivity and acknowledgment.)[12] Macbeth carries a dangerous "extra" (the surplus value created by outstanding valor, success, extreme recognition), and this "extra" must be appropriated by ontological presence. This gesture is an organizing feature of the scene (1.4). The neutralization of the "extra" involves the cutting-back of what is outstanding, what stands out. Duncan extends his arms, and as he completes his embrace the sensation is that the closure brings the aggressive "extra" into the transcendental circle of royal presence. The unit "would thou hadst less deserv'd" (1.4.18) is spoken as a compliment, but a literal reading is not absurd: things in a sense *would* be easier had Macbeth deserved less. No malevolence or grudge need be conjectured in order to produce this sensation. If Macbeth had deserved less there would no doubt be better "proportion" (1.4.19) between presence and its other.

It should be seen, then, that Shakespeare's language here can achieve three quite different effects on three quite different levels. On an ethical level of polite dialogue, Duncan is in fact strengthening our sense of him as Macbeth's superior; for whereas Macbeth is already destabilized by a weird inner turmoil with morally dubious overtones, Duncan is shown to be a generous man who can afford to praise a fellow human as his superior without in any way being duplicitous or untrue to himself. Second, on a psychological level of mere subjective interaction, the two men exchange rather trivial items of polite discourse, showing us a region of mutual courtly respect that is necessary for the preparation of its murderous violation. Third, and on the level that I am calling ontodramatic, the imagery, rather than pointing to the "political thoughts" of the two subjects, throws the men into separate ontodramatic zones: having seen Macbeth behave so differently in the battle scenes (without any courtly restraint at all, without paying his respects to the "enemy slave") we sense that *this* Macbeth is not the whole man, indeed not even the real man. Thus language here creates three different Duncans: one who is superior (through sublime generosity), one who is equal (through courtly politeness), and one who is inferior (through ontological centeredness).

5.3 The Traitor Man

Macbeth, insofar as it is to be apprehended historically, is not primarily interesting through topical allusions but through the historical question that we have already looked at, the question of "man." Even before the moment when players arrive at the court to provide dramatic entertainment, that court and throne are already charged with the dramaturgy of the new historical power that is being staged: the achievement of the modern self. Macbeth all on his own engineers the absolute implications of such a historical staging, but when he interacts with his wife the sweep of historical suggestions is not lessened. The play emerges in the period of great uncertainty following a female government of England that had lasted for almost half a century. Elizabeth's quaint attitude to men is too well known to need comment at this point. Obviously the figure of the father as well as that of the husband are made to tremble in any appraisal of the world of Elizabethan courtliness, and the ramifications of such a historical tremulation cannot be *identified* by any scientific critique since their complexity recedes infinitely out of the grasp of finite types of inquiry (investigations built on "historical fact"). In any event it is pretty clear that the question of "man" (in "history" as well as in our play) to a certain extent spaces itself out in terms of the main ambiguity of this word: man as human being, man as male rather than female. All kinds of "forces" make this ambiguity suggestive to us today in restrospect—not only the immense shadow cast by Elizabeth, not only the massive burning of witches, but also such things as the change from boy actors to actresses during the Restoration. There are *no actresses* in the play *Macbeth*; yet the role of actresses in it is overwhelming. Curiously, furthermore, all these actresses in *Macbeth*—so fully present, so fully absent—press down and in upon the hero precisely by focusing him as "man." In fact this word "man" in a number of ways monitors most of the tensions that the play uses to build toward its spell:

The Traitor Man

I dare do all that may become a man:
Who dares do more, is none. (1.7.46–47)

And, to be more than what you were, you would
Be so much more the man. (1.7.50–51)

Bring forth men-children only! (1.7.73)

My husband? (2.2.13)

Are you a man? (3.4.57)

What! quite unmann'd in folly? (3.4.72)

What man dare, I dare (3.4.98)

I am a man again. (3.4.7)

Be bloody, bold, and resolute: laugh to scorn
The power of man, for none of woman born
Shall harm Macbeth. (4.1.79–81)

He was a gentleman on whom I built
An absolute trust— (1.4.13–14)

No man's life was to be trusted . . . (2.3.103)

Who can be . . .
Loyal and neutral, in a moment? No man (2.3.106–7)

Fawkes's Gunpowder Plot is of course not unrelated to this solicitation of "man," for it had now been suggested to popular consciousness (and no doubt also to the king himself!) that the order of man as currently defined could be blown sky-high at any moment. *Man*, as the transcendental pinnacle of the political scenario, is in fact curiously absent (potentially or materially) during a long historical sequence: he is replaced by woman during the reign of Elizabeth, is potentially blown sky-high during the Jacobean era, gets beheaded as the Puritans come to power, and gets abstracted into republicanism during the Commonwealth. That females should be systematically burnt to death during the reign of a female monarch is in this context somewhat poignant. Various historical slidings "coincide" here in patterns that are disturbing not only for feminists but for any reviewer concerned with the historical role of the feminine. Where is woman most *dramatically present*: in the exclusively male acting performed before the Tudor queen or in the "mixed" acting performed for that womanizer and patron, Charles II? What has happened to "woman" at the end of this period of transition—now that the concern with *burning* her has significantly diminished? What was distilled in that burning? And, more dangerously: what, in woman, is *no longer* of burning interest, worth the burning/distillation?

The Gunpowder Plot, let there be no mistake, was a shock. It brought vividly into popular imagination the possibility of the total absence of the state: the possibility of the absence of order but also the possibility of the absence of an order. Yet in *Macbeth* woman is not only one who cunningly negotiates the possibility of treason, but also one who resents treason and resents man as its agent.

> Son. Was my father a traitor, mother?
> L. Macd. Ay, that he was.
> Son. What is a traitor?
>
> (4.2.44–46)

In this exchange between Lady Macduff and her son, both of them left to the wolves by their politically active father, we see how Shakespeare refuses to allow us to treat the various levels of the drama separately or abstractly: we might like to discuss politics and Jacobean treason at one seminar, and then to discuss "the question of man" at another seminar; but in *Macbeth* these apparently separate issues are intertwined—and structurally so, logically so. Sooner or later the politico-historical issue has to be opened up in terms of its "metaphysical" correlative; sooner or later the airy speculations about "man" have to touch ground in the messy and intricate details of political fact and historical uncertainty.

Although Lady Macduff deserves much more attention than she is usually granted in criticism, and although she is here engaged in the very discourse where the question of "treason" merges absolutely with the hyperontological dimension of the play ("What is a traitor?" 4.1.46), it is clear that her feminine role is less complex than that of Lady Macbeth since she unilaterally represents her own sex and its particular interests. Morally speaking she is Lady Macbeth's superior; indeed she is in a sense the most ethically likeable character in the entire play (at least for a twentieth-century spectator), for her absolutely limpid assessment of the masculine hemisphere as a world of military and political cruelty is an opinion that, as it were, she has to shoulder all by herself. She is, marginally, and precisely therefore gloriously, the play's true martyr—the only person (to pick up the recent imagery) that the play actually burns.

But if Lady Macbeth and Lady Macduff are separated by the fact that the former lady activates cross-gender forces that the latter lady only touches passively (4.2.38–40), they are united by the irony they both use to subvert masculinity. Lady Macduff's irony (4.2.27–31) is simple and classical because it so dialectically opposes feminity and masculinity, private and public, family and state.[13] What is "wisdom" in the political world of men is from her viewpoint perfectly irrational:

> L. Macd. Wisdom! to leave his wife, to leave his babes,
> His mansion, and his titles, in a place
> From whence himself does fly? He loves us not:
> He wants the natural touch;
>
> (4.2.6–9)

Unlike Lady Macbeth, Lady Macduff can represent the family principle in a pure way, and Shakespeare centers this difference between the two women by calling attention to the childlessness of Lady Macbeth. In fact this very childlessness in the Macbeth family surfaces for the Macduff family when Macduff eventually hears that his family has been annihilated by Macbeth: "He has no children" (4.3.216). Yet, curiously, it is precisely this absence of the child (its negation, removal, and finalized distancing) that Lady Macbeth utilizes to implement the force of her own female irony—again directed toward the male.

> I have given suck, and know
> How tender 'tis to love the babe that milks me:
> I would, while it was smiling in my face,
> Have pluck'd my nipple from his boneless gums,
> And dash'd the brains out, had I so sworn
> As you have done to this.
>
> (1.7.54–59)

Here the family's baby, indeed what *makes* it a family (a blood-unit knit into conspiracy and togetherness in conspiracy), is strangely absent in two ways: the child no longer exists (which is why Macbeth has no heirs) and its projection in the mother's discourse is a negative projection: the child is present at the breast in terms of a negation of that presence. Now this rupture of the family through the rupture of the family dialectic (child/mother but by implication also mother/father, wife/husband) is the very thing that negotiates the tragic conundrum. Yet this familiar rupture is not itself dialectical, is neither cause nor effect. The child-absence (in the Macbethian lineage) is the source of a certain (murderous) tension, yet in *completing* that tension (and making murder materialize as an actual intention and project), the family has to "restore" its baby, rescue it from negativity and return it to dialectical presence: the husband/child's smiling and milking *at* the mother's nipple. The absence of the child here is absolutely necessary for the tragic propulsion, but so is the absence of the absence of the child. Yet these two things—the absence and the absence of the absence—cannot be firmly distinguished from one another in Lady Macbeth's discourse, do not "face" one another dialectically—as the smiling eyes face those of the mother. That is perhaps why Lady Macbeth's words are so terribly frightening: we would like to imagine that some enormous change comes over the woman that first milks the babe and *then* dashes its brains out; but we feel with this dreadful woman that the tender milking somehow already is full of that horrible sense of infinite power that will crack the skull and spill out the brains. The word "boneless" in "boneless gums" is of strategic importance in this rupture of dialectic, for whereas the skull that is to be cracked is a bone and an uncracked one, the lack of bone in the gums (an object of tender contemplation for the mother) suggests a bone-absence that is already prematurely being supervised by the mother—and in the name of love.

The lovers then (for this is what they continue to be, 1.7.40–41, 73) need to be at once absent from their child and present to it, need to negotiate its absence, but also to idealize its self-presence within the horizon of desire created by that negotiation.

As I remarked some time ago, the really dialectical and idealizing power of Lady Macbeth works for presence and self-presence: she completes the transition to metaphysical servitude by furthering the Truth-oriented project that the Weird Sisters had set in motion. The baby imagery marks the definitive phase of this general persuasion. It is the time when Macbeth is *appropriated* in the name of imperial presence. Emotionally speaking, the scene is obviously one where the dependency of the child on its mother parallels Macbeth's dependence on Truth/presence. Stevie Davies puts this well:

> Here is the . . . remembered helplessness of babyhood dependent on the all-powerful, hunger-filling love of a mother who may offer or abstain from offering the means of life; who lifts the infant to soar through vertiginous heights and leans it back as if to drop in infinite space, impressing it with the fear of having its brains "dashed out". More specifically, Macbeth works through the male experience of his continuing bond with the feminine as a condition of dependency, threatening to his autonomy.[14]

The important word here, I think, is "all-powerful": the mother is all-powerful and so is Lady Macbeth. Curiously, Lady Macbeth comes to be all-powerful toward Macbeth, and this notion clashes with the image of Macbeth given to us in the opening scenes. There, as magnificent fighter, he himself was all-powerful. But Lady Macbeth does not really want to negate this "athletic" and sociopolitical all-powerfulness; rather, she wants to appropriate it, domesticate it, make it present, ontologize it. Macbeth, now shown most of the time indoors, in the home ruled by woman, is made to contract and shrink. One type of all-powerfulness gives way to another, and the all-powerfulness that wins is the all-powerfulness of ontological presence. Davies's review (above) is absolutely correct and relevant, but of course fathers also play these "threatening" games with their babies. What the mother uniquely controls is the breast. Because, as Lacan suggests, the breast can menace with its absence (much in the way that Truth can in *Macbeth*), it becomes a "peak" of deprivation, the very image of absolute withholding.[15] Herman Rapaport observes that the breast in anaclitic terms becomes an object for the drive of infant sexuality to lean on,[16] and this object is a symbolic "prop," something like an actual "stage prop."[17]

As the smiling infant "leans" on Lady Macbeth's breast, so Macbeth "leans" on Lady Macbeth—leans on presence. In fact, but only for a short moment, he *is* that milking babe, he *is* a creature possessing the nipple of full presence itself. As Bayley has emphasized, Macbeth is in an important sense Lady Macbeth's child, fed with her ownmost milk.[18] Indeed, Lady Macbeth has already drawn attention to her breasts as the site of power, and the appropriative act of making the breast the vessel of synthesis where the forces of the genders coalesce is prefigured in preparatory units of discourse. On the one hand, Macbeth is "too full o'th'milk of human kindness" (1.5.17); on the other hand, Lady Macbeth wants negativity to come to her "woman's breasts, / And take [her] milk for gall" (1.5.47–48). But because Lady Macbeth's proximity to the actual murder is a liquid proximity, one made humid by liquids (she smears the grooms, she prepares their nightcaps), the milk/gall of her breasts gets diluted into all kinds of fields of suggestion. And all these saturated areas, soaked as it were in and by her breastmilk, become areas that give us the sense of her operative presence. She appropriates not only Macbeth but an entire scenario where thought and action now come to presence themselves inside the order and regime of presence. The world itself is now for a while a place that is nourished by Lady Macbeth. Her project to drench the chamberlains by preparing their drinks cannot be firmly distinguished from her milking of the boneless infant or from her preparation of the premurder drink for Macbeth (2.1.31–32): all-powerfulness is now the transformation of the world in terms of her own will-to-nourish. It is as if she is going to give suck to the grooms, for they too are somehow smiling and boneless, "drenched" helplessly in "swinish sleep" (1.7.68–69).

The self-centeredness in Lady Macbeth's desire shows up on several occasions: "my dispatch" (1.5.68), "Leave all the rest to me" (1.5.73), and so on. But although Lady Macbeth's desire always works through empirical channels and toward empirical goals, its appropriative thrust is not itself empirical. She does not only take possession of murder as an empirical possibility, she also ontologizes murder. In fact she ontologizes everything, and her breast is nothing but the magnetic center of affect for all such ontological desire.

This difference between her empirical purposefulness and her ontologizing desire can be gauged by considering an absurd misreading of her intentions: Dover Wilson's odd notion that "my keen knife" is a unit revealing that "she intends to do the deed herself."[19]

> Come, thick Night,
> And pall thee in the dunnest smoke of Hell,
> That my keen knife see not the wound it makes,
> Nor Heaven peep through the blanket of the dark,
> To cry, "Hold, hold!"
>
> (1.5.50–54)

What Shakespeare is working with, here, is not the empirical level of possible fact but the sensation of an all-powerful appropriation. It is not a question of her wanting to perform the murder, but of her wanting to possess the sensation of its performance. It is not a question of her holding the knife, but of her holding the holding of the knife. In a sense this involves the suggestion that Macbeth does not really "hold" the knife (except in a strictly empirical sense)—and this is of course exactly what we have recognized in the earlier section discussing the dagger of intentionality.

Macbeth is in this general context a passive figure, almost an instrument that Lady Macbeth manipulates in order to complete a specific task. This instrumentality can be sensed just a few seconds before Macbeth's emergence from Duncan's chamber. At this moment Shakespeare makes us feel that Lady Macbeth has not only organized the entire butchery, but that she also looks upon Macbeth's participation in that operation as the mere passive completion of a ready-made project. All he has to do, as it were, is to press the button: the rest will follow automatically (indeed happily so for the rest of their lives), for she has thought of everything and fixed all the structures:

> I laid their daggers ready;
> He could not miss'em.—Had he not resembled
> My father as he slept, I had done't.
>
> (2.2.11–13)

Having looked at the first half of this section earlier, we might consider the second one. Lady Macbeth's commentary is interesting, here, for empirical positivism goes really wrong when trying to establish what is referentially true. Such positivism posits (1) a resemblance between Duncan and Lady Macbeth's father, (2) her perception of this resemblance in the chamber, (3) a secret tenderness (for fatherly gentlemen in general) in the depths of her being, (4) a desire in her to effectuate the deed herself, and (5) her failure of nerve at the decisive moment. Marvin Rosenberg tells us that there was something that she saw in Duncan's face[20] and that the lady now emerges from the experience with the quite new knowledge that she really cannot kill (MM, 322).

I find this type of reading anachronistic (relevant only for modern novels) and absurd for the simple reason that Shakespeare is not working here either with a detailed depiction of empirical action (exactly how she behaved in the chamber) or with a detailed depiction of empirical thought (exactly what she experienced in the chamber). The chief purpose of the description of the perfect readiness of the daggers is to emphasize the absence of physical impediments: all that separates Macbeth from murder is a small bodily gesture and so the current deferral, marking an immense dramatic hesitation, cannot be caused by practical obstacles. The notion of the father resemblance seems to me to be thrown in here to explain why such an utterly satanic woman should have at all bothered to let the execution of the deed be a matter for another person. But this token reason for her personal absence from the murderous act of course only covers up a much more structurally necessary reason. The murder itself would in no way satisfy the desire underlying her project. Her entire will to power moves through Macbeth. He could not be replaced by another man, and least of all by herself, since her appropriative power over Macbeth is quite as important as her power over Duncan. Without the Shakespearean emphasis on this power of wife over husband, the next Shakespearean move does not work at all—for this move is of course the showing of the absolute emptying of this power. Her anxious "My husband?" (the Folio question mark should be retained, 2.2.13) signals the expectation of a grand welcoming, perhaps brief celebration, in which her appropriation of his free negativity would be utterly finalized, indeed crowned. But that hypothetical finalization of her appropriation is of course immediately shown to be extravagantly illusory: we see and hear Macbeth's absence from Lady Macbeth and from the general project with which he so passionately ought to be identified. In terms of empirical fact, the question "My husband?" is answered in the affirmative: it *is* Macbeth who emerges from the chamber, and this Macbeth *is* the man who has done the deed for her—pleased her in this way just as much as he manages to please her in bed (1.7.40–41). But in ontodramatic terms, the question "My husband?" is answered in the negative. What ought to emerge from the chamber is an utterly ontologized man: man as Man. What ought to emerge from the chamber, precisely following the telos of action as family dialectic, is *the husband*. But if Macbeth, as we saw Bayley argue, is unfit "for the play," he is also unfit for the role of "husband." Indeed, as I shall try to show in the next chapter, he is unfit for husbandry in general—for what restricts itself, dialectically, within the house and property of a possible ontology.

Lady Macbeth's anxiety is in this context significant. Sensing the gap between her ontologized conception of murder and her husband's (non)conception of it, she tries to quickly bridge the widening gap between them by pathetically offering to establish some melodramatically intimate blood-communion: "My hands are of your colour" (2.2.63). But as we see, the gulf between man and woman expands with astonishing rapidity. Normative critics tend to want to rationalize (and thus suppress) this quick alienation between wife and husband by concocting some theory about the common guilt that they share. But while Macbeth's reactions are vaguely suggestive of something that looks like guilt, Lady Macbeth's anxiety is in no way reducible to the notion of guilt. Nor is it reducible to mere worry about her husband's strange conduct. What rapidly hollows her out, unjoining her self-confidence, is the growing awareness that her ontologization of events is totally out of touch with her husband's utterly different experience of them.

5.4 Thickening Brightness

If the Weird Sisters "de-ontologize" the drama from the outset, making the disconcertingness of play more forceful than logical presence or metaphysical centeredness, all moves seeking to ontologize action sooner or later seem self-defeating. Duncan is thus "doomed" from the outset, and not merely from the viewpoint of plot. So is Lady Macbeth. These characters, through their hyperontological emptiness, or failure to engage with originary contradiction, are not really in touch with the play's total energy pattern but only become actual in it in terms of "plot." Macbeth of course is also doomed, certainly by the plot. Yet in a sense he escapes one kind of doom—almost an aesthetic one—by living out the full conditions of possibility for the drama: negativity as pure play. Although he for a long time struggles against this sensitivity of his for what is weird and playful, trying instead to achieve metaphysical status as a logical component of "plot," he eventually (as I shall argue in the next chapter) accedes to a kind of loss of meaning which is the play's own strange "meaning." More than tragedy is involved here, and there are worse fates in the play *Macbeth* than that of being tragic in it.

Now before Shakespeare embarks on this final stage of his venture, the one negotiating the emptying of tragic Macbeth and the emptying of tragic momentum, there comes a critical phase in which all the violent energies of (the) play seem to draw toward a premature closure. This happens in act 4—a place where "meaning" and "plot" have as it were already run their full courses and where Shakespeare, precisely in order to manifest the transgression of meaning/plot, has to work himself round the logic of what now threatens his artistic freedom.

One part of Shakespeare's difficulties here is created by the need to satisfy stereotyped demands of theatrical expectation: villains have to be punished and new heroes have to be rewarded. Shakespeare cannot suddenly achieve this prescribed pattern at the very end of his work, with a moral thunderbolt in the very last scene: he obviously has to prepare his audience for moral "order" just as he once had to prepare it for the rupture of order. But it seems here as if Shakespeare, uncomfortable with this entire stabilization of his complex conception, wanted to get it out of the way as soon as possible. In fact Macbeth emerges as more of an inhuman villain in act 4 (4.3.55–60) than he does in act 5, and the new heroes are nowhere more saintly and snow-white than they are in this fourth act (4.3.21–24, 114–31). The problem, however, is that the play has organized itself, ontodramatically, as that which cannot "tolerate" the dialectically simple. Nothing canny really looks convincing in the hyperontological world of Macbeth—as we indeed saw a while ago when reviewing Duncan's polite encounter with victorious Macbeth. But this law that the uncanny must always triumph over the canny in Macbeth is not a question of emotionality: Shakespeare does not only play on our emotions in order to achieve his dramatic hypnosis, he plays on our logic. Logic itself *plays* in Macbeth, and it plays with logic. This logical play, nearly always working toward originary equivocation and originary contradiction, now cannot leave act 4 alone—cannot stop itself from toying with premature dialectical "either/or-ness" and cannot indeed prevent itself from doing most damage in those very areas where dialectical sanctity reigns supreme. Shakespeare's rhetoric now upsets the moral and logical dialectic that act 4 celebrates, unbalancing the characters that plot forwards as the pinnacles of goodness. What now emerges, through rhetoric rather than "meaning," is an entirely wicked Macduff and an entirely wicked Malcolm. Both of these types of wickedness are from the viewpoint of "meaning" and "structure" quite harmless and provisional; Shakespeare's plot quickly withdraws the wicked shadow that momentarily darkens the play's heroes, permitting them to emerge unscathed from the obscuration and to move forward toward their righteous actions in act 5. Yet, as I shall argue, something *remains* after this Shakespearean negation of the negation; some parts of the obscurity of Macduff and Malcolm cannot be salvaged by the neutralization of negativity. There is an element of negativity and contradiction in the men that cannot truly be taken back into reassuring "meaning"; we may be entitled to feel that there is somehow more suggestive truth in the provisional obscurity of the characters than in the perfunctory negation that eventually lightens it. In fact the characters themselves seem to come to this very intuition. I shall concentrate here on Malcolm rather than Macduff, since our previous discussion of Lady Macduff has already outlined a critique of Macduff: all we need to do in order to sense what *remains* disturbing and unsatisfying in the character and presence of Macduff is to empathize with his wife and "see" him from her perspective. From this perspective, indeed, Macduff is not a fully self-present character. He has fled; and this flight is in a sense not only his absence from his home but his absence from his character—from the fulness of the character "Macduff" as it would have emerged in a slightly different play, the kind of smooth construct some critics (and characters!) are yearning for.

Thematic criticism often complains that 4.3 is uninteresting, and this conclusion is not very surprising given the fact that there is little to thematize, no thematic movement that is not more poetically and adroitly stated elsewhere. Chambers thus complains that the scene is "tedious," Grierson that it is "dull and forced,"[21] while Knight holds that its "function" is that of "choric commentary"—to make explicit "the evil which Macbeth has caused" (KM, 122). Partly, no doubt, the lack of critical enthusiasm is produced by knowledge of how closely Shakespeare has followed Holinshed's *Chronicles* (4.3.44–96, 101–32). Yet this imitative proximity deters only the thematizing critic, the one basically uninterested in language and obsessed with "moral content" and "moral dialectic." It would not be difficult to show that all the important ontodramatic slidings in the scene are a function of Shakespeare's writing, not Holinshed's. In fact, as Bradley remarks, it is important to recognize what is affirmative in the fourth act: although there is a drop of dramatic tension, as in many tragedies that "fall off" in act 4,[22] the slackening that might be experienced in this vulnerable phase is compensated by the surreptitious opening of new avenues of signification.[23]

Malcolm is an equivocator. He first tells Macduff that his thoughts "cannot transpose" the truth of Macduff ("That which you are," 4.3.21), and he follows up this assurance, anchored in rapturous ontotheological commitment (4.3.22–24), with an astonishingly lengthy equivocation on the topic of his own temperamental constitution (4.3.46–102). He concludes this excessive disquisition on excess by forwarding an assurance that is as solid as it could be: "I am as I have spoken" (4.3.102). Expressed in a deadpan manner, this untruth is as "sincere" as the very different: "That which you are my thoughts cannot transpose" (4.3.21). It is in this context not particularly surprising that Macduff should find Malcolm's final negation of his negations (4.3.114 ff.) somewhat hard to stomach (4.3.139); for during a considerable lapse of time, Malcolm has been saying two utterly contradictory things: (1) that Truth after all is Truth, no matter what you say; (2) that the very proposition *Truth = Truth* is suspect. On one side there is Malcolm's honesty and Malcolm's dissimulation, the real Malcolm versus the provisional mask. On the other side there is Malcolm's hesitation between his absolute intuition of Macduff as an honest fellow and his politic testing of this absolutely honest friend in a shrewdly elaborate political gamesmanship. But can these two sides be firmly distinguished from one another? Can a man who so radically distrusts his own intuition look convincing when he sets up a provisional dialectic between his "real" and his "false" ego? If a man equivocates with his own trust (4.3.21–31), can he then be fully trusted as one who can distinguish between his soul and his mask, his truth and his playacting? What reason has Macduff now to absolutely trust this master equivocator? Would not such immediate trust reflect the very naiveté that Malcolm was working off—the very naiveté that threw trusting Duncan first into the treacherous grip of the first Thane of Cawdor, then into the treacherous grip of the second Thane of Cawdor? Where in this world is there absolute foothold, absolutely nonsliding, nonchanging, nonequivocating Truth?

The very theological image that Malcolm employs to dismiss the structural equivocation of course only deepens and radicalizes it into something universal and cosmic.

> That which you are my thoughts cannot transpose:
> Angels are bright still, though the brightest fell:
> Though all things foul would wear the brows of grace,
> Yet Grace must still look so.
>
> (4.3.21–24)

Thickening Brightness

The thesis that angels are still bright though the brightest fell is logically unstable. The brightest angel, by being the brightest, was the most angelic angel among the angels (cf. *Measure for Measure*, 3.1.185). His fall, far from betokening a flaw in the margin of the angelic paradigm, betokens the originary equivocation, unrest, and structural weakness of that very paradigm. As the subsequent lines on "grace" suggest, it is of course still possible to maintain the unflawed goodness of a pure godhead uncontaminated by "things foul"; Lucifer is the source of treacherous evil, not God, and the untreacherous angels continue (like the untreacherous thanes) to be innocent in spite of the misguided villainy of their leading hero. But as Malcolm, Shakespeare, Macduff, and the spectator full well realize, an insurmountable contradiction remains. Why did the godhead create Lucifer, treachery, and fall from brightness in the first place? Was not the godhead the source of the source of his own contamination? Lucifer seems to stand vis-à-vis God as evil Macbeth stands against Malcolm/Duncan; but just as some structural weakness in the godhead caused him to permit the existence of Lucifer/Satan, so some structural weakness in the monarchial authority of Duncan caused him to place his destiny in the untruth and untrustworthiness of the Thanes of Cawdor. Malcolm, it would now seem, is about to stage a deflection from the trusting innocence of Duncan. Malcolm will not read all brows of grace as brows of grace. But does this necessary distrust not already establish the purity of Grace/Kingship/Truth as somehow dislodged and disrupted? The fact that Malcolm, as God's image on earth, has to resort to the knavery (dissimulation) of the evil ones seems to bring him structurally down from the realm of ethereal, unsoiled purity to which he should belong. In his testing of Macduff he has himself to wear the brows of "things foul," and his *perfection in that acting* (good enough to fool Macduff) endows him with the very qualities he is out to reject: untruth's perfect imitation of truth.

The idea that "the *brightest* fell" (4.3.22) seems to me to engage with the tragic depth-formula not simply by suggesting that the brightest fell in spite of his superlative brightness but by suggesting that the brightest fell *because* of his superlative brightness. Superlative brightness, brightness pushed exceedingly far, brightness that is pure excess, "must," structurally, turn over into its opposite. Ontodramatically speaking, the unit "the brightest fell" thus belongs to the same sensual movement as "Light thickens" (3.2.50). As the light beams crowd they stifle one another, smothering the luminosity they seek to produce.

Malcolm suggests that there is something in Truth, in its inner substance and material, that never equivocates. True truth presences its presence as truth: "Yet Grace must *still* look so" (4.3.24). That which is bright and truthful will in the final outcome necessarily appear as such, will necessarily *identify* itself and shine forth as this its own true appearing. But the reason why profounder aspects of our dramatic attention are unmoved by this argumentation is not only that the entire equivocating depth-formula has advanced an opposite cosmic paradigm, but also that this very reassuring thesis is promulgated in a sequence of rather mechanical and dogmatically naive propositions. The notion that Truth is Truth, Malcolm Malcolm, Good Good, Grace Grace, and brightness brightness belongs to an ontodramatic nexus that act 4 is paying lip service to in the construction of a banal moral dialectic within the cultural code of signification. To this nexus belong the notion of the sanctimony of legendary King Edward, "this good King" (4.3.147) with the powers of miraculous healing, the parallel notion of the sanctimony of Malcolm, a youth who never has told a single lie in his entire life (4.3.130), never felt the prick of egoism (4.3.127), nor touched the opposite sex in the heat of desire (4.3.126)—and finally the notion of Macbeth as Satan himself. It may now be objected that Shakespeare is writing for an audience that took the moral dialectic seriously; but as Robert Ornstein once pointed out, the moral and providential platitudes that the Elizabethans and Jacobeans liked to see in print were not the piloting ideas at the forefront of their awareness.[24]

Macbeth, in this closing phase of the moral code, is more evil than the citizens of Hell (4.3.55):

> Macd.   Not in the legions
>   Of horrid Hell can come a devil more damn'd
>   In evils, to top Macbeth.
> Mal.   I grant him bloody,
>   Luxurious, avaricious, false, deceitful,
>   Sudden, malicious, smacking of every sin
>   That has a name;
>
> (4.3.55–60)

There may be a modicum of truth in Muir's remark that Malcolm is now exaggerating for the sake of enhancing his argument (KM, 125), but the fact that these extravagantly negative epithets are

Thickening Brightness 153

joined by others—including the standard reference to Macbeth as "the tyrant" (5.2.11)—nevertheless clarifies the main schematization forwarded by the cultural code: equivocation is reduced and the dramatic figures emerge as either villains or heroic saints. Because of this narrowing of the tragic ideology, what is interesting is not so much the commonplace dramatic "content" but on the contrary what language now itself has decided to think.

The general equivocation at the beginning of 4.3 is maintained when Malcolm begins his long playacting, centered on the notion that he really lacks all moderation of character. As Rosenberg observes, King James hardly had a reputation for the royal virtues listed in this scene (4.3.92–94), and it is possible that Shakespeare is indirectly reproving His Majesty (*MM*, 548–49 n.). Since James was known as a drunkard, and since the current disquisition on excess parallels the ironic discourse on excess in the Porter's scene where the "equivocator" was indeed drink, it is likely that the entire excess nexus should be considered in some significant relation to the issue of monarchial absolutism. Apart from this dimension of general implication, a further analogy exists between the presencing of excess in the two scenes. The Porter, we recall, was crucially involved with the ideological purist (the Jesuit) as one who was prepared to soil himself utterly in order to reach his final purity of purpose: "Faith, here's an equivocator, that could swear in both the scales against either scale; who committed treason enough for God's sake" (2.3.8–11). Now Malcolm, in a sense following this doctrine that the end justifies the means, is himself at this moment in 4.3 one who swears in both scales against either scale. Also, like the Porter's "equivocator," he actualizes all this double talk "for God's sake." In other words, it is the holy cause of the crusade against black Macbeth that justifies various less-than-honest and less-than-true manipulations on the part of the saintlike apostles of justice and goodness.

What is perhaps most alarming—and indeed most astonishing—in this sliding is Macduff's politic cooperation with its mundane relativism. In fact he does not seem to care all that much about the intrinsic goodness that Malcolm may or may not have; Malcolm is for him merely a political alternative to horrid Macbeth, and Macduff is prepared to let Malcolm become an alarmingly ugly ruler before he finally decides that he will not do as a replacement for Macbeth. Vile sexual arrogance and recklessness do not disqualify Malcolm (4.3.60–66), nor do devastating avarice and probable destruction of feudal property (4.3.79–84). Indeed, Macduff not only accepts these monstrous forms of sinfulness in "Malcolm"; he is also prepared to be a go-between and courtly pimp, one who will find the right channels for the princely perversions (4.3.67–76). Some shabby political compromise to cover up the monarchial flaws by no means upsets Macduff's sense of correct political purpose (4.3.84–90). The rather gruesome political realist that looms darkly behind Macduff's chivalrous facade can also be glimpsed in the spontaneous reaction to the news of the massacre of his family: "He has no children" (4.3.216). It is faintly possible that he is here contemplating the fact that Macbeth might have moderated his violence had he himself had tender babes to care for; but this common critical rationalization seems to deliberately obscure the very obvious suggestion that Macduff wishes to inflict a comparable injury on his enemy.

In summary, then, I am saying that the general ontodramatic signification in most of act 4 works in order to create a world where the firm line between good and evil is shown to be oscillating and dangerously fictitious. "Sinful Macduff" is not only a man who experiences the conflict between opposite duties, but also one who in fact encourages monumental greed and lechery. Fear "not yet / To take upon you what is yours," he tells Malcolm, when the prince has spoken of the bottomless abyss of his voluptousness and of a desire that would overbrim all "continent impediments" (4.3.64–70). Macduff insinuates that deception will be a legitimate means of placing Malcolm's "boundless intemperance" beneath the outer shell of feigned decorum and true restraint ("And yet seem cold," 4.3.72). One terrible sin is "portable" if some modest counterweight is thrown into the balance (4.3.89–90). Does Macduff emerge spiritually unscathed from this political pragmatism? In what elusive regions of dramatic awareness does the spectator store this unsettling information? Do these manipulative gestures, in men who are free from true agony of the soul, in any way work to enhance our recognition of the peculiar tragic status of the play's hero? The self-perversion, states Malcom, is his primordial falsehood: "my first false speaking / Was this upon myself" (4.3.130–31). But that is the problem! If he goes to this perverse extreme in his *first* imaginative effort in the sphere of erotic and malicious excess, what will the succeeding instances look like? What does this tragedy consistently show if not the tragic fall of a spotless hero who becomes the victim of the transcendental intensity of his own excessive imagination?

6

6.1 The Notion of Expenditure

In this concluding phase of analysis I am going to discuss the fifth and final act of *Macbeth*. Again, my terminology will be Continental, and as I speak of "lordship" and "sovereignty," I will be following the Nietzschean cue given by Georges Bataille and taken up by Jacques Derrida: the notion of unconditional expenditure. One way of looking at act 5 is to say that Shakespeare here is rounding off his drama and "setting things right." But in a sense dialectical closure of the ethical and normative type is achieved already in act 4—and thus it could be argued that Shakespeare now has time and space to create something new and unforeseen. In fact it may be suggested that act 5 contains the most daring slidings in the entire play, and that language is nowhere more fascinating and "Shakespearean" than here.

Bataille's term "lordship" encompasses mastery (in the Hegelian sense) as well as servitude (in the Hegelian sense)—and thus Bataille's "sovereignty," by opposing "lordship," opposes the entire closed system in which the production of meaning is negotiated by the ontological dialectic of mastery-versus-servitude (see the list of terms, p. 233). If the fighting and victorious thanes of act 1 suggest mastery (the production of dialectical recognition as "golden opinions"), and if Macbeth's mania for certainty in the crowning of metaphysical Truth suggests anguished servitude, act 5 may be thought of as an arena where this opposition between absolute fearlessness and absolute fear has been dismantled, or deconstructed. The "struggle to death" produces dialectical meaning in act 1 (victory is a consequence of innumerable duels on the battlefield), but as Macbeth abandons such extrovert activity for the introverted quest for Certitude/Truth/Presence, the dialectical process of meaning-production does not get cancelled; on the contrary, it gets internalized into the elation of an equally dialectical state: one where the hero is at war with his own doubt rather than with the negativity of the external enemy. Act 5 terminates this dialectically oriented epoch, opening the very different epoch of sovereignty. The long period of Macbeth's incarceration is over; he is now once more an outdoor man, a fighter. Lady Macbeth's domesticating powers of appropriation are completely gone, and so are the dialectical deliberations that display the linguistic surfaces of soliloquies as dialectical constructs. But if servitude in the sense of metaphysical paralysis is mainly in the past, so in a sense is also heroic mastery. For although Macbeth now is about to return to the military world of the fighting thanes, his presence in that fighting—as I shall presently be arguing—has suffered a drastic sea change.

According to Bataille it is impossible to reduce human activity to processes like production and conservation;[1] humans secure subsistence and survival in order to engage in activities that have nothing to do with subsistence or survival but that instead have to do with free expenditure.[2] The element of unproductive expenditure is always there in society—even in times and places of extreme poverty.[3] Glory, what Macbeth produced in act 1, is an example of such an unproductive value: "glory, appearing in sometimes sinister and sometimes brilliant form, has never ceased to dominate social existence."[4] Glory, then, following Bataille, is a form of free expenditure and unproductive production; glory is a part of sovereignty. But how does this tally with the idea that glorious Macbeth produced meaning and dialectical recognition in act 1—with the fact that the glorious fighting *produced* a victory that meant the subsistence of Duncan, Scotland, and the dialectical State in general? As I have already remarked on numerous occasions, glory, while being something that promotes meaning and conserves presence, is not reducible to such things. There was an element of excess in Macbeth's glorious fighting, indeed an element of glorious excess in his glory, that was somehow "unnecessary"—that overshot what Duncan (and in fact Scotland) could calmly review and really cope with. There was an intensity in Macbeth's athletic action that, precisely following Bataille, was the joy of free expenditure. This free excess could just barely be contained within the diplomatic atmosphere of Duncan's court, could just barely be harnessed by the dialectical waverings of Macbeth's metaphysical reveries; but in act 5 this excess as such leaps out into thought and language, and it is this particular upsurge that now interests me in the following discussions.

One is close here to the question of unthinkability reviewed at the opening of this book, for rationality—in the normal, dialectical sense—is one of the things that sovereign expenditure transgresses. Human life, writes Bataille, "cannot in any way be limited to the closed systems assigned to it by reasonable conceptions"; such systems are brittle shells that life itself bursts open as it constitutes itself through "[t]he immense travail of recklessness, discharge, and upheaval."[5] Art can of course reflect such a sovereign transgression of logical closure, since, as symbolic expenditure, literature and theater can stage a form of tragic loss that is not a loss that meaning can altogether appropriate.[6] If the symbolic principle itself is loss, the aesthetic experience approximates a condition of toxic excitation where the impulse to utilize material or moral goods rationally is rejected.[7] Because, as *Macbeth* shows, there exists at the basis of life a principle of irreducible insufficiency,[8] logic constantly recentering itself on (its own) moderation and platitude tends to work against the grain of reality: against the element of endless supplementarity that the closure of meaning never can neutralize.

As I shall presently try to show, the notion of expenditure is crucial in *Macbeth*, and quite explicitly so. But the tension between various types of expenditure is not only internal to the play "itself," but also conspicuous in the economic realities of its times. These economic oscillations are at once minute, comprising changes from one year to another, and vast, spanning entire eras of government. The first type of oscillation is reflected in the Porter's scene, with its various references to the fluctuating demands and supplies of corn. Also, there is "economic" thinking in the Porter's discussion of the unhappy tailor. In this way Shakespeare makes us feel that the principle of insufficiency is universal rather than particular—that what afflicts Macbeth in a major way has afflicted others in less grand fashion. The tailor is one who is obsessed with increasing profits, and therefore obsessed with the idea of abridgement. He steals material from the various fixed quantities of cloth defined by his contract with the purchaser; but when fashions change so that the tight-fitting "French hose" (2.3.14) has replaced the baggy breeches of an earlier epoch, the tailor finds that the margin for cheating is reduced: the new mode of production has eliminated the element of free expenditure in the use of cloth, and the tailor's illegal profit is based, in its own criminal fashion, on such "free expenditure."

If these types of minute shifts in real-life economies get indirectly dramatized in Shakespeare's play, so do the more sweeping changes—most of them centered on King James. This fairly free-spending monarch is, perhaps tragically, caught in a vast historical sliding that works against his temperament and against the fortune of his heirs. Clearly, England was moving from one type of spending to another. The English nobility began to cut down on the excesses of their lifestyle in the early seventeenth century: the "economy" moved away from the medieval code of public openhandedness toward a world of increasing privacy.[9] Yet the aristocratic excess that *Macbeth* tangentially discusses (4.3) was still a significant aspect of social reality. In the 1580s and 1590s such recklessness was conspicuous, Rutland spending at a rate of £12,000 a year, and the ninth Earl of Northumberland running up £15,000 worth of debts in a year and a half.[10] Curiously, James's general spending created more animosity than Elizabeth's non-spending (toward the end of her reign), for James's generosity was selective and arbitrary, while Elizabeth's senile meanness was universal and therefore homogeneous.[11] What we find then, to use Bataille's terminology, is not a restricted economy facing a general one (free and unconditional), but a general economy of restriction (Elizabeth's) facing a restricted economy of general spending (James's).

The engagement of this toxic monarch with "unproductive" types of expenditure (hunting, drinking, "gaming" in general—possibly including the act of *hunting* witches) is rather poignant in this context. In his list of activities forwarding unconditional expenditure (free from the production of meaning as rational utility) Bataille mentions the purchase of expensive jewels, the sacrifice of blood in various cults, and the participation in competitive games that are expensive to stage.[12] Bataille also argues that modern bourgeois society has crushed the age-old human tendency to engage affirmatively and spontaneously in the "free forms of unproductive social expenditure."[13] Expenditure as such has disappeared from the horizon of cultural activity. Suppressed as an excessive and ecstatic event, such a movement has become reified so that it today organizes itself inside the controlled and closed systems of modern economy. As infinitude, wealth complies to the boring conventions of shop-window display.[14] The dresses, jewels, and cars that wait for the sinister industrialist as he steps outside his bank belong to the unfreedom of dialectical lordship rather than to the affirmativeness of sovereign spending. Such items are logical units inside a narrowly rationalist conception of expenditure, one that is "humiliating" and utterly inglorious.[15]

The Notion of Expenditure 159

I think it is quite obvious that *Macbeth* activates this type of tension between restricted and free expenditure (between a restricted and a "general" economy)—and I now move rapidly on to discuss this very tension as an organizational principle for ontodramatic signification.

We might begin, as a matter of mere coincidence, with the idea of the connection between jewelry and expenditure (discussed by Bataille, above). This part of the play has little to do with the action of act 5, but I linger over some preparatory sections before actually engaging fully with that final act. Here in act 2, some time before the murder, Banquo speaks to Macbeth of Duncan's retiring gesture of royal expenditure: he has sent a fine gift to Lady Macbeth as token of friendship and trust.

> Who's there?
> *Macb.* A friend.
> *Ban.* What, Sir! not yet at rest? The King's a-bed:
> He hath been in unusual pleasure, and
> Sent forth great largess to your offices.
> This diamond he greets your wife withal,
> By the name of most kind hostess, and shut up
> In measureless content.
>
> (2.1.10–17)

Ontodramatically speaking, the most interesting unit here is "shut up / In measureless content," and I suggest we consider it in relation to the lines that Banquo speaks a few seconds earlier:

> Hold, take my sword. —There's husbandry in heaven;
> Their candles are all out. —Take thee that too.
> A heavy summons lies like lead upon me,
> And yet I would not sleep: merciful Powers!
> Restrain in me the cursed thoughts that nature
> Gives way to in repose! —Give me my sword.
>
> (2.1.4–9)

It should be said, first, that Banquo's "cursed thoughts" hardly refer us to any lurking maliciousness in him, as some critics think; it is rather unlikely that Shakespeare at all would care to besmirch the gracious ancestor of King James. The words are instead spoken as choric commentary on cosmic instability and anticipate not only the dreadfulness of murder but also the sense of cosmic disorder that emerges from the postmurder discussion between Rosse and the Old Man (2.4.4–20). If we turn to ontodramatic signification we see that the unit "shut up / In measureless content" (2.1.16–17) first of all reaches out to "husbandry in heaven" (2.1.4).

Heaven is normally conceived as the site of infinity. Heaven is infinity's home. But "husbandry"—the implementation of a restricted economy—suggests finitude, an organized abridgement. The notion that there is some thrift up in the heavens is faintly absurd, and Shakespeare is of course aware of this. The gods do not need to balance their accounts. The lack of light in the heavens, this lack of light that first seems to denote the absence of God's searching eye, is a lack that produces a feeling that no one is up there watching you. Yet at the same time an opposite effect is created: because it is so dark up there, they (or he, God) can see the world down below all that much better. The impression is similar to the sensation created by the hypnotic sensory deprivation encircling Macbeth during the Murther/Tarquin soliloquy, when he begs the stones not to prate of his presence. On the one hand the silence grants the privilege of a cosmic vacuum in which only the criminal and the crime strictly speaking *exist*; on the other hand the silence throws upon the entire universe the burden of an absolute attention and attentiveness. Theatrically speaking, the reference to the lack of moonlight and starlight serves the purpose of presencing a sense of pitch-black darkness; the description gives imaginative support to a spectator who in the playhouse would be witnessing the action in broad daylight. But ontodramatically speaking, the absent moonlight and starlight signify a world from which the powers of Light have temporarily been withdrawn as well as a world that presents divine surveillance in terms of its absence.

The contradiction in the unit "shut up / In measureless content" appears to rehearse this general sense of stricture in the Absolute promoted by heaven's husbandry. The "measureless," as that which cannot be measured, is infinite; but "shut up" suggests a finite closure or enclosure—depending on whether we read this unit as "concluded" (Steevens) or as "wrapped in" (Chambers). The contradiction might seem unimportant, for the meaning is after all clear and simple: the infinitude of "measureless" refers to monarchial bounty and a subjective state of mind, while "shut up" merely depicts the ending of a speech act or, more likely, the king's act of shutting himself up in his room for the night. But while this contradiction remains banal and critically speaking futile on an empirical level of dramatic understanding, it by no means remains so on an ontodramatic level.

The idea that Duncan shut up in "measureless content" (2.1.17) evokes a sense of fulness—and as ontodramatic sensation this fulness was first encountered in 1.4.[16] There his "plenteous joys, / Wanton in fulness, seek to hide themselves / In drops of sorrow" (1.4.33–35). Here, in our current scene (2.1), it is as if the "diamond" that is delivered from Duncan's inner chamber of measureless content (2.1.15) is a crystallized form of such a monarchial teardrop, spilling over from the selfsame fount of "unusual pleasure" (2.1.13). Yet whereas Macbeth, in his "vanishing" moments of ecstatic bliss, seems to have known truly unusual pleasure, Duncan's unusual pleasure is profoundly usual. The unusualness of his pleasure belongs to the norm of the usual, not the unusual. The "pleasure," as in the "wanton" fulness (1.4.34), far from being wanton, is absolutely chaste: absolutely mastered in terms of checked and self-regularized desire. The chastity I am defining now is no moral chastity but an ontological one. Ordered and reserved forces are strengthening the closed systems they consolidate—and "shut up" merely finalizes the sensation of such closure and control of expenditure. In the play's first dramatization of heroic rewards, the king certainly seems to spend himself absolutely, but the monarchial gifts are of course ordered in their measurelessness according to a fixed formula that measures Malcolm as "Prince of Cumberland" and the rest as nondescript props:

> We will establish our estate upon
> Our eldest, Malcolm; whom we name hereafter
> The Prince of Cumberland: which honour must
> Not unaccompanied invest him only,
> But signs of nobleness, like stars, shall shine
> On all deservers.
>
> (1.4.37–42)

It is not necessary, as I have argued throughout, to posit some politically manipulative Duncan behind this power discourse. The law of economic stricture ontologizes itself as well as its own language—so that the husbandry of the absolute head of state no more belongs strictly to Duncan here than it belongs to the person Malcolm in the stylized finale:

> We *shall not spend a large expense* of time,
> Before we *reckon* with your several loves,
> *And make us even with you.* My Thanes and kinsmen,
> Henceforth be Earls; the first that ever Scotland

>   In such an honour nam'd. What's more to do,
>   Which would be planted newly with the time,—
>   . . . .
>   by the grace of Grace,
>   We will perform *in measure*, time, and place.
>   So thanks to all at once, and to each one,
>   Whom we invite to see us crown'd at Scone.
>
>   (5.9.26–41)

On this night of starless "husbandry," then (2.1.4), the retiring king has "[s]ent forth great largess" (2.1.14) within a closed economy of "shut up" freedom that distributes the radiance of its currency in the manner of royal generosity in act 1: "signs of nobleness, *like stars*, shall shine / On all deservers (1.4.41–42). The king falls asleep in a world that is absolutely secure, in a world of absolute self-presence. He falls asleep in *himself*. Measurelessly.

Now when act 5 foregrounds Macbeth's conquerors in terms of heroic presence, there is not only an ontological emphasis on meaning as restricted economy but also on the dialectical nature of this productive economy:

> SCENE 9—*Within the castle.*
>
> *Retreat. Flourish. Enter, with drum and colours, Malcolm, old Siward, Rosse, Thanes, and Soldiers.*
>
> Mal. I would the friends we miss were safe arriv'd.
> Siw. Some must go off; and yet, by these I see,
>   So great a day as this is cheaply bought.
> Mal. Macduff is missing, and your noble son.
> Rosse. Your son, my Lord, has paid a soldier's debt:
>   He only liv'd but till he was man;
>   The which no sooner had his prowess confirm'd,
>   In the unshrinking station where he fought,
>   But like a man he died.
> Siw.   Then he is dead?
> Rosse. Ay, and brought off the field. Your cause of sorrow
>   Must not be measur'd by his worth, for then
>   It hath no end.
> Siw.   Had he his hurts before?
> Rosse. Ay, on the front.
> Siw.   Why then, God's soldier be he!
>   Had I as many sons as I have hairs,
>   I would not wish them to a fairer death:
>   And so, his knell is knoll'd.

> Mal.   He's worth more sorrow,
>   And that I'll spend for him.
> Siw.   He's worth no more;
>   They say he parted well and paid his score:
>   And so, God be with him!
>
>   (5.9.1–19)

Dialectic reigns. Meaning-versus-nonmeaning fits perfectly into the opposition frontal wound versus rear wound. Transcendental truth faces untranscendental untruth symmetrically and reassuringly: as recto and verso, positive and negative, good and evil, right and wrong. The "economic" thinking of heroic recognition is conspicuously restricted, but also conspicuously economic: the great day is "cheaply bought," and in this buying-and-selling of Truth/Meaning/Honor young Siward "has paid a soldier's debt." The economic restriction, moreover, is not passive and implicit but quite active and explicit: as soon as youthful[17] Malcolm offers to turn restricted mourning into unrestricted mourning, Siward, as the essence of normative heroic orderliness, intervenes and brings back things to their proper focus and logical proportion. An absolute expenditure in general is out of the question. Having become dialectically recognized in the proper manner and according to just proportions, his son's epoch of productivity is terminated. "He's worth no more" (5.9.17). The son has "paid" his destined score, and having been amply rewarded by Meaning/God/Truth, he cannot expect *more than that.* By definition, divine and transcendental recognition, however small, has already infinitized its productive potential. To ask for more than infinity is absurd.

The phallocentricity of all this heroic masculinity is of course oppressive for most modern audiences. The male hemisphere, as far as action goes, has taken over completely. Woman, in act 5, is only present in her absence. Lady Macbeth can only walk into act 5 when she is asleep, and her offstage dying in 5.5 only helps to finalize this sense of the marginalization of her presence. The news of her death enters action like a small footnote, a tiny pebble dropped into an ocean of unfeminine awareness.[18]

Yet if femininity has disappeared from act 5 in an empirical sense, it may not have done so in a more important one—the ontodramatic. The fact that Macbeth has negotiated his entire dramatic existence in the vicinity of the sisters and of his wife lends him a form of heroism in act 5 that is not exclusively heroic. His masculinity may still be masculinity—but unlike the solidly forthright manliness of venerable knights like Old Siward it comes across as unstable and self-ironic. Certainly, Macbeth is still classically masterful in that he can distinguish between "honour" and "mouth-honour" (5.3.25–27), that he can unflinchingly meet young Siward's challenge to the duel (5.7.5–11), and that he can finally participate in a dialectically organized struggle to death with Macduff. When masterful Macduff commands him to yield (5.8.23) and Macbeth understands that yielding implies the ultimate soiling of heroic dignity and heroic recognition, the reassembly of what is heroically dormant is striking. What characterizes heroic masters fighting for recognition characterizes Macbeth to the bitter end: the refusal ever to surrender:

> I will try the last: before my body
> I throw my warlike shield: lay on, Macduff;
> And damn'd be him that first cries, "Hold, enough!"
> (5.8.32–34)

But in spite of this apparent reacceptance of the dialectical conditions of possibility for the production of meaning, there is the sensation of a subtle unbalancing of that world of meaning. Recklessness has defined Macbeth all along, but Macbethian recklessness evades ipseity by constantly sliding into new modes of suggestion. As athletic "vanishing," masterful recklessness in act 1 promoted the sensation of speed and fearlessness; in the reversed world of the drama's middle portions, recklessness was servile rather than masterful—a function of desperation and fear: "let the frame of things disjoint" (3.2.16); "come, fate, into the list, / And champion me to th'utterance!" (3.1.70–71). But as military recklessness now reappears ("Blow, wind! come, wrack! / At least we'll die with harness on our back," 5.5.51–52), it is neither masterful nor servile. It is, as I will be arguing (still following Bataille's terminology), sovereign: sovereign recklessness. Here the disinclination to fight (5.7.2; 5.8.5–6; 5.8.22) is not the function of a (dialectical) negation of heroic courage, nor a function of servile anguish and retreat to metaphysical reverie. Undecided, but not indifferent to the dialectical poles, sovereign recklessness opens up what Shakespeare now forces us to think beyond what the drama hitherto has demanded of thinking.

6.2 Sovereignty

The state of sovereignty—if it is a state—is so delicate and volatile that it is probably entirely missed in many productions and readings. Yet the potential for what is sovereign has been written into the dramatic text as the condition of possibility for its finest moments of poetic and dramatic excitement. This delicacy of sovereignty, its presence in space as vanishing and in time as transgression, makes the critical task of preparing the ground for its identification peculiarly troublesome—"sovereignty" being what strictly speaking eludes identity and identification. In such a venture one runs the constant risk of overstating one's case, of *showing* sovereignty, of triumphantly claiming one has collar'd it (as Dickens would say). Yet, paradoxically, sovereignty only yields up what is sovereign by means of some overstating—some extraordinary emphasis that calls attention to that which has passed beyond moderation and platitudes. One could not gently *coax* sovereignty into the provisional reality of its possible appearing; as something wild rather than tame, sovereignty has to be worried out of its retreat by the hounds and terriers of the most obstinate inquiry.

Jacques Derrida follows Georges Bataille closely in his essay "From Restricted to General Economy: A Hegelianism without Reserve" (WD, 215–77). In Nietzschean style, "free" negativity is something quasi-heroic, quasi-pagan: a noble "expenditure" (271), an "expenditure without reserve" (268), a "gay affirmation of death" (274), an "awakening to death" (276), a "sovereign affirmation of the play outside meaning" (274), an "excess of nonmeaning" (273), an "exceeding energy as such" (271), an "absolute unknowledge" (268), a sovereign silence (262–63) producing ecstasy (263) and ecstatic poetry (261), something that does not want to greedily maintain its own self, clutch itself, govern itself, watch itself, master itself (264), become recognized (265). But this desire to burst the ontological circularity of a restricted economy is not only conspicuous in Derrida's commentry on Bataille but also in works of general theoretical inquiry like *Glas* where, it will be remembered, "[t]he contraction, the economic restriction forms the annulus of the selfsame, of the self-return, of reappropriation. The economy restricts itself; the sacrifice sacrifices itself."[19] The sacrifice is not a real sacrifice, not a sacrifice, and thus can be said to sacrifice what is truly sacrificial, to sacrifice sacrifice. The sacrificial expenditure calculates its dividends and returns, all that returns to it in terms of meaning. To give here means to hypocritically guard and keep.[20] What joyously escapes lordship and the harvesting of meaning is thus what rational productivity happens to neglect. As sovereign trace, the item that liberates itself from the logical calculations of the apparatus of productivity is what by chance remains outside its masterful onslaught: "The [sovereign] sacrifice . . . is total, holds back no enjoyment, except . . . through abandoned laughter. If it leaves behind a chance survivor, it does so unbeknownst to itself, like the flower of the fields after the harvest" (WD, 266). A very different "sovereign flower" appears in *Macbeth*, act 5:

> Cath.   Well; march we on,
> To give obedience where 'tis truly ow'd:
> Meet we the med'cine of the sickly weal;
> And with him pour we, in our country's purge,
> Each drop of us.
> Len.   *Or so much as it needs*
> *To dew the sovereign flower, and drown the weeds.*
>   (5.2.25–30)

Here the "sovereign flower" (5.2.30), far from belonging to "sovereignty" (in Bataille's sense), belongs to lordship: to a restricted and dialectical economy where all loss is related to the measuring of profit and all profit to the measuring of loss. We saw earlier how Old Siward quickly and rationally turned Malcolm's general expenditure of emotion into a restricted one (5.9.16–17), and here the selfsame pattern is evident. The general outpouring first proposed (by Cathness) quickly checks its sovereign excess, transforming its affirmation of absolute sacrificial loss into the moderate and calculated measure of a restricted outpouring: excess as such is changed into the right excess, the appropriate excess, the most fitting excess—the degree of excess that the situation logically demands. *Glas* again: "Always *already*, the [pseudo-sacrificial] gift . . . calculates on two registers the expenditures and the receipts."[21]

We see once more here how Shakespeare is working throughout the play with the notion of the *watery drop* and how this image comes to negotiate the economic thinking of the play by signifying the excess of an absolute outpouring as well as the sublation and retention of such outpouring. The watery source of these various "drops" seems to be the monarchial expenditure that we have already discussed: "Wanton in fulness," Duncan's joys sought to "hide themselves" inside the gentle flow of a trickle of tears (1.4.33–35). Our sympathies for Duncan are not diminished by this weeping of his; on the contrary, he has all our respect. Yet the timidity of his expenditures—which is ontodramatically the timidity of the spending, not of Duncan—comes into overall interaction with the sensation of other re-

Sovereignty

stricted outpourings. Here in the passage just quoted from act 5 we see how the "sovereign flower" (5.2.30) of dialectical mastery only can grow inside a restricted economy where it escapes from the risk of drowning. It must be dewed, not flooded. Mastery transforms the possibility of the flood into the reasonableness of a nurturant economy, into a fit sprinkling that calculates the pattern of its dispersal: that which spares the "sovereign flower" must annul the weeds (5.2.29–30). Whereas act 1, through the dread of its battle scenes, gave us the sensation of an absolute noncaution (1.2.40–41), act 5 now presences the world of heroic fighting as a site where the product of dialectical struggle (dialectical meaning as social reputation) is more important than the ecstasy of the competitive game itself. Caution has now intervened so as to ensure that the heroic engagement is productive in the correct sense: the production of unproductive values must be marginalized. This becalming of heroic recklessness, the foregrounding of the conquering thanes as agents of dialectical moderation, is an important ontodramatic move in the play, for it helps to make Macbeth emerge into the "sovereign" state that I shall presently be discussing as his final tragic status. Sovereign Macbeth as he finally appears thus negates the cautionary rationality of the wise thanes as well as the servile Macbeth that anxiously nursed his mania for certainty in act 3 and act 4.

The medicinal "drop" dewing the sovereign flower (5.2.30) is not only related ontodramatically to the gentle monarchial expenditures that we have just discussed but also to the entire ontodramatic nexus of fluids as equivocating liquids: drugs as drinks, drinks as drugs—all that is pharmaceutically and economically undecided. Like the Derridean "pharmakon," the drug becomes a dangerous supplement, complicating our sense of the line of demarcation between inside and outside, cure and disease. We have already looked at the equivocating potential of the pharmakon/drink/drug when Lady Macbeth medicined the drink of the grooms prior to the murder of Duncan: "That which hath made them drunk hath made me bold: / What hath quench'd them hath given me fire" (2.2.1–2). In that premurder scene, then, we saw a degree of self-ministering in Lady Macbeth; and such self-ministering is a notion of cardinal importance in act 5 too.

How does your patient, Doctor?
Doct. Not so sick, my Lord,

> As she is troubled with thick-coming fancies,
> That keep her from her rest.
> *Macb.*   Cure her of that:
> Canst thou not minister to a mind diseas'd,
> Pluck from the memory a rooted sorrow,
> Raze out the written troubles of the brain,
> And with some sweet oblivious antidote
> Cleanse the stuff'd bosom of that perilous stuff
> Which weighs upon the heart?
> *Doct.*   Therein the patient
> Must minister to himself.
> *Macb.* Throw physic to the dogs; I'll none of it.—
> Come, put mine armour on; give me my staff.—
>
> (5.3.37–48)

It might be worth noting in passing here that the unit "written troubles" reflects the notion of *writing* as troublesomeness as it appeared earlier in the servile effort to eliminate "rubs" and "botches" from transcendental "clearness" (3.1.132–33). But the most important movement is obviously the feeling that Macbeth himself is drawn into the pharmaceutic problematic (and not merely his ailing wife). Moreover, we see that the unit "Throw physic to the dogs" indicates a general dismissal of the pharmakon as supplement. Not only is Macbeth moving toward a frame of mind where the antidote fails to operate, to *be* an antidote; he is also moving toward a sovereign state of awareness in which what is thrown to the dogs is the entire dialectical world where remedy and poison face one another symmetrically and reassuringly. At this point, in other words, he is already stepping into the sliding that finally dumps him in the absolute loss of meaning ("Signifying nothing") that is affirmed in the play's sovereign soliloquy: "To-morrow, and to-morrow, and to-morrow" (5.5.19–28). Macbeth's discussion of the "purgative drug" (5.3.55) with the Doctor is monitored from a point where not only drugs but also doctors are viewed in a somewhat comical light: as if through an invisible glass wall separating two worlds. In this absolutely translucent mutual alienation there is, to be sure, a degree of envy in Macbeth—envy of a world where an "antidote" still is an antidote, where *pro* and *con* still mean. Yet equally, and alongside this sadly remote envy, there is also a kind of sovereign pity for the Doctor: so that Macbeth, in maintaining conversation with him, is like an adult talking to a child from a superior sphere of experience and insight. Not patronizingly, perhaps, but with a kind of muted sagacity, outwardly modulated as reckless buoyancy, or simulated gusto.

Underlying Macbeth's sense of sovereign nonmeaning and of the futility of the auto-purgation suggested by the Doctor is his awareness of a general cosmic organization that forbids and disrupts ontological mastery of the remedy/pharmakon/drug/supplement. What gets implemented as remedy, he has tragically learned, swings round in its very curative operation, transforming itself into the poisonous. As undecidability, the pharmakon upsets the world it should medicine. The sensitive spectator now notices the appreciable intensification of the sovereign affirmation as Macbeth renews his gay engagement with the pharmakon. He has thrown physic to the dogs (5.3.47), but in spite of this utter and absolute dismissal of the pharmakon, he cannot help himself from picking it up again.

> Throw physic to the dogs; I'll none of it.—
> Come, put mine armour on; give me my staff.—
> Seyton, send out—Doctor, the Thanes fly from me.—
> Come, sir, despatch.—If thou couldst, Doctor, cast
> The water of my land, find her disease,
> And purge it to a sound and pristine health,
> I would applaud thee to the very echo,
> That should applaud again. —Pull't off, I say.—
> What rhubarb, cyme or what purgative drug,
> Would scour these English hence?
>
> (5.3.47–56)

If sovereignty at all could make a first appearance as unit or pointlike linguistic occurence, its gay materialization in *Macbeth* would undoubtedly emerge in "rhubarb" and in "cyme." "Sovereignty," bursting through the walls of Meaning/Truth, spends itself in an absolutely unproductive discharge that is the joy of language signifying a bliss indistinguishable from a loss of meaning. Unlike the inquiry into the well-being of Lady Macbeth that took place a moment ago, the entire passage just quoted is the ontodramatic equivalent of a tremendous burst of laughter. This laughter, as "sovereign laughter" (in Bataille's sense), would not be "normal," dialectical laughter, laughter that signals comic relief in a to-and-fro between the solemn and the amused, the tragic pressure and the release of that tragic pressure—but instead laughter "close to anguish" (WD, 252), instrumental in the desire "to fold discourse into strange shapes" through an absolute, superfluous, nonmeaningful, gay excess (253): rhubarb and cyme.

The Doctor is here drastically marginalized, and so is also all the enigma that "his" pharmakon organizes; what instead is centered is the business of the day—getting the armor in its right position, getting ready for more dialectical struggles to death. But in a sense the Doctor, precisely by being marginalized, is focused with an unprecedented intensity—that which the margin alone facilitates and makes possible. Conversely, the actual dialectical business of the day is in the way, is a tiresome obstacle, a center of physical struggle that is strangely entangled by the obviousness of its centeredness. (By being so immediately available and necessary, the armor provisionally obstructs its own purposiveness as its impatient owner hurries ahead of his own action.)

The game is up, and the Doctor understands that Macbeth's questions are "rhetorical questions" as we say. There is no real way of answering Macbeth's request for a "purgative drug" to scour the English hence. But while the Doctor actually understands this particular dimension of what is "rhetorical," he is outside the possibility of grasping what is sovereign in the rhetorical affirmation. He can understand the spiritual exhaustion in Macbeth and that "rhubarb" and "cyme" signal a linguistically absurd movement, a loss of "sincere meaning." But what the Doctor never can fully appreciate is the sovereign sensation of freedom achieved in and through this loss: that "rhubarb" and "cyme" now are set *entirely* free into the gaiety of language. They now mean, just through their linguistic and dramatic situatedness, the immeasurable ruination of meaning. "Rhubarb" and "cyme" get written into a peculiar delicate spacing that addresses itself to a sovereign "beyond-reason."[22]

The jubilation that is here negotiated is not ostentatious, or even strictly speaking tangible and present. There is no pause or interval in which Macbeth lets the sovereign moment crystallize. By definition, the sovereign moment is not something that can crystallize. By definition, the sovereign moment is not a moment. It comes, and in that coming it is gone. It vanishes, and is vanishing. In this zone of linguistic hyperactivity, the "[s]overeign transgression" (*WD*, 268), as an ecstatic "transgression of discourse" (274), is so instantaneous and the burst-through so pure that it is Macbeth the (dialectical) master that laughs but Macbeth the (nondialectical) sovereign who *has* laughed. "Laughter," then (as discourse dismantling the opposition be-

Sovereignty

tween sincerity and irony), does not "illustrate" or "reflect" anything—least of all sovereignty—but is instead the staging of the sovereign (non)moment itself, something neither active nor passive. The sovereign laughter of act 5, organizing itself around the unit "Our castle's strength / Will laugh a siege to scorn" (5.5.2–3), thus reanimates and perfects what we identified from the outset as the crucial element of "vanishing" in *Macbeth*.[23] Although "vanishing," as we see below, can be discussed in temporal terms, it is not itself reducible to temporal thought but belongs, precisely, to the unthinkability that the temporal attitude of Western awareness has excluded from its mind:

> And the *instant*—the temporal mode of the sovereign operation—is not a *point* of full and unpenetrated presence: it slides and *eludes* us between two presences; it is difference as the affirmative elusion of presence. It does not give itself but is *stolen*, carries itself off in a movement which is simultaneously one of violent effraction and of vanishing flight. The instant is the *furtive*. (WD, 263)

> [Q]uickly, furtively, . . . as betrayal or as detachment, drily, laughter bursts out. And yet, in privileged moments that are less moments than the always rapidly sketched movements of experience; rare, discrete and light movements, without triumphant stupidity, far from public view, very close to that at which laughter laughs: close to anguish. (WD, 252)

The instability of the purgative drug (as pharmakon/supplement) in *Macbeth* in general and in act 5 in particular is of course related to the instability of "drink" as discussed by the Porter in 2.3. What the Porter says there about the ultimate essence of drink is that it does not have one. Drink equivocates, dissolving the identity of the drinker but also dissolving any proper identity that it could itself wish to have. Drink, like the pharmakon, determines itself in terms of indetermination.[24] But this equivocation in the drink/drug/supplement/pharmakon/medicine cannot possibly be separated from the structure of the play as a whole, least of all from its meaning; for that meaning, centered on the oracular and uncanny conception of Truth, is itself centrally caught in the equivocating depth-formula of the supplement. Truth, as constantly needed supplement, is the hero's equivocator: it makes Macbeth, and it mars Macbeth. It sets him on, and it takes him off. It persuades him, but it just as much disheartens him. It makes him stand to, and not stand to. In conclusion, it equivocates him in a sleep, and, giving him the lie, leaves him. The pharmakon provokes and unprovokes, "it makes him, and it mars him"; and this making/marring does not merely structure sexual and physical desire (2.3.31–35) but also desire in general as it is foregrounded in the play as the energy of its supplementary drive. Lady Macbeth: "They [time and place] have *made* themselves, and that their fitness now / Does *unmake* you" (1.7.53–54). As drink displaces presence (as well as itself as proper essence) for the Porter, so the murderous opportunity (as we saw at the outset) cannot be made viable in this play in terms of sheer presence. For Lady Macbeth "murder" might be ontologized and centered in such fashion, but for the hero it is essential that murder become less and less thinkable as the presence of its natural availability and more and more thinkable as the unreality of that availability. For the hero it is essential that murder lacks an essence. As the Porter playfully ontologizes drink by naming and identifying the knowable appearing of its essential phenomenology, we see that Shakespeare is focusing the displacement of ontologized centeredness on more planes than one. The project of *determining* drink and giving it a stable essence/identity is as futile and absurd as the project of "determining" murder and appropriating it as a "thing" one could logically manage and leave behind:

> and drink, Sir, is a great provoker of three things.
> *Macd.* What three things does drink especially provoke?
> *Port.* Marry, Sir, nose-painting, sleep, and urine.
> (2.3.25–27)

Drink can of course not produce any finite set of consequences; it organizes itself so that its production of consequences is structurally infinite—that is, not very structural at all. The soliloquy on "consequences" has engaged with this very indefinition of consequentiality ("trammel up the consequence," 1.7.3) suggesting to us that a review of "consequences" in terms of their restricted economy is futile since the supplementary chain will unleash effects beyond the horizon of what the logical mind can foresee or calculate. Similarly, the aftereffects of the drink/drug, though a pragmatic issue for a porter with a hangover, cannot be essentialized, since the lack of foreseeable definition and proper identity will withdraw what is properly self-present in that area of risk. *Propriety* in general is drawn away, drink spreading uncontrollably into what is improper, unknown, and unknowable.

6.3 Tragic Simulacrum

G. I. Duthie once observed that Macbeth's situation in act 5 is logically paradoxical. The hero "is violently defending something (his life) which he has come to regard as totally valueless to him. So even at the end, as far as he is concerned, opposites coexist in the same action—the noble and the absurd, the sublime and the ridiculous."[25] Macbeth of course regarded his life as "valueless" in the fighting of act 1 too (and that is why act 1 and act 5 negotiate a curious resemblance); yet while the current sense of absent life-value is produced by the absolute emptying of the epoch of meaning, the act of treating empirical existence as "valueless" in act 1 was produced by the absolutely opposite gesture of subordinating mere "life" to the ideals that fighting for one's country implied. But what is most important in Duthie's commentary is the idea of the coexistence of polar opposites: that Macbeth seeks to preserve what no longer is really worth preserving—and that this collapse of a world of dialectically organized possibilities itself creates two opposite impressions that normally are mutually exclusive: "the sublime and the ridiculous."

Macbeth continues to be aware of the difference between winning and losing, overcoming his enemies and being disgraced by their triumph. He still in a sense wants to win, as the final combat with Macduff indicates, and as the final disappointment at prophecy's hollowness proves. On the other hand, though, there is in Macbeth the expanding recognition of an odd coimplication between failure and success. Such a recognition would seem to be "sovereign" in its nature (still following Bataille's terminology): mastery "becomes sovereign when it ceases to fear failure" (WD, 265). The sovereign fails "by failing absolutely, which is simultaneously to lose the very meaning of failure by gaining nonservility" (ibid.). This is exactly what happens to Macbeth in act 5. Although he continues to experience significant moments of pure dread, and although fear continues to structure the ontodramatic terrain, the overriding concern is not to avoid failure, as it was in the middle acts.[26] As notion, failure came to dominate Macbeth's mind as soon as prophecy suggested Truth as crowning metaphysical possibility; conversely, the loss of the fear of failure (and thus the act of "gaining nonservility") coincides with the gradual loss of the faith in (metaphysical) Truth. Macbeth is thus "restored" to the preservile state of being fearless and of having faith in his fearlessness; but since that fearlessness was already dialectically nourished by a forestructure of metaphysical truth, viz., heroic truth, the new type of sovereign and nonservile loss of faith in Truth also undermines fearlessness in its ancient guise. In fact Macbeth now emerges into a strange territory where fear and fearlessness are as dialectically unclear in their oppositional function as are failure and success. What has to be *thought* now, as the condition of possibility for sovereign signification in the hyperontological sphere of act 5, is a world where these opposites are "real" but where their reality is displaced from dialectical norms.

As I have indicated on two separate occasions in this chapter, "sovereignty" cannot be easily identified in terms of logical space or temporal locus: as "vanishing" it tends to slip away from the grasp of critical appropriation, and as "moment" it tends to mock our normal sense of temporality. But to these logical and temporal difficulties one could add a spatial one, one already hinted at in the reference to the danger of locating "sovereignty" within any lexical unit or attaching it firmly to any linguistic structure. Here in act 5 the spatial elusiveness is not only a critical "difficulty," however, but also the very condition of possibility for the material appearing of the sovereign as dramatic figure: as a man ready to fight, die, and stage his tragic fortitude.

While the original struggle to death, as the originary site for the first production of dialectical meaning, promotes annihilation and nothingness, the absolute defiance of all solid "human" presence and biological empiricalness,[27] that readiness for annihilation—as we saw in act 1—does not imply invisibility. On the contrary, the "nothingness"[28] into which fighting masters disappear (as the realm and horizon of their deathward desire) is the most visible thing in the world. Nothing could be more visible than Macbeth's fighting in act 1, because glory is nothing but recognition, and recognition is nothing if it is not recognized as such—if it is not recognized as glory: immediately, ostentatiously, absolutely, universally, and indisputably. One disputes, engages in the deathward duel, to emerge from it in terms of the indisputable: absolutely visible through one's death or absolutely visible through one's triumph. Macbeth *appears* to us, as "Macbeth," in and through the struggle to death of act 1. Indeed, the struggle to death is classically what high-philosophy has identified as the originary ontological site for the appearing of appearing, for phenomenology. Unlike animals, humans self-consciously stage the business of appearing as the business of producing meaning, so that becoming-visible and becoming-meaningful (in the idealist sense) converge in the transcendental locus where human recognition is originally produced. Macbeth becomes meaningful for his heroic society in the place where he becomes absolutely visible (the battlefield), and therefore any disruption of his meaningfulness (at least in his own consciousness) must somehow involve a dislocation of the sense of what a battlefield is, what a struggle to death is. Now, Shakespeare, I believe, has a pretty shrewd idea of the importance of this dramatic dislocation of the struggle to death, and I now proceed to examine the fracturing of its phenomenology in terms of a fracturing of its (dialectical) visibility. The dramatic and technical problem that Shakespeare (and in a sense Macbeth) now faces might be summed up as follows: how can the fighter become "visible" in a dialectical struggle to death if he no longer truly participates in dialectic, if his "visibility" no longer is a dialectical visibility (a phenomenological appearing), if he no longer really struggles? This problem may be put in optical terms (What *is* visibility when it is no longer dialectical? How is a nondialectical visibility at all visible?), and I therefore first turn to a discussion of a theory of problematized vision in order to prepare the ground for the subsequent exposition.

In *Truth and Method*, Hans-Georg Gadamer discusses our tendency to invariance in seeing and reading. Seeing, the author remarks, means differentiation; and during the small lapse of time when we are hesitating between differing forms of optical discrimination, trying various versions as while figuring out trick pictures, we fail for a while to perceive what is there. "The trick picture is, as it were, the artificial perpetuation of this hesitation, the 'agony' of seeing. The same is true of a literary work."[29] Now the transitions that *snap* Macbeth in and out of sovereignty (or that snap the spectator in and out of the possibility of apprehending sovereign Macbeth as visible) are transitions, precisely, that create the doubleness, equivocation, and hesitation that here are discussed in terms of the "agony" of seeing. In the trick picture, the hesitations are *immediate*, and so are the hesitations that simultaneously negotiate the opposed possibilities of lordship and sovereignty in act 5. Language, like signification and dramatic presence, here acquires the quality of the moiré, so that "difference," as dialectical oppositionality, gets smoothed out into what is fluidly undulating. The uncertainty of vision here becomes ours as much as that of the hero, his as much as ours. Because of this opened sphere of simulacrum—surface playing with surface, light with light, as in shot silk—there are now in a sense *only* hesitations. As in the trick picture, the discontinuity of hesitation is flattened out, becoming the actual surface of what is seen. Hesitation and its object merge. Equivocation and its site of staging dissolve into one another. Seeing and theater are one (cf. 5.5.34).

Simulacrum may now perhaps be understood as a function of those very "immediate" spacings that cause the trick picture to be at once possible and impossible as singular identity. The transitions that "snap" Macbeth "into" sovereignty and then "back" to lordship are transitions, indeed, that call forth no interface. The interface, while operative as difference, is not itself there as a dialectical dividing line. No tangible, self-present line of demarcation can be scientifically identified; such a line, while being crucially effective, cannot be retrieved as such. It is a "trace" following and preceding action, yet it has no traceable habitation. The interface is part and parcel of the (optional) figures themselves, one of the innumerable sinuous lines that make up their lineaments. Hence the transitions between gestalt and gestalt, while mediated (by the contralateral gestalt) are absolutely immediate. The erasure of one silhouette *is* the burgeoning appearance of its structural twin.

Thus, if "sovereign" Macbeth is "invisible," hidden inside, behind, or in front of masterful Macbeth, "he" is not hidden dialectically. He is no shadow persona or alter ego, he has no existence separate from the wrathful and volcanic master who despotically urges his men to hang out banners, man the battlements, bring his armor, and so on. The lord and the "sovereign" do not alternate, they hesitate. They defer one another. Simultaneously. We can—as spectators or critics—only produce the one by recognizing the other. We can only *slip*. All that possibly could supply us with the required foothold is an uncommon attentiveness turned toward Shakespeare's language itself.

The sovereign simulacrum, as trick, displaced visibility, and visionary agony, belongs with sovereign laughter to the general organization of sovereign gaiety. What gaiety? The one that is not release or comic relief, that is no "support" for what soberly frames it—but the one that unproductively and unconditionally affirms the pure sacrifice of meaning. Nothing beyond the optional pictures themselves, their play, is gained by knowing the law of their indecision—nothing, that is, except their *trick*. As sliding, this sovereign gaiety can be represented by the angle, by the introduction of the visibility of an invisible angulation. Olivier's Macbeth wore his crown slightly tilted and off-balance. Once the epoch of this tilting and minute dissymmetry has been inaugurated, meaning itself can vanish in an anguished burst of laughter that, precisely, no longer can *betoken* anguish. Laughter now betokens nothing. Laughter now betokens laughter; and thus, even in its first burst, it has affirmed the simulacrum. Laughter that betokens laughter now simulates laughter that betokens. Amusement is hollow not because it itself lacks substance but because it reverberates endlessly at its own free will (cf. "I would applaud thee to the very echo / That should applaud again," 5.3.53–54). The "amusement," of course, can take many different courses, all of them more or less "sovereign." McKellan provided savage laughter to edge his cosmic disgust as the "tomorrow" soliloquy finally suggested life as a great joke (*MM*, 619–20), and several actors lapse into brutal laughter as Macbeth tells the Doctor to throw physic to the dogs (*MM*, 603).

Laughter, now, is the space where the simulacrum is about to be staged:

> This burst of laughter makes the difference between lordship and sovereignty shine, without *showing* it however and, above all, without saying it. Sovereignty, as we shall verify, is more and less than lordship, more or less free than it, for example; and what we are saying about the predicate "freedom" can be extended to every characteristic of lordship. Simultaneously more and less a lordship than lordship, sovereignty is totally other. . . . [S]overeignty is no longer a figure in the continuous chain of [meaningful, "Hegelian"] phenomenology. *Resembling* a phenomenological figure, *trait for trait*, sovereignty is the absolute alteration of all of them. And this difference would not be produced if the analogy was limited to a given abstract characteristic. Far from being an abstract negativity [as Hegel called "pointless" sacrifice], sovereignty (the absolute degree of putting at stake), rather, must make the seriousness of meaning appear as an abstraction [of lesser worth] inscribed in [the bliss and glory of affirmative] play. Laughter, which constitutes sovereignty in its relation to death, is not a [dialectical] negativity [among a logically organized set of symmetrically negative terms], as has been said [by Sartre and others]. And it laughs at itself, a "major" laughter laughs at a "minor" laughter. [T]he sovereign operation . . . must simulate, after a fashion, the absolute risk [of the struggle to death], and it must laugh at this simulacrum. In the comedy that it thereby plays for itself [a tale full of sound and fury?], the burst of laughter is the almost-nothing into which meaning sinks, absolutely. (*WD*, 256; emphasis added, except for *"showing"*)

Is this not a recapitulation of what happens ontodramatically in act 5?—that Macbeth "must simulate, after a fashion, the absolute risk," quite earnestly, but that in the serious reengagement with that lethal risk, he "must laugh at this simulacrum."

As *Theater Quarterly* reviews Olivier's rendition of "Well, then, now" (3.1.74), there is a discussion of a linguistic all-powerfulness that anticipates my future lines of approach to linguistic sovereignty in act 5. Here Macbeth, already as impatient as he is for most of the time in act 5, confronts the prospective murderers. (Notice the "gay angulation" mentioned earlier.) Ontodramatically, this section clearly belongs to what we have been discussing as "sovereign laughter."

> He stood centre-stage, in his vivid red gown, black-bearded, with his crown at a mere suggestion of an angle on his head.... Olivier glanced arrogantly from one [murderer] to the other, crooked the index finger of each hand in terrible invitation, and made "well" into a question. He paused. The murderers looked at one another. The index fingers swept downwards and pointed straight at the floor on each side of him. He said "then" as a command. They moved slowly towards him like frightened stoats. Almost humorously, but with an edge of impatience, he said "now" and an act of hypnosis was completed. (*MM*, 400–401)

What is interesting here is Olivier's ability to compress the lord ("as a command") and the sovereign ("Almost humorously") into one another—suggesting the precarious dividing line that I have already discussed. It is also important to notice the smallness of the linguistic unit ("Well then, now") carrying the burden of this entire ontodramatic complexity. As I now turn to a fascinating section of act 5, I focus a further minute linguistic unit with comparable powers of signification.

> *Macb.* Bring me no more reports; let them fly all:
> Till Birnam wood remove to Dunsinane,
> I cannot taint with fear. What's the boy Malcolm?
> Was he not born of woman? The spirits that know
> All mortal consequence have pronounc'd me thus:
> "Fear not, Macbeth; no man that's born of woman
> Shall e'er have power upon thee." —Then fly, false Thanes,
> And mingle with the English epicures:
> The mind I sway by, and the heart I bear,
> Shall never sag with doubt, nor shake with fear.
> *Enter a Servant.*
> The devil damn thee black, thou cream-fac'd loon!
> Where gott'st thou that goose look?
> *Serv.* There is ten thousand—

Tragic Simulacrum

Macb.   Geese, villain?
Serv.   Soldiers, Sir.
Macb. Go prick thy face, and over-red thy fear,
  Thou lily-liver'd boy. What soldiers, patch?
  Death of thy soul! those linen cheeks of thine
  Are counsellors to fear. What soldiers, whey-face?
Serv. The English force, so please you.
Macb. Take thy face hence. *[Exit Servant.]*—Seyton!—I am sick at
  heart
  When I behold—Seyton, I say!—This push
  Will cheer me ever, or disseat me now.
                                                             (5.3.1–21)

What interests me, from the viewpoint of "sovereignty," is now the linguistic unit "Geese." In terms of mere meaning, of course, interpretation is simple. Macbeth is in an extremely impatient mood and cannot wait for the boy's reply: he reanimates his previous expression "goose look" by transforming it into "Geese." Macbeth is telling the Servant that his extreme fear is as ridiculous as such a linguistic absurdity. From this rationalist perspective, moreover, Macbeth is simply bullying people about; his blustering egocentricity deafens his more human environment, and his coarsened sensibility no longer has time for any exchange (even of information) that is truly dialogic. But I think such a reading might itself run the risk of being accused of coarsened sensibility. It is more likely that Shakespeare is working, linguistically, with the kind of "gay angulation" that we saw Olivier discover in "Well then, now." According to the reviewer, we may recall, Olivier's crown was placed not at an angle but at "a mere *suggestion* of an angle." This remark can hardly refer itself to a mere mathematical appreciation of a geometric datum. What is being discussed, surely, is our equivocating sense of a structural incertitude. The angle is there all right; but equally it is not. In other words, the angle partakes of the evasive, furtive quality that belongs to sovereignty in general. It is a "trick," an illusion if you like. It should not be emphasized or foregrounded. Nor should it be suppressed or concealed. It should be suggested.

   Following this cue I am not going to say that the unit "Geese" *is* a "unit of sovereign gaiety"; but I am going to *suggest* that "Geese" indeed can be considered as a linguistic prop for the difficult dramatic staging of sovereign Macbeth. There is a suggestion of gay laughter in "Geese," and this suggestion is not a gesture marking something tentative or half-hearted. The suggestion is absolute, *qua* suggestion.

It is clear from the speech that precedes the Servant's entry that Macbeth feels the panic of servile fear as his enemies close in upon him, and that his references to his prophetic invulnerability aim at boosting up an artificial kind of courage. Macbeth's last words before the Servant's appearance are: "the heart I bear, / Shall never sag with doubt, nor shake with fear (5.3.9–10). The boy's face, however, is of course a reminder of the shallowness of this provisional fearlessness. In the countenance of this servile employee, the master finds the overt signs of his own thinly concealed dread. It is this clash that accounts for the violence of Macbeth's greeting: "The devil damn thee black, thou cream-fac'd loon!" (5.3.11). But as Olivier showed in his rendition of "Well then, now," several different moods can be negotiated by a very small linguistic unit, and when Shakespere's linguistic powers are working at full throttle, language is not merely a vehicle of "expression" but one of multiplex differentiation. As the servant boy defers his answer, dreading his master's reaction, there is time enough for Macbeth to perceive a slight shift in his tragic situatedness and to gauge the kind of situational absurdity that he acknowledged in the final stages of the paramedical dialogue with the Doctor (5.3.50–56).

"Geese," now, becomes a reckless signifier, something that belongs to the free and unconditional expenditure of language rather than to expressiveness. "Geese" is strictly speaking superfluous—and few writers beside Shakespeare would have decided to place it here.[30] There is certainly violence in the hero's outburst—"Geese, *villain?*—but this violence is hardly an interpersonal one any longer. The linguistic violence is not really something negotiated between two subjects or characters as part of the commerce of their verbal interchange. The linguistic violence, rather, is almost directed at language itself: as if Macbeth now has dived into *it* to at once discover and lose the ultimate sense of what signification can signify. The yearning for signification here is desperate, yet it is already fraught with the depletion of signification ("Signifying nothing," 5.5.28) encountered in the "to-morrow" soliloquy. "Geese," signifying nothing, partakes of sovereign loss here; but the loss, being glorious, unrestricted, and gay, can still be valued and appreciated in terms of the unproductivity that it affirms. Nonsignification, being merely the brief candle of a single word's vanishing appearance, has still not yet reached the quasi-methaphysical level of linguistic amplification where soliloquy will give it the status, almost, of a transcendental signified. Already, however, Macbeth seems to lack patience for "meaning"; he is no longer willing to wait (as the Weird Sisters have made him wait) for the fulness of meaning as the complete presence of its idealization.

>   Where gott'st thou that goose look?
> Serv. There is ten thousand—
> *Macb.*   Geese, villain?
>   (5.3.12–13)

Macbeth runs *through* meaning (much as he formerly ran through the enemy slave), vanishing into its transgression and prematurely enjoying its linguistic richness before the materialization of the signifying moment that could supply that linguistic richness with its noetic substance. It appears that Macbeth is impatient for meaning; it appears that he cannot tolerate the deferral of meaning created by the Servant's hesitation. Yet it could also be argued that Macbeth himself now defers meaning, and that the current passage indicates the quaint desire to infinitize such deferral. Macbeth's attitude hardly speeds up the process of communication, and he probably realizes that. The show of impatient longing for the right facts somehow conceals a desire to indulge in self-referential modes of discourse—as we once saw in the medical digression with the Doctor and as we here see in the extensive and "unnecessary" digression on the poor boy's complexion. These—largely linguistic—round trips now in themselves seem to interest Macbeth, as if they could divert his attention from the painfulness of the future, or as if his future, already, has slipped into the oracular linguistic mystery that the witches once controlled but that now no longer is uniquely reserved for their exclusively personal copyright.

6.4 Cosmetics

Macbeth, insofar as he is now enjoying the gaiety of language rather than the mastery of it, is progressively becoming initiated into the law of originary contradiction that witchcraft/language from the outset darkly outlined as the enigmatic and paradoxical principle of cosmic organization. On the level of mere action and meaning, to be sure, he is stubbornly and thickheadedly resenting this contradictoriness (since it ruins what is dialectical in him, especially monarchial self-presence): weird discourse is double-talk, "th'equivocation of the fiend, / That lies like truth" (5.5.43–44). But on the level of language, on the level of *its* action, a highly intelligent and evermore sensitized Macbeth is gradually appreciating the glory and might of everything he has been resisting. From this viewpoint, his relinquishment of the desire to control the all-powerfulness of language (to control its irreducibly rich contradictoriness and flatten it into meaning) is indistinguishable from his abandonment of dialectical mastery and entry into "sovereignty." Sovereignty, as the abandonment of the desire to control the world (especially in terms of linguistic mastery), is also the abandonment of the servile fear of the world (and language) as the uncontrollable—as something "larger" than the cogito. As Birnam Wood now moves toward Macbeth, there is given to us precisely this sense of the final triumph of world over cogito. This triumph, let it be noted, is also a linguistic triumph: for Birnam Wood is not merely a collection of twigs and branches but also the materialization of the linguistic all-powerfulness that marked its threat and reality from the outset. As witchcraft's broth was indistinguishable from the language/receipe that was its constitutional source, so the transgressive horror of the advent of Birnam Wood is indistinguishable from the linguistic paradoxicality (ultimately Shakespeare's) that is its condition of dramatic possibility. As Macbeth now *receives* "Birnam Wood," and particularly its advance/advent, he is finally uncrowned as master and finally emancipated as visionary sovereign subjected, without subjection, to linguistic spectacle.

As it comes toward astonished Macbeth (in imagination more than in actual sight, 5.5.35–40), the moving greenery forms a symmetrically reversed counterpart of the hallucinated dagger that once showed him the way to Duncan's chamber. I am in no way implying that Birnam Wood too is a hallucination. What I am saying is that the outward movement (away from Macbeth) that characterized the pointing dagger (2.1.42) is a hyperontological equivalent of the inward movement (toward Macbeth) that characterizes the mobile forest (5.5.35). Why? Because what moves toward Macbeth is not the forest, but its movement. As I argued in the section on the "dagger of intentionality," the pointing weapon does not bridge a gap between a subjective volition that is already on its feet, full of desiring movement, and a target that is to feel the full brunt of this coiled mobility; on the contrary, the pointing dagger *is* mobile pointing/willing itself, and it takes into *itself* the movement-toward-murder that in fact was absolutely absent in inert Macbeth. When Macbeth now sees the moving forest, he theatrically and empirically speaking perceives something fixed that now has become unfixed; but ontodramatically speaking, the hyperontological sensation is that Macbeth feels the radical and absolute emergence of unfixity itself. This unfixity, as the originary unfixity that the play promotes as the main principle of its hyperlogical and dramatic organization, is as I have said an overwhelmingly linguistic unfixity—for all that has become restless in *Macbeth* has become so through the linguistic conundrum that the Weird Sisters first implemented to set tragic action and the quest for metaphysical closure in motion.

The coimplication of tragic unfixity and linguistic unfixity can be gauged by considering the way in which sovereign gaiety already has "invaded" Birnam Wood as one of its constituent aspects. An ordinary wood is held up by trees, while Birnam Wood is held up by soldiers; but the soldiers, by having been inadvertently referred to by Macbeth as "Geese" ("Geese, villian? / Soldiers, Sir," 5.3.13) are already part of a gay linguistic merry-go-round that none of the participating parties can hope to master or supervise. What is uncanny about Birnam Wood is that the soldiers have *become* the wood (otherwise one could not say that "[t]he *wood* began to move," 5.5.35). But in this world where five acts of Shakespearean technology have accustomed us to the feeling that language empowers more than "fact" can empower, soldiers have also "become" geese. The unit "Geese" has already become integral to the general metonymy that is displacing a fixed, "nonlinguistic" reality—so that the vital world of the play, already touched by magic through the introductory machinations of witchcraft, finally emerges as a theater for a quasi-Ovidian gaiety and transformational recklessness.

No longer a producer of meaning (5.5.18–28) and no longer fully sincere in the quest for self-crowning within metaphysical Truth, Macbeth now nevertheless takes part in military transactions and heroic duels that necessarily display the ontological production of meaning. That type of "participation," we have already remarked, is a constructional absurdity for the hero; yet, ironically, he has no choice, for his withdrawal from the struggle to death would become just as much a unit of meaning within dialectical recognition as would be his full and active participation: he would become idealistically *meaningful,* in an act of withdrawal, as a dialectically negative term—as one with wounds in the back rather than in the front (metaphorically speaking).

Insofar as he is "sovereign," then, insofar as he is one who no longer desires to appear (as the master did), to become dialectically visible, Macbeth now finds that it is, ironically, only the essentialist realm of appearing that will constitute itself as the possible site and sovereign locus for his nonappearing. The sovereign appears in the struggle to death among masters yearning for appearing; yet the sovereign appears there in order to disappear. Like children hiding inside the metal shells of knightly armors in museums or exhibition galleries, Macbeth steals back into heroic mastery as doppelgänger and alien. We sense therefore that there are moments when armor is cumbersome in more senses than one: when Macbeth, like a play actor, is surreptitiously aware of his own hot bustle as something faintly ridiculous, uncannily unreal. He stops, as if beside himself, observing his energetic participation in a game that someone else has devised, and whose hero is an utter fool.

But no fake is involved here. It is a fight to death. While Macbeth no longer is "honest" and sincere in the act of engaging with the culturally preordained ritual of struggling to death in order to produce idealist truth and heroic meaning, he still is no dialectical "opposite" of the heroic fighter: we cannot say that he is "dishonest," that he "fakes" his presence in the struggle to death by "pretending" to be part of its visibility. Where one's own life and blood are at stake, one cannot "pretend." Or if one can pretend, one can only do so seriously; just as, if one can be seriously "there" (in the fight), one can only be there gaily (a single burst of laughter away from anguish proper). As something cumbersome (throughout all of act 5), the struggle to death is now simulacrum. But the simulacrum, not being simply an imitation, is not the mere absence or untruth of the deathward struggle. It is its absolute purity: *its* truth rather than the truth of the essentialist truth it was intended to produce (dialectical meaning). Gaiety, as that which the struggle now itself furthers, is not the activity of the less-than-serious. The play *Macbeth* does not end the way it ends by dropping off in any manner from the seriousness of its inquiry, by concocting some slightly frivolous end game. What has to be taken seriously now is on the contrary the pressure put on what is serious. Transactions, bloody as they remain, still involve serious sacrifice; but the seriousness of the predicament is now that there is no longer sacrifice (in deathward struggle) for the sake of meaning, but sacrifice *of* meaning (*WD*, 257).

This rather serious projection of simulacrum into the bloody business of sacrifice may be appreciated by looking at a passage where Shakespeare has deliberately called attention to the simulacrum as such—to a use of cosmetics that is not only nonfrivolous but also nondialectical. Blood here, and indeed deathward blood, is the cosmetic substance. Macbeth now asks the boy servant *to bring forth blood as cosmetics:*

> the heart I bear,
> Shall never sag with doubt, nor shake with fear.
> *Enter a Servant.*
> The devil damn thee black, thou cream-fac'd loon!
> Where gott'st thou that goose look?
> Serv. There is ten thousand—
> Macb.   Geese, villain?
> Serv.   Soldiers, Sir.
> Macb. Go prick thy face, and over-red thy fear,
> Thou lily-liver'd boy.
>
> (5.3.9–15)

The blood-production is of course not empirical, or empirically interesting. There is not a jot of purposive command in Macbeth's taunting exhortation: he in no way expects the boy servant to actually run away and paint his cheeks red with his own blood. Instead the very notion of makeup and cosmetic simulacrum betokens an indirect recognition of the entire process of ontodramatic reorganization that I have been discussing around the hero in terms of "sovereignty" as a displacement of ontological mastery. On the one hand "over-redding" natural fear is a notion that refers us back to the hero's own precarious predicament: he has just patched up the self-confidence that has been shattered by the recent abundance of "reports" (5.3.1) indicating the negative trend of his military fortunes, and Macbeth cannot bear the idea that his companions in misfortune will be unable to join up with him in concealing the fear of death. On the other hand "over-redding" opens up the entire realm of further ontodramatic experimentation by drawing attention to the paradoxicality that now afflicts all genuine struggle to death. War paint must now come into operation: but in preparing the fighter for his deathward struggle, it will neither conceal him from the fight in terms of camouflage nor *simply* enhance him as one more painted figure in the picture of war. This picture, by now something of a trick picture, will require of cosmetics that it too be something of a trick.

At the end of his tether, Macbeth (as we have seen) gives way to the kind of cruel impatience that most of us give way to in times of crisis and extreme strain. Shakespeare, in fact, through Macbeth's "poor player" soliloquy, is voicing a certain inner fatigue known to all actors and players: a fatigue growing from the immense strain of having to freshly open, as the absolutely fresh, what strictly speaking lost its empirical freshness ages ago. The renewed performance of "to-morrow" must tomorrow celebrate the very freshness that it empirically speaking will be pushing further from freshness. "To-morrow, and to-morrow, and to-morrow." The piling of performances is deadening. That is, as long as the individual performance is considered as an empirical event in a strictly empirical (that is linear) temporality. But is "to-morrow" empirical? Is the performance empirical? Worse: is "to-morrow" temporal?

Just as Macbeth's exhaustion in act 5 can be taken as the sign of his spiritual decrepitude as *well* as the sign of his passport to sovereign ecstasy, and just as an actor's inner fatigue can betoken his dramatic decline as *well* as his arrival at the horizon of absolute self-renewal and self-transgression, so the "to-morrow" of the tomorrow soliloquy can signal a resigned sense of closure as *well* as an enjoyment of sovereign expenditure. Precisely because Macbeth knows his fate by now, just as the player knows his lines and as the worshipper knows his ritual, he can enter the sovereign realm of free "un-knowledge" (*WD*, 263) where what is now unconcealed a minute ago seemed neither new nor unconcealed. Once this inward boosting within empirical fatigue is apprehended, the supplementary performance no longer becomes the rehearsing of (a given) identity. Not even two "identical" performances are from this perspective the rehearsing of an identity, a fixed and ready-written pattern. The supplementary performance, by engaging with the logic of supplementarity, cannot confirm, entirely, the identity of that which it supplements.

The infelicity of the poor player now continues to produce the most felicitous linguistic affirmations and play actings. The poor player, in order to be fully able to clarify his impoverishment, must negate it with the monumental enrichment of his own staged effort. If theater engages with the miraculous, this is its moment.

> *Sey.* The Queen, my Lord, is dead.
> *Macb.* She should have died hereafter:
>   There would have been a time for such a word.—
>   To-morrow, and to-morrow, and to-morrow,
>   Creeps in this petty pace from day to day,
>   To the last syllable of recorded time;
>   And all our yesterdays have lighted fools
>   The way to dusty death. Out, out, brief candle!
>   Life's but a walking shadow; a poor player,
>   That struts and frets his hour upon the stage,
>   And then is heard no more: it is a tale
>   Told by an idiot, full of sound and fury,
>   Signifying nothing.
>   (5.5.16–28)

For a vanishing second Macbeth holds Lady Macbeth at the forefront of his attention; but there is quickly a fracture of this field of attention, and what then supervenes is distinctly something that follows a metamorphosis. There is a radical ascent from subjectivity to nonsubjectivity, from personality to universality: from, one is tempted to say, Macbeth to Shakespeare. Macbeth himself, one could argue, is not untouched by the beauty in the purity of his closure.

7

7.1 The Ontological Fallacy

As I suggested in the introductory pages of this book, what is being deconstructed in this venture is not only *Macbeth* as an originary and pure thing-in-itself, but what criticism has made of *Macbeth*. I therefore move toward the conclusion of my efforts by first comparing my own reading of the play with its ontologizing opposite. Marvin Rosenberg's *Masks of Macbeth* will serve as an excellent example of the ontologization of *Macbeth*—not because the criticism is weak and full of errors (it is not), but because its numerous insights and strengths communicate themselves across a field of discursive traits that inadvertently ontologize everything they encounter.

The favorite move of the ontotheological critic is to combine "dialectic" and "harmony," to create the sense of a reassuring to-and-fro *as* the full resonance of what is pleasingly oscillating in reverberating harmonies. As we shall see in a moment, Marvin Rosenberg is a Shakespeare critic who uses this technique in order to ontologize the conflict in *Macbeth* between the Apollonian and the Dionysian; but he is by no means alone in this determination to ontologize dialectic and to dialecticize ontology. Rosenberg's British equivalent is perhaps Michael Long, a critic who deliberately twists Nietzsche's conception of tragedy by minimizing the importance of Nietzsche's own criticism of *The Birth of Tragedy*.[1] Long tells us that *Macbeth* is an Apollonian play (*US*, 229), and that Macbeth's criminality consists in his violation of the gentle Apollonian order of the community (233). According to this model, that of a juvenile Nietzsche still under the influence of Schopenhauer and romantic German music, the Apollonian vision is a happy lyrical state that avoids the rigid extreme of the Socratic man (18) as well as the "witches' brew" (*US*, 20; *BT*, 40) of Dionysiac brutishness. "Apollonianism" (*US*, 234) is a wondrous "stability" in nature and man (235), and this stability is a classical "balance" (237) where there is synthetical interaction between Apollo and Dionysus (229), and where the play's contact with its own center of "fulness" itself is profoundly "dialectical" (238).

In Michael Long's essentialist play, therefore, it is Apollo who rules. Shakespeare is basically Apollonian, but so are dramatic figures whose intrinsic "royalty" sweetens the air (235). Duncan and Banquo are the Apollonian equals of Cordelia (236). Shakespeare is ultimately giving us an "Apollonian" vision of what is "humane" (241), and his literary achievement must clearly be a space where words run together "harmoniously" (234). Macbeth's fate is thus not that of falling *into* the trap of the Apollonian, but of abandoning the Apollonian. Whereas we have been studying a Macbeth who is from the outset caught in the tumultuous, Michael Long sees "tumult" and "frenzy" as latecomers that deprive the hero of true "creative possibilities" (240). There is very much "life" in Macbeth, but unfortunately he gives over all his "imaginative intensity" to its "counterfeit" (239).

It might be argued, however, that the critic's reductive notion of "imaginative intensity" (above) is premature, rigid, and Socratic. If the full imaginative potential of the Dionysiac is not grasped, as in the case of Nietzsche's immature *Birth of Tragedy*, imaginative intensity is only perceived in places mastered by Apollonian sweetness. In such a sentimental and obsessively lyrical predicament, one risks missing the play's finest achievement: William Shakespeare's ability to *increase* his hero's imaginative intensity as both of them (Macbeth and Shakespeare) slide into the non-Apollonian tumult that concludes the tragic frenzy. If, as Long argues, pure Dionysiac energy is a "substitute" for real imaginative power (*US*, 239), and if Macbeth's "imaginative intensity" becomes that of a "hideous counterfeit" (ibid.), then the imaginative intensity of the Thane of Cawdor and the imaginative intensity of William Shakespeare must be two entirely different things. (For surely the dramatist's own imaginative intensity cannot itself be a "hideous counterfeit.") But if these imaginative paths, the genuine one of Shakespeare and the counterfeit one of Macbeth, diverge so radically, how do all of us manage to arrive together at that single point of dramatic imagination in act 5 (the to-morrow soliloquy) where theatrical energy and tragic energy are one and the same experience?—where the climax of Shakespeare's intensity is also the climax of Macbeth's intensity, but where also the climax of (imaginative) intensity is identical—for both—with the climax of (imaginative) exhaustion? How does Michael Long know that Macbethian intensity is counterfeit? Is it really possible, once Shakespeare has taken us this far, to still go on wisely proclaiming that intensity and exhaustion are opposites? Is not exhaustion too a form of intensity?—for Macbeth, for Shakespeare; for us. And is not that, in a sense, the greatest intensity that the play creates?

Is not that imaginative exhaustion exactly what somehow besets the hero from the outset?—as if his wild imaginings did not peter out into their pictorial and linguistic exhaustedness, but instead always already used such exhausting as primary fuel. And is not the real failure of "imaginative intensity" the critical act of failing to imagine this breakdown of the dialectic of imagination?

In the "Attempt at a Self-Criticism" that Nietzsche came to attach to The Birth of Tragedy, we see that the "profound metaphysics of music" borrowed from Schopenhauer (BT, 51) now embarrasses him. Socratic puritans have of course always favored a rational "musicality" that would restore an ideally original intuition of the just relation between sound and sense,[2] and when Nietzsche eventually rejects his own sentimental notion of lyrical "union" and "identity" (49), he is deliberately rejecting a "musical mood" (ibid.) that is too metaphysical and mellifluously puritanical to cope with strong Dionysiac otherness (25). Thus the Schopenhauerian slant provided by Michael Long to illuminate Nietzsche's critical thinking on Apollo-versus-Dionysus is the very sentimental and musical bias that Nietzsche wanted to get rid of in mature retrospect: "I obscured and spoiled Dionysian premonitions with Schopenhauerian formulations" (24). In sum, "the rapture of the Dionysian state with its annihilation of the ordinary bounds and limits of existence" (59) has virtually nothing to do with the "sentimental" and "saccharine" (19) philosophy of those who find Nietzsche's first theory of tragedy to be the lyrical essence of the profound. The weak, saccharine text, paradigmatically, is " 'music' for those dedicated to music" (ibid.).

If "Dionysian man" according to Nietzsche resembles a Shakespearean hero (BT, 60), and if the "witches' brew" (40) involves a sense of nonsaccharine, "Dionysian music" (ibid.), this music of a stronger kind cannot be based on the notion of the individualistic outpourings of the Apollonian lyrist (36). There is always something tame and "plastic" about the energies of Apollo (35); and therefore the attempt to define a work (Macbeth, The Birth of Tragedy) in terms of "a piece of music" is to insult it (26). That is precisely what Nietzsche does with his own juvenile text in his

The Ontological Fallacy

criticism: "Is it not itself . . . a piece of music, *German* music? But listen: . . ." (ibid.). Insofar, then, as this current enterprise offers resistance to the habit of ontologists to discuss Shakespeare *primarily* in terms of "a piece of music," we too will perhaps be sceptically saying: "But listen: . . . ." The target of attack here is not the critics, but their rhetoric; not music, but musicality. The love of music is perfectly legitimate, has its own horizon of suggestive infinitudes. And a work like Rosenberg's *Masks of Macbeth*, far from being a lower-order achievement, is a most impressive piece of solid research. What is at stake, then, is a hidden musical rationale that *itself* must be unmasked. As a critical paradigm operative mainly on the rhetorical level of the act of criticism, such a rationale systematically overlooks the "ontological difference" between music and literature.

You can, if your name is Giuseppe Verdi, create a musical *Macbeth*. You can, with a certain amount of violence and goodwill, turn *Macbeth* into music. But you cannot turn Shakespeare into music. There is no general "musical Shakespeare." And even a musical *Macbeth* would contain a nonmusical remainder. This remainder could never itself become (a) musical. It could never resonate. The nonmusical remainder, music of a kind, is not "music" for those dedicated to music. And this is partly so because the nonmusical remainder *is* not at all.

Rosenberg's master concept is "polyphony." In his critical enterprise, "polyphony" promotes harmless polysemia—what Derridean deconstruction views as an obstruction of signification as free dissemination.[3] Rosenberg's "polyphony" seeks to appropriate Shakespearean signification: meaning is pluralized so as to become plural meaning, the pluralization in no way threatening the self-presence of present meaning, but only increasing that presence by multiplying it. As Barthes once put it, ontological liberalism "magnanimously" wishes to acknowledge a spectrum of subtruths, each constituting a "share" of truth.[4] There is a generous "conceding" of meanings within a truth-economy, as long as the "migration" of meanings creates no "vanishing" of presence.[5] Against Rosenberg's "polyphony," which consistently brings all "notes" on stage, onto the platform where Shakespeare is present to Shakespeare as his drama's absolute proximity to its meaning, one would have to forward Barthes' alternative conception: alongside each utterance, various "off-stage" voices can be heard.[6]

Rosenberg's musical imagery gives his critical enterprise a strong ontological bias. What bias? Presence. Because "polyphony" consistently operates as a centripetal, essentialist, framing, enclosing, gathering, centering, unifying, homogenizing, and inwardizing concept, the critical text in an overwhelming way comes to project *Macbeth* as a drama commensurate with a centered ontology—which, as it happens, is precisely the ontology that *Macbeth* is displacing and questioning in almost every move of its linguistic action. It matters little, in this context, that Rosenberg in his liberal tolerance is open to an entire spectrum of critical options, from the most centripetal and inwardizing to the most centrifugal and dissociative. Since even the noninwardizing options are brought under the unifying rubric of centering "polyphony," the descriptions of Shakespeare's decentering dimensions in fact come to work for centering. This movement to appropriate the decentering as centering in the very act of seeming to do the opposite is reinforced by the tendency of Rosenberg's rhetoric to employ centering images of fusion and synthesis to map diffusion and nonsynthesis. In this way Rosenberg's text inadvertently works for an obstruction of the kind of "fractured" critical model tentatively advanced by Grove, Bayley, and others. This obstruction is completed also in those sections where Rosenberg is sympathetically reviewing interpretations favoring fracture, displacement, diffusion, and dissemination. As we shall see, the various features of Rosenberg's attitude help us to focus dramatic traits that will enhance our understanding of the role played, or not played, by character in *Macbeth*.

"Polyphony" spearheads an entire army of music-oriented notions: "harmonics," "resonance" (*MM*, 98), "pastoral note" (245), "mixed notes" (255), "multiple tones" (182), "countering tones" (190), "modulating tone" (196), and so forth. Such musical orientation also slips into less stylized stretches of critical discourse: "accords with" (196), "resonates" (260), "sounded" (196), and so on. As an organizing principle the musical becomes indistinguishable from the self-harmonized, the harmonically self-present. Rosenberg's rhetoric has a distinct leaning toward images and phrases suggesting fusion, inwardization, and cohesion: polar opposites "must" come to "interlock" (60), the "coherence" (61) of a total stage personality (60) being promoted by what unifies the tragic identity (61). Rosenberg has a general desire to see equivocation as something framed by the comprehensive vision of dramatist, spectator, and hero. He sees equivocation as an ongoing to-and-fro (which he calls "dialectic") *within* character, *within* creative vision, *within* our changing conception of the play's movement. Thus "ambivalence" is a "double force" that shunts attention between "extremes of characterization," the servility of murderous desire alternating with the mastery of conscience's "reins" (265)—all of this *inside* a more or less unified field of tragic awareness. Whereas I conceive equivocation as cause, and contradictory panels of awareness as functions of that original equivocation, Rosenberg always starts out from some unity, seeing equivocation as a secondary problem troubling unified self-presence. Persistently, pluralism is the projection of the nonplural (of self-unified presence) into the shape and form of the plural. Plurality, in other words, is never really achieved, for what falls into plural forms of self-expression itself remains constant beneath mutability. The unity of character breaks into "multiple aspects" only to be "fused" in a complex "polyphony" that reassures us as the "profoundly comprehensible" (105).

The quoted words belong to a single sentence, suggesting how intimate is the connection in Rosenberg's thought between "polyphony" and inward movement toward the calm of fusion. In fact the master concept "polyphony" *is* fusion: being that which unites all other critical concepts under the formula of a single notion as well as being itself a notion promoting presence as self-cohesion. But although the music analogy helps to bring Marvin Rosenberg's own vast achievement together as a satisfying whole, I am not at all sure that it does the same for Shakespeare. In fact the very idea of linking the plurality of Shakespearean signification to the plurality of musical suggestion is quite misleading. Music and drama, to be sure, are temporal; but is that shared temporality equal or equivalent? Both music and drama are temporal art forms, but does that mean that the understanding of the temporal quality of the one enhances our comprehension of the temporal quality of the other? Rosenberg frequently uses "polyphony" to suggest a musical now in which the marvelous richness of the character's plurality is rendered as the harmonic immediacy of his self-present presence. In seducing Macbeth into murder, Lady Macbeth has managed to pluck across "his strings" so as to sound all the "multiple notes" of "his polyphony" (275). I have no wish to dispute the richness of Macbeth's multiple character, nor any wish to dispute Lady Macbeth's ability to quickly probe a whole range of delicate levels in his being. What I *do* wish to dispute is the secret ontology that Rosenberg's essentialist rhetoric smuggles into the critical review. In no way does the richness of Shakespearean signification come over as the polyphony of music comes over: as a multiplicity of notes unified in the now of a note-blending chord, as complementary atoms of sound fusing in time into a molecule of immediate presence. In no way whatsoever do the various subpersonalities of Macbeth lie alongside one another as strings conjointly vibrating on the face of a single instrument. Indeed, the character "Macbeth" is effective because his various potentials of tragic presence are never actualized at once, never synchronic. We feel the empty ("soundless") space between the disparate segments of his awareness as he shifts between incompatible levels in moments of split-second self-violence.

The presence of Shakespeare's tragic hero is in an important sense dependent on his lack of full self-presence, and the presence to one another of the protagonists is in an important sense a function of their failure to be absolutely present to one another, to "understand" one another. In this particular play, it may well be that Lady Macbeth bases her seduction on the fact that she fully "understands" her husband—she knows him well enough to realize that he will be unable to resist the strategy designating him as unmanly coward; but as we have seen, the whole point is that this very connectivist "understanding" of him is tragically circumscribed by a much more significant and powerful nonunderstanding.

"Polyphony" thus creates various types of analytical distortion. In addition, as I have observed, "polyphony" has the crucial extra disadvantage of suggesting that words burst upon us from Shakespeare's characters much in the way that notes burst upon us from some philharmonic orchestra. Obsessed as it is with "orchestration" (*MM*, 177), Rosenberg's musical criticism looks like an ideology. One sometimes suspects that the critic brings in "polyphony" everywhere simply to prevent a very crisis of interpretation, to always make sure that otherness is not experienced *as* otherness. If the ever-present "polyphony" is not there to guide and reassure us, it is instead "intricate polyphony" (195), "complex polyphony" (158, 178, 257, 268), or the pleonastically overdetermined "many-toned polyphony" (205).

Rosenberg conceives character as something that can possess, own, and master "polyphony" as a property helpfully constituting its essence. The character indeed becomes character in terms of polyphony. The becoming-character of character is the becoming-polyphony of *his* music: his internal resonance in the chamber of his own self-presence. When Rosenberg speaks of Lady Macbeth, he speaks of "her polyphony" (197, 268), if it is

The Ontological Fallacy 195

not "the Lady's polyphony" (71). Similarly, Macbeth is endowed with "his polyphony" (275), and the drama generally with "Shakespeare's polyphony" (163). The parts of the character fall *into* character, polyphony orchestrating all its "deep notes" (276).

"Dialectic," insofar as it engages with character, is for Marvin Rosenberg a mere tidal motion *within* character, the tension, as it were, between the east and west of a tragic hero's personality. He speaks of Lady Macbeth's "polar extremes" (205), of "double" in "He's here in double trust" (1.7.12) as a "reverberating double" symptomatic of the "ongoing dialectic" (*MM*, 259). The "polyphony" in or of a character is virtually the same for Rosenberg as the "dialectic" in or of a character (176). In both cases, the movement intensifies presence as the presence of the character, intensifies the character as self-presence. The more Shakespeare manages to portray "polyphony" and "dialectic" as a dynamic aspect of character, the more real and present does that character become as a tragic human unit. As a movement *inside* character, "dialectic" only extends the east-west latitude of the character, increasing his size by widening his humane self-presence. In the "dialectical design" of *Macbeth* (269), "dialectic" comes to signify all kinds of interaction, but never originary otherness.

Orchestrated in this way, the musical norms of Rosenberg's review coax us into faith in a world that has nothing to do with the world of vanishing staged in *Macbeth*. The hyperontology of *Macbeth* does not show a world of presence and presences to which is added, as it happens, a modicum of tragic vanishing; on the contrary, the very vanishing-from-presence is paradigmatic, and all illusion of presence is either the very deception that leads the hero to his tragic fall or else a kind of closure that Shakespeare employs in order to finally stabilize his tragic vision as something palatable within the commonplace ethical expectations of contemporary decorum. There is, to be sure, "dialectic" in linguistic complexes as well as in musical complexes, inasmuch as conflicting extremes of suggestion are made to combine in various patterns of intricate presencing; yet there remains in linguistic dissonance a crucial aspect of nonpresence that music (however dissonant) never can achieve—and it is precisely this all-important element of irreducible nonpresence that enables us to enjoy *Macbeth* as something different from plenary speech, as something radically Shakespearean. (Disastrously, Macbeth in 3.4 *attempts* plenary speech.)

No musical now can fully escape from traces of (its own) reverbatory presence. But in Shakespearean language things are different. The conflicting strands of tragic discourse can mark a quick absence from the space of the now they seem to fully occupy. Nothing is, but what is not. If we consider the mode of presencing effectuated by the unit "nothing is, but what is not" (1.3.142), we see on the one hand that each "half" of the unit marks (its) presence: the subunit "is" *is*, and the subunit "is not" *is*. Each subunit exists at the time it is spoken, hits the ear of the spectator and the speaker in a pure now. But since "is-ness" itself is at stake in the drama, in the hero, and in the very conflictual texture of this pronouncement ("nothing is, but what is not"), each will-to-be-present in the two subunits is a will observing, as it were, its own will-to-presence, its own (hyper)ontological "weight." (There is no place in *Macbeth* where this ontological voiding has not already started.) Hence the two subunits, far from being atoms merging into a Rosenbergian molecule of essentialist meaning and dialectical presence, are items of signification that problematize, obstruct, and alter this very becoming-presence of "meaning." This obstruction of plenary speech is by no means confined to the hero; it works its way into every nook and cranny of the drama. Those who (like Lady Macbeth) wish to stand at the furthest remove from this disruption of plenary speech are in a sense those who suffer most from its powers of dislocation (witness Lady Macbeth's discourse in the sleepwalking scene); and conversely those who (like Macbeth) try to match the absence of plenary speech with the unthinkable attentiveness that this absence seems to call for are somehow redeemed by the privilege of becoming (vanishing) participants in its free negativity. What we are left with is not at all any polyphonic character enriched by the vastness of polyphony: the tonal range of subjectivity from horizon to horizon, from Macbethian "is" to Macbethian "is not." We get the very reverse of this. We get first and foremost the *gap* between "is" and "is not"; and Macbeth, far from being a ready-made and fully constituted given exploring the extreme horizons of his possible being, is a man falling through this abyss and horrendous spacing: his "own" difference. Sound, as any kind of musical immediacy, seems to be the very thing that Macbeth does not have direct access to in this situation. Even the sound of his own name ("Glamis," "Cawdor," but also "Macbeth") is quickly becoming an alien entity—so that we begin to feel that the hero actually has to begin to *strain* to catch the sound of his name. As "spacing" radicalizes itself during the course of the play, so "hearing" weakens itself; one could discuss the entire career of

Macbeth, including his dialogues with his wife, in terms of a hearing problem, the growing difficulty of hearing.

The very things that Marvin Rosenberg sees Macbeth as deploying through rich "character" are in my view absent from Macbeth. This absence is crucially evident to the hero himself. It is precisely because he senses that the not-Macbeth is more central than "Macbeth" that he listens to his own "dialectic" from a significant distance—the horizon of reverie—hearing his inner struggle as mock-dialectic in the very moment of presencing it, hearing the pros and cons of murder fully aware of the fact that pro- and con- no longer signify as they should. I am tempted to use inverted commas for "hearing" here ("*hearing* his inner struggle," "*hearing* the pros and cons of murder"), for it must once more be emphasized that the originary other (implemented by the Weird Sisters) immediately removes Macbeth from "hearing" in the ordinary sense. If Macbeth is capable of hearing, then not-Macbeth is capable of not-hearing. I write "capable of," since not-hearing here is not a defect or a simple minus. To be capable of not-hearing is in Shakespeare's world not the same thing as being incapable of hearing. Let us say, if you prefer simplicity, that one hearing replaces another, faces another. And that the difference between these two hearings itself cannot be heard. Only one of the Macbeths can "hear" such a difference: the non-hearing Macbeth who does *not* hear.[7] Not-Macbeth.

Rosenberg never comes anywhere near this not-Macbeth who neither hears nor lacks hearing. "Polyphony" takes care of that. "Polyphony," by promoting the mastering notion of inner dialectic, ensures the philosophical perpetuation of the interpretation of Macbeth as someone adhering obstinately to the ontological sphere of Western belongingness. Inner dialectic is a stage and working platform on which the Western mind labors for truth— for *its* truth; but against this notion one would have to oppose the quite different view that *Macbeth* is very much about the reduction of this stage and platform into a kind of defunct screen of banal meaning in which the tidal motions of ordinary dialectical "sense" move ritualistically through dreamy phases of predictable and fantastically uninteresting change. Subjectivity now— and this is the very first spacing of *Shakespeare's* (rather than the West's) sense of the tragic—is centrally activated by the sense *of its own absence*. Saying that much is not to claim that subjectivity and dialectic (or even plenary speech) are entirely wiped out; that is a ridiculous claim. What is being asserted, instead, is that we can never get right into the hero's particular tragedy, if we cling to the common rationalization that unitizes him as being nothing but a self-present subject capable (under strain) of certain extremes of dialectical subjectivity.

7.2 The Desire of Apollo

According to a classical critical paradigm, best exemplified perhaps by the works of Lily Campbell, Shakespeare's tragic heroes are "slaves of passion."[8] It may be objected, however, that Shakespeare transgresses this innocent conception of "tragic passion," and that it is this very Shakespearean transgression that makes the tragedies works of genius rather than just rhetorically spectacular exemplifications of popular wisdom, Elizabethan ethics, and Christian humanism.

Marvin Rosenberg, our ontological point of critical reference, uses the "Apollonian-Dionysian dialectic" (*MM*, 99) to suggest a traditional conflict between impulses of human "innocence" and the evil passions of a "Dionysian storm" (261). If mastery and servitude are at stake in the drama, this is so only in the most banal and commonsensical sense: the struggle for dominance is for Rosenberg nothing but a tug-of-war in which the Apollonian tries to master the Dionysian, to "manage" and "tame" desire in order to bring it into the servile state of being "subdued" (261). Hence the "If it were done" soliloquy that begins 1.7 is seen as a struggle between the rising heat of desire and the cooling rationalism of humane tenderness. Murder is said to be the function of Dionysian impulsiveness while, at the other extreme in the soliloquy's "dialectic," the impulse *not* to murder is said to be a function of Apollonian restraint in the name of compassion and self-control. The murdering Macbeth is in this reading a Macbeth losing control, shown to be off-balance, while the nonmurdering Macbeth is described as the balanced man. Two main factors ensure this reading: first, the general impact of a cultural code conceiving goodness in terms of restraint, evil in terms of the loss of restraint; second, the play's apparent subscription to such a code—for instance in the conflict between restraint and nonrestraint in the scene where an entirely licentious Malcolm opposes an entirely nonlicentious Malcolm (4.3). It seems, in other words, that the play explicitly opposes passion and mastery of passion, and that this opposition gets dramatized as the tragic macrostructure: Macbeth is shown as one who enters tragedy by losing mastery over desire.

But is it likely that the greatest tragedy we have in this way centers itself on the crude dialectical problematic shown off as the conspicuous constructional formula of conventionalized ideology? As we have seen, it is possible, and somehow indeed necessary, to reverse this formula and to systematically undo all the reassuring assumptions that belong to it. Far from viewing Macbeth as a man whose tragedy involves the movement from a state of balance to a state of imbalance, we have permitted ourselves to consider his movement in an absolutely opposite direction: from imbalance to balance. Balance, or balancing, is his tragedy. Balance was presenced to him as an ideal through the prophecy of the sisters. Prior to that moment of the presencing of Truth as absolute balance of self in the absolute balance of Truth, Macbeth was shown to be paradigmatically off-balance: off-balance in every Dionysiac second of his fluid, athletic movement. As I have demonstrated, the hyperontology of 1.2 is one of pure excess. But the ideology that Macbeth embodies after the presencing of Truth is an ontology that progressively moves in the direction of balance, presence, and desired stability. (This stability is frantically desired, desired frantically; but it still remains a stability, a balance.) This progression is heightened first by Lady Macbeth and then by the act of murder. Macbeth seeks to *balance the equation of Truth*, as we have seen, and the moments of his most searching soliloquy are moments when he trembles at the realization that this balance is withheld: the great soliloquy that opens 1.7 amounts to the realization that promised Truth seems to break its promise of absolute balance; and it is this, in the final analysis, that puts the hero off.

Marvin Rosenberg uses the word "equation" to designate a happy state of affairs in which the dramatist is supposed to be bringing the "dialectic" between characters or in character into a satisfying state of rich equilibrium (*MM*, 67, 72, 75, 85, 229, 232). And since he sees "dialectic" as a mere tug-of-war between extremes of inner being, it is clear that the Apollonian/Dionysian conflict for him must become the staging of a struggle between a hot and a cool subpersonality. "Doubling" (221) in the hero is the result of Lady Macbeth's invocation of spirits, "Hyde" becoming the Dionysian hemisphere of her Jekyll/Hyde structure. Thus the persona—for Macbeth as well as for Lady Macbeth—"doubles" in the premurder ecstasy, so that a disjunction is effectuated between the Apollonian and the Dionysian, between "conscience" and "will," the "knowing" and the "doing," the "eye" and the "hand" (224, 269).

Although this dialectical scheme at first looks attractive, we need to recognize that the tragic fall in *Macbeth* delineates something infinitely more sophisticated. So does Shakespeare's language.

The problem, in this tragedy, is that desire comes from the "wrong" hemisphere. It should come from the Dionysian, but in fact comes from the Apollonian. The heroic Macbeth of 1.2 was extremely Dionysian. But with the appearance of the Weird Sisters, and with the appearance of Truth on the screen of his mind, Macbeth is immediately shown as one cooling off uncharacteristically into an Apollonian serenity. His friends, struck by the vanishing of the Dionysian persona, are quite alarmed at this sea-change. Desire, being from the outset linked to the ideality of Truth through prophecy, is always already Apollonian in Macbeth. This is precisely why Macbeth has to consciously work himself up into a Dionysian state of murder to be at all capable of effectuating a deed that is so detestable. A fine actor will be able to show this Apollonian substratum throughout. Shakespeare emphasizes it also at the time of murder. In fact the rousement for murder, we have seen, is very different in Macbeth and Lady Macbeth. Rosenberg is right when he claims that Lady Macbeth and Macbeth conjointly need to become Dionysian in order to effectuate murder (*MM*, 221), but he is wrong in assuming a kind of structural analogy in this metamorphosis (224). Because Lady Macbeth never has encountered the sisters, she has not encountered prophecy as Truth; hence she can invoke "spirits" without in any way engaging the Apollonian hemisphere (quest for Truth) that Macbeth always engages with in *his* contacts with spirits. For her, a rapport with the demonic certainly is a rapport with the passion of desire. But for Macbeth this entire dimension of supernatural soliciting is quite different, in an important sense inverted. His desire has an Apollonian source, and the fact that Lady Macbeth momentarily can bring him over to her cruder involvement with desire as Dionysian passion only heightens our sense of Macbeth's Apollonian involvement: Shakespeare shows us how the very "Dionysian" passion of murder itself fails to bring over Macbeth into that hemisphere. *After the appearance of the sisters in 1.3 Macbeth is never for a single moment in the Dionysian hemisphere.* Even the anguished vanishings that promote his most servile form of cosmic fear are movements monitored from the mastering throne of promised Truth.

As I have shown, Rosenberg's entire criticism is monitored through the mastering concepts of his musical analogy: "polyphony," "orchestration," "resonance," "harmonics," and so forth. The result is a sense of a mastery of meaning through presence, and a sense of meaning as mastering presence. Music, never being absent from its sonorous plentitude in the "now" of the ear, works for presence. This emphasis on presence is reinforced by Rosenberg's treatment of the Apollonian/Dionysian "dialectic." Apollo, as Rosenberg must know, is the god of music; and hence it is significant that the critic should envisage tragic conflict as a struggle between Apollonian reason and Dionysian emotion: the musical-rational is good and controlled (normally deploying itself in terms of harmony), mastering what is darkly subversive, passionate, and evil. Evil, in this classical apparatus, is quite literally dis-cord. And goodness is conversely sonorous, melodic, truth in tune with itself. In Rosenberg's rhetoric, the "control" exerted by "reason" checks the "Dionysian symptoms" that threaten its mastery (*MM*, 255), so that in the soliloquy of 1.7 "emotional words" are a "load" charging the "cool prudence" of the Apollonian Macbeth (258). We get the impression, then, that the pacific equanimity of the musically harmonious Apollo is threatened by "Dionysian violence" (74). Rosenberg can now analyze the soliloquy opening 1.7 as an inwardized tug-of-war between the nonmurdering Apollo-Macbeth and the murderous Dionysus-Macbeth, whose "Dionysian storm" is tantamount to the "violence" of Macbeth's feelings (261).

Rosenberg's entitative thinking is of course typical of essentialist criticism, and much Shakespeare criticism is mastered by such bipartite schematization. I deny the relevance of the mechanical analysis and posit an inverted paradigm. Apollo is the murderer. Apollo, as it happens, is not merely the god of music, but more importantly also the god of prophecy. I repeat, therefore, that Truth is the trigger of tragic desire in *Macbeth*—and that Lady Macbeth's conventionalized desire counterpoints it. It baffles her as much as it baffles the audience—as much as it has baffled criticism. With Macbeth things are slightly different; for while he is on the one hand just as confounded as all the rest of us, he is on the other hand not confounded at all. What is monstrous has arisen "naturally" in him—he recognizes it as coextensive with his own thought. It is Macbeth's fate to find that otherness sojourns in him both naturally and monstrously, and it is this doubleness that opens up the space of the tragic archetrace: that murder and the resistance to it must be co-originative.

The role of the "philosophical" in *Macbeth* can only be gauged once we in this way have emancipated ourselves from the classical schematizations of essentialist critics. Rosenberg devotes an entire subsection to "Macbeth-Philosopher" (*MM*, 100–107). The "philosopher" is one of the "masks" of Macbeth. But only one mask in a set of masks, one note in a general polyphony. We have seen how Rosenberg's commitment to pluralism as a balance of dialectically negotiated extremes creates a considerable overdetermination in his analysis. Since embracing any single option (sounding any single note, wearing any single mask) would be to endanger the multiplicity and dialectical "equation" sought everywhere, no unique extreme is ever wholeheartedly affirmed, wholeheartedly explored. And what characterizes Macbeth—indeed Shakespeare—is an ability to engage absolutely, fully, and excessively with a particular extreme. The "philosophical" is a case in point. Far from being an "aspect," dimension, or extreme of "character" in Macbeth, the "philosophical" is the entire world of Apollonian Truth that he absolutely and totally immerses himself in after the prophecy—after Apollo's promise of Macbeth to Macbeth as the light of golden Truth, worn on his head. (Apollo, incidentally, was also the sun god.) The witches may themselves be darkness, but the promise they presence to Macbeth does not shine in terms of their obscurity, but in terms of golden brightness—a place in the sun. The "philosopher" in Macbeth is for Rosenberg an extreme of character and temperament in the hero, one of the "deep notes" in his character design (*MM*, 276). Thus "philosophy" is seen merely as a trait of character, the hero's congenital tendency to fall into a brown study, to introvert. The point, however, is that Truth (as presenced in 1.3) has effectuated a cataclysmic change in Macbeth, so that after prophecy there is in an important sense no Macbethian action that is not a function of a "philosophical" stance, that is not philosophical action. This is what I have designated as "servitude." All servitude (in this sense) involves building security round an Apollonian cogito. Rosenberg speaks of the hero's inward struggle, and the "philosophical" Macbeth takes part in this struggle as one of its combatants. The "philosophical" Macbeth would from such a viewpoint either be the reasoning penchant of the hero's psyche or else the "good," Apollonian hemisphere of its "dialectic." But, we must ask again, is it an "inward struggle?" Can it be said that "philosophical Macbeth" is some kind of "part" of his total temperament?

If we argue instead that the entire monarchial exaltation of the name "Macbeth" immediately involves everything the play foregrounds as "philosophical," then we can quickly recognize that the awesome power of the drama springs from the ability of the ascent to political Truth to combine itself with the general Apollonian desire *to know all that can be known about "Macbeth."* The prophecy materializes the first aspect of imperial Truth rather quickly (with the crowning of Macbeth), but for Macbeth to reach the finalized truth of Macbeth, he must travel to the very end of his destiny; he only gets the final answer to his absolutely exhausted truth at the moment when Macduff proves not to have been born of woman. "Philosophic" (or Apollonian) Macbeth—the one marked by prophecy—has to move through his entire career on stage to reach the philosophic Truth of his name; hence the ideality of the play as such (the career of its ideal performance) is in an interesting sense identical with the ideality of Truth that is promised in prophecy. We await the truth of "Macbeth" with the same beating heart as the hero. Not as murderers, but as philosophers. Not in our greedy Dionysian will to power, but in an Apollonian fixation on Truth as the spellbinding destiny of our spectatorship. If a deconstruction, I may add, could completely elude such a spell, there would not have been a powerful spell there to begin with.

The reason why a play like *Macbeth* is a challenge to an actor like Garrick or Olivier is that spectacular thought intuits a level of dramatic intensity—made possible by the language of the dramatist—where commonplace logic is transgressed. Rosenberg mentions a review in the London *Times* where Olivier is depicted as facing the problem of "reconciling" the tremendous forces unleashed by tragic strain; but it is hard to see how any strong reconciliation can take place in that imaginary polyphonic center where all extremes get happily "fused" (MM, 105). What is involved in the extreme efforts of dramatic thought—whether at the limits of writing or at the limits of acting—is a rending of common ontological tension ("thesis versus antithesis") and the attainment of a level of dialectical interaction that is no longer strictly bipartite—that is no longer strictly dialectical. The "reconciliation," far from being equatorial or centered, takes place in a realm of pure excess: linguistic, intellectual, imaginative, physical. And thus the reason why Olivier/Macbeth can "reconcile" the fighter and the philosopher is that Olivier/ Macbeth, unlike the dialectical critic, does not have to think in terms of center, presence, or fusion as compromise. The fighter is uncompromising (1.2), and so is the philosopher. The "philosopher" (someone more than just a political gambler) has been promised *absolute* Truth in prophecy, and he will continue to hold the stage—as one hundred percent "philosopher"—until he has attained that absolute (Macbeth as finally knowing what he knows in act 5). There is no negotiation at all between extremes in the normal sense of a harmonious, essentialist interbalancing of opposites. The distance between fighter and philosopher is in no way a distance between two "aspects" of the "character" Macbeth. It is a spacing between two Macbeths: what we have been calling the master and the slave. For the effective materialization of each of these men, there must be an absolute affirmation of excess, the difference being that in the case of the master excess has to be outward-bound, while in the case of the slave it has to be inward-bound. Of course, as I have argued, there is introduced into philosophic servitude an element of "balance" that is absent in the hyperontological world of heroic fighting (1.2) where extravagance and a degree of reckless insanity pay off handsomely. But the "balance" I have discussed as central to the prophecy of Truth is not the function of an equation of "character," but a transcendental property idealized as part of Truth.

7.3 Shakespeare's Other

What we have been moving away from in the foregoing pages has been an ontologizing conception of Shakespearean language as plenary speech, an essentialist conception of Shakespearean meaning as the sonorous presence of a complexly melodic truth. As Michael Goldman has observed by calling attention to numerous tongue-twisters and dense entanglements in the discourse of *Macbeth*,[9] the "Macbeth-sound is not a coloration or a harmony."[10] The important ontodramatic zone discussed in this book in terms of *the cut* is an example of something that, precisely by not being an entity, is perfectly meaningless from the melodic viewpoint.[11] Yet *the cut* is a highly suggestive notion against the background of the alternative critical imagery forwarded by Goldman: density. As he points out, neighboring units "smother" one another in this tropical realm of thick growth—so that in the *Macbethian* language forest, no melodic universal can really hope to reach and synthesize all the "unassimilated residues of sound and sense."¹² In such a situation of density, we have to cut our way forward; but language too—crossing its own paths as it were—itself participates in this jungly nihilation.

If entitative and dialectical thought is allowed to take over *Macbeth* and to administrate its power in terms of ontologized meaning, we lose not only the peculiar aesthetic and hyperlogical ingenuity of this particular plot, but also the sense of how Shakespeare's highly original language interacts with it. If the *villain* in the drama is Dionysus, it can never continue to cast the full power of its spell—which, constructionally as well as linguistically, is highly Dionysian. A play that shows us that we are slaves of passion cannot take us to the extreme limit of the possible; nor can it take us into unthinkability. But the imaginative and dramatic encounter with Dionysus is precisely a stretching to the extreme limit of the thinkable. What "remains" of Macbeth (in act 5) after his Apollonian quest (conducted in the shadow of prophecy/Truth) is highly Dionysian; but how are we to experience that Dionysian remainder in terms of the Dionysian (in terms of free joyous excess), if the servile block of tragic disaster that it disengages itself from itself is Dionysian? If Dionysian rather than Apollonian (i.e., essentialist) Macbeth has committed the crime, then clearly there is nothing that is really Dionysian left to admire in the hero: no Nietzschean dimension of unorchestrated negativity left behind for us as a (non)structural remainder.

Any "remainder" in *Macbeth*, if it is to appear as a positive remainder, must be Dionysian, non-Apollonian. It cannot be a leftover that Truth/Apollo could have retrieved if it/he had worked more carefully. The glorious remainder cannot be "true," cannot simply mean. But if the glorious remainder—what we have already discussed in terms of "sovereignty" and "gay laughter"—is Dionysian, it is also linguistic: a linguistic or hyperlinguistic remainder. As we have seen, indeed, what is hyperlinguistic in Shakespeare comes over as Dionysian excess, as pure intensity. By affirming intensity as such, the hyperlinguistic resource of Shakespeare's language demands of actor and spectator what it demands of hero and critic: the experience of the sensation of an absolute strain, a total commitment, an extraordinary readiness for the extreme limit. The intensity of language is here a function of the violence of its intense engagement with (rather than against) negativity. The language that we think of as peculiarly Shakespearean thus builds toward itself according to a grammar of absence, or what Derrida has called a "graphematics of undecidables."[13] Such a language is by nature Dionysian and nonclassical, its negative "stir" (the fracas of its active nihilation/cutting) creating the enduring sensation of savage unpredictability. Language here is in a special sense dangerous—as we indeed saw in the articulatory efforts of the bleeding Captain ("my gashes cry for help. / So well thy words become thee, as thy wounds," 1.2.43–44). Articulation itself implies the risk of absolute spending, of loss in the most unconditional sense. After ten minutes everyone in the audience realizes that Macbeth is dangerous; but after ten minutes everyone in the audience also senses that language itself is dangerous.

Like equivocation, then, negativity is inseparable from tragic speech. Negativity, whether as "cut" or "vanishing," whether as death or imaginative transgression, does not "surround" presence (or dramatic entities) in the form of a circular "ditch"[14] (or reassuring moat) to be contemplated from the fortified "inside" of the tranquil cogito. Always, the waters of absence and negativity have already entered the tragic subject, and they persist in re-marking their intrusion as oddly originary. In Venetian fashion such dark waters—as the arteries and veins of thought, but also as the traffic of signification—hold the system together by cutting it up. Through its curious and baroque projection of originary negativity, its Venetian ability to let its avenues of meaning become flooded by absent meaning, *Macbeth* thus permits Shakespeare to infinitize the conflictual nature of all human discourse and to launch that dark potential into the unthinkability of lasting tragedy.

The sense of *Macbeth* as a transgressive play is negotiated by language; but it is of course not only language that is transgressive in *Macbeth*, not only language that transgresses. (A grotesque misunderstanding of this book would be to view it as a language-over-performance venture, as if we in any way ourselves could choose between these alternatives.) As Marjorie Garber has pointed out, "[t]he play is itself transgressive, and insists upon the posing of pertinent thought-troubling questions."[15] The notion of *Macbeth* as an "unlucky" play is not entirely unconnected with this sense of the transgressive.[16] The play is obsessively concerned with taboo: with things that should not be thought or heard, with "boundaries that should not be crossed—and are."[17] Garber calls attention to taboo as it also works in the area of vision: the Waiting-Gentlewoman who has seen Lady Macbeth's nocturnal performance is asked to repress what she has witnessed ("you have known what you should not," 5.1.44).[18] "The whole play is in one sense at least a parade of forbidden images gazed upon at peril"[19]—"a fatal journey from the familiar to the forbidden."[20] Again, I would like to add, we need to focus the tendency of motions "inside" the play to be dangerously operative also outside it. The stage history of the play, its peculiar effect on actors and actresses, may be viewed as such a tendency of the drama to spill itself far beyond its "own" proper margins; in addition, it will be remembered, I argued that a certain type of criticism (represented provisionally by John Dover Wilson) risks getting drawn into the tragic patterns of deception that the play itself discusses. But the curious ability of the critical outside (criticism) to be drawn into the problematic of the originary inside (*Macbeth*) also involves the question of taboo and forbidden seeing (reviewed by Garber). Not only actors but also critics have felt the need to protect themselves against *what should not have been revealed*. Also to the critic the play might seem to say: "you have known what you should not." Also for the critic there might exist this need (felt by the superstitious actor) to retreat behind a screen where the forbidden no longer is in full view. Also for the critic there might exist a natural tendency to screen off what we just saw Garber call "the posing of pertinent thought-troubling questions." In these pages it is in that case this very type of screening that we have tried to resist and overcome. If Garber is right in describing *Macbeth* as a journey from the familiar to the forbidden, it is only natural that institutionalized criticism often will seek to reverse this movement. In that event one directly or indirectly covers up what is happening in *Macbeth*. Writes Garber: "There *is* something uncanny going on here."[21]

As I have tried to argue in my reading of *Macbeth*, the sense of the really uncanny in the play is related to various types of inversion and reversal—particularly in the field of causation. Classical logic and classical criticism cannot manage such "non-logical" causation, since the mechanisms that operate fail to be comprehensible inside the logical paradigm of entitative thinking. Jonathan Culler draws attention to this type of problematized causation when he discusses meaning in *Oedipus* in terms of cause rather than effect. The "force of meaning" is itself a sufficient cause for the creation of tragic fate.[22] Tragic fall is in such cases dependent on the exceptional readiness of the hero to believe in the meaning of his situation, in the point of his story.

Meaning, or what I have called Truth in this investigation, is itself a temptation—and especially so when the hero is subject to prophecy. According to Culler, Oedipus leaps to various conclusions based not on evidence "but on the force of meaning, the interweaving of prophesies and the demands of narrative coherence. The convergence of discursive forces makes it essential that he become the murderer."[23] Thus, as in my reading of *Macbeth*, "the crucial event is the product of demands of signification. Here meaning is not the effect of a prior event but its cause."[24] This line of thinking is no doubt related to what I foregrounded some time ago: that "the ideality of the play as such (the career of its ideal performance) is in an interesting sense identical with the ideality of Truth that is promised in prophecy." This type of Macbethian convergence becomes poignant in the light of Culler's remarks on *Oedipus*: "Moreover, it is essential to the force of the play that Oedipus . . . accede to the demands of narrative coherence. . . . If he were to resist the logic of signification . . . Oedipus would not acquire the necessary tragic stature."[25]

The Macbeth/Oedipus analogy is illuminating, but only up to a point. For whereas it is true that Macbeth too cannot "resist the logic of signification," it is also true that he can and does resist it. As I have tried to argue, the opposition resistance/nonresistance is itself deconstructed in *Macbeth*, in itself has to be resisted.

Culler then goes on to point out that the "contrary logic" created by the new interpretative move does not replace an "incorrect" reading with a "correct" one.[26] Instead we face "two logics" that cannot be reconciled.[27] We end up in a situation of "double reading" where "narratological analysis" is at once possible and impossible.[28] It would thus be tempting to say that we too end up in this situation of "double reading," so that—on a somewhat different level of logical extraction—we would need to keep the traditional reading of *Macbeth* as a parallel entity running alongside the present interpretation. Yet the neat oppositional play created by the "double reading" paradigm is always to a certain extent already disrupted in *Macbeth* through the fact that the hero perpetually is in a position where he himself performs an ongoing "narratological analysis." This "narratological analysis" effectuated by Macbeth—his critical seminars on the subject of his own fate—cannot be situated in any entitative space at all: can take place neither inside nor outside "the story of Macbeth." On the one hand he is distinctly outside his own narrative, outside the discursive forces converging to shape his destiny as tragic signification; on the other hand this outsideness already somehow always belongs to the logic of signification, to his story. Macbeth can neither rectify his fate, nor avoid rectifying it.

Yet, as Baudrillard points out in his own discussion of Oedipal fatality,[29] otherness needs to be thought of in terms of an alterity that is far more radical than the alterity managed by theories of the subject—and there are moments in *Macbeth* when even the most weird notions of causality must give way to the far more disturbing idea of pure noncausality. From this viewpoint—that of "an event *without precedent*"[30]—there is a difference between destiny in the weak sense and destiny in the strong sense. Weak destiny is still a form of what Baudrillard calls "*histoire*";[31] the notion of "story" is still relevant, and therefore discussions of "narratological analysis" still remain illuminating. In the case of weak destiny, psychoanalysis continues to be a possible mode of clarification: the story/dream/fabrication is still a "symptom," the clue and rational pointer to something preceding it and explaining it.[32] In the case of strong destiny, however, the initiative has *completely* slipped over to the object: the dream, the surprise, the prophecy . . . the event. You do not dream the dream; it dreams you.

> What psychoanalysis has not grasped is that fortunately something really other always happens to us, an event *without precedent*, which inaugurates not a history or story, but a destiny and which, by lacking a precedent, liberates us from such origination and such (hi)story. This event without precedent is seduction, is also without origin, comes from elsewhere, always arrives unexpectedly, and is a pure event that in one fell swoop obliterates all the determinations of the conscious and the unconscious.[33]

The seductive "surprise," Baudrillard continues, turns you into an object of sovereign choice; and this elect object ["*object d'élection*"]—that you have already become, that now replaces you with its own mineral quality—is not a subject.[34] Only subjects have stories and histories; only subjects are *fully* open to "narratological analysis." From the viewpoint of a theory of seduction, the "mineral object" ["*objet minéral*"][35]—a function in *Macbeth* of the mineral gold[36]—does not merely take us into the territory of the forbidden, thus giving us opportunity for rationalizing the logical causes for taboo and violation. Instead the transgressive process is primarily perceived as an initiation.[37] The emphasis of our understanding shifts violently: from the subjective to the objective, from subject to fate, from a theory of the subject to a theory of the "mineral." (I take "the mineral" here to mean clinically pure otherness, otherness free from everything, including psychoanalytical and nonpsychoanalytical causation.) The shift from subject to "object" amounts to the shift from Macbeth to prophecy, from narrative to gold. No longer are we in that case (that of gold as Truth and that of Truth as a mineral) mainly interested in the subject's mode of transgression, nor in the boundary that is transgressed. To be interested in these two things, we would still need to have the subject at the center of our field of vigilance. What now instead would magnetize our powers of concentration (as well as those of the hero; part man, but already also part gold, part mineral) would be the seductive object itself—the actual territory that seduction and initiation open. This territory is now no longer just the forbidden, but the given, *what the play* (the seduction) *gives*. This gift, provided by destiny and seduction, is neither human nor abstract; it is mineral. What is given is neither personal nor truthful. It is Truth.

Truth in this special sense is an event. Or a destiny. It has no cause. It is the pure "eruption" of otherness.[38] Yet this noncausal purity, the "mineral object" that breaks up everything through the solidity of its surprise, does not merely betoken the irrational—some situation, dilemma, or predicament where we throw all our powers of reasoning overboard. It is not enough for the story to be nonsensical or illogical in order to be seductive— the unexpected enchainings of language must engineer the ironic performance.[39] We, like the hero, have to reason ourselves through language and causation toward that point where pure otherness has already commenced the initiation into the hyperlinguistic and hypercausal. The inequality or dissymmetry in this situation is that language, by always anticipating the seductive powers of its hyperlinguistic reservoir, in some way "knows" more.[40] Not only more than the subject, but more than itself. In such a climate, language only needs the tiniest phrases ("Hail Macbeth!", etc.) to disidentify the subject through the nonidentity of the seductive entity.[41] As long as it is purely "exterior," the minute phrase will be infinitely disruptive. Each phrase coming from the pure outside is peculiarly effective because it corresponds to no natural other with which we could oppose it. We assist it with the gestures that would have helped us to resist it in other circumstances.[42]

I think it is evident that *Macbeth* must be understood in terms of the question of otherness, and in terms of an otherness that radicalizes itself infinitely. But in that case, we do not only have to find a theory of the infinite radicalization of otherness, but also permit theory to follow this cue, to itself radicalize its notions of how otherness could radicalize itself. Hegel, as Derrida realized, is a kind of starting point here, for his theory of otherness is one of the most audacious and awesome notions ever conceived: that each thing "is" the otherness of itself, its "own" other. (All antithesis is "there" from the outset, "inside" the thesis.)[43] Derrida in the final analysis challenges this notion on the grounds that it is not radical enough: precisely by recentering itself in the "itself," the other is tamed and brought back into ipseity. Derrida's notion of the "supplement" seeks to avoid this recentering, eternally pushing otherness beyond the reach of the logical center that organizes its activity. Both of these conceptions of radical otherness have been encountered in this survey: Macbeth's ability to see each entity as the symmetrical opposite of itself (murder *is* nonmurder, Macbeth *is* not-Macbeth), but also his ability to intuit supplementarity as otherness perpetually on the move away from the reaching center that desires mastery over it. Yet, as I have already suggested, the possibility of radicalizing a theory of otherness does not really stop with the recognition of the importance of the play of the supplement. Some deconstructions are based on the notion that patient scrutiny of the sign will provide us with quasi-scientific certainty about the various "laws" governing the production of signification: the "supplement," "différance," "hymen," and so forth. As if, given the field of semiotic inquiry, literary critics would forever be the patient Louis Pasteurs of textual analysis; as if the literary scholar would forever be bending over his tweezers and his microscope with the fastidious reverence of a man of the laboratory. What may be opposed to this mode of procedure, and precisely for the purpose of radicalizing a theory of otherness, would be something far less neat and (in many quarters) far more disturbing. I am tempted to simply call this other notion of the other "the miraculous." Miracles are the extreme limit of the possibility of otherness, of the possibility of the other. And literature is full of miracles.

The power of the "miracle" is partly derived from its simplicity, or apparent simplicity: our sense (like that of the hero) that it *immediately* is beyond the pales of analysis. But the power of the "miracle" is also derived from its proportions, its engagement with the sublime.

It is (to transvalue a Hegelian tag) the "Unhappy Consciousness" who will fail to recognize or acknowledge the miraculous *qua* miraculous. Psychoanalysis, as Baudrillard correctly argues, is thus the Unhappy Consciousness of the sign.[44] The sense of the miraculous that empowers the sign in dreaming is reduced by psychoanalysis, so that the sign becomes the rationally explained symptom of something else (the operations of the unconscious, and so forth). The sign is brought down from the level of the noncausal and miraculous to the level of causal explanation. Baudrillard then goes on to clarify the striking power of the miraculous as it works when seen free from this type of rationalization, and the analytical outline, I suggest, is highly relevant for an understanding of Macbeth. Macbeth, by being sucked into the higher-order system of initiation, is one who can be defined as entering the area and sense of the miraculous (and not merely the world of doom, as has often been argued):

> [T]hings come to organize themselves in terms of the miraculous [*comme par miracle*]—we all have experience of that, including our experience of the written and spoken word, for words have the same compulsion, once left to play freely, to arrange themselves as destiny; language as such can in this way come to engulf itself in a single phrase, through a seductive effect which precipitates the floating signs toward a central enchainment.[45]

Shakespeare, on my view, becomes increasingly preoccupied with the notion and experience of the miraculous during the final phase of his dramatic career—and I see the "romances" as the final and necessary consequence of that preoccupation. The Reformation obviously did its best to minimize this sense of the miraculous, destroying nearly all of those miracle plays that helped to shape the general dramatic awareness of the medieval consciousness; and this tendency of the austere Protestant mind to obliterate the traces of the sense of the miraculous is still operative in many contemporary academies—so that we determine to always replace the sense of wonder at the mystery of the other with a rational explanation that accounts for the wonder but not for the sense of it. *Macbeth*, in spite of its sinister subject matter, adumbrates a sense of the miraculous that *Antony and Cleopatra* will develop further, and that the romances will turn into a dominant imaginative energy. (Through the gruesomeness of its constructional premises, *Macbeth* retains the advantage over the romances—and perhaps also over *Antony and Cleopatra*—that it does not need to deliberately secularize its sense of the miraculous.)

Shakespeare's Other 213

For us, but also for the hero, the sense of the miraculous outdoes the sense of doom, because the absurd overbidding of grotesque and negative events fails to create a sense of higher order that itself is grotesque or negative: the haunting necessity that Macbeth intuits as an alternative to mere "Chance" (1.3.144–45) is of the highest order of beauty, the weird interlacing of unlikely events projecting catastrophe itself as a site of exquisite pleasure.[46] If theory too must become haunted by such fatal pleasure,[47] the poststructuralist notion of the "general other" (TM, 103) does not quite do the job.[48] The miraculous other is not general, is not scientifically available everywhere at short notice.

To *hope for the miraculous*—which is what any hero does, any spectator, any reader opening the first pages of a book—is to want to be a gambler and a player. And who is Macbeth if not a figure nourishing such hope? Who is Macbeth if not this heroic spectator opening the first pages of his own book?

> We are all gamblers. That is, what we are most intensely hoping for is that sometimes the slow-moving rational enchainments will unmake themselves, and that, even if only for a brief moment, an unprecedented unfolding of an other order could supervene, a marvelous overbidding in events, an extraordinary succession, as if predestined, of the smallest details, where one has the impression that things, hitherto maintained artificially at a distance through a [rational] contract of [logical] succession and causation, immediately find themselves not delivered to chance, but spontaneously converging and concurring at the same level of intensity through their singular enchainment.[49]

The sense of the miraculous, in this type of theory, involves the sense of magic. Thus Baudrillard speaks of the strategy of fatal gambling as the desire to effectuate a provocation that will turn the de-intoxicating process of rational causation into the intoxicating escalation of magical enchainments.[50] This connection between the miraculous and the magical is of course conspicuous in *Macbeth*, Shakespeare utilizing the magical aura of witchcraft to negotiate his entire drama through a sense of magical enchainment. Again it becomes interesting to relate this dramatic and theoretical procedure (that of magic and the miraculous) to Culler's discussion of reversed causation (mentioned above): the notion that "meaning" can assert itself as cause rather than effect, the hero (Oedipus) somehow obeying the power of the converging forces of (his) narratological relevance. Oedipus completes his tragedy by catching up with the full significance of his own narratological import. But from the viewpoint of our rather different theoretical perspective, *Macbeth* is organized by a *failure* of the hero ever to "catch up."

This failure, as it now operates in our theoretical apparatus, is negotiated by the fact that narratological coherence for us cannot be thought of as a single unified entity. There is one "story" on the level of rational meaning and another "story" (sense of narratological completion) on the level of initiation into the miraculous. "Destiny" here itself splits up: being either the "tragic fate" of the hero, or else his status as an object of beauty in the higher-order system of magical enchainment. Whereas the former fate is organized narratologically in terms of causal enchainments of a logical kind, whether straightforward or problematical, the latter fate is not only organized narratologically. It is organized, rather, through an excess of signification that produces an order of pure magical appearances, what Baudrillard calls an order of the "symbolic."[51] The order of the symbolic is not empowered by syntax, narratological truth, or any ordinary convergence of meaning. The order of the symbolic is instead empowered by appearances, magical appearances. What makes the appearances magical (which incidentally is also what makes the appearances appearances, pure appearances) is their lack of an ability to converge except on the level of the miraculous.

Thus, following this line of thinking, there is a "gap" between appearances and (their) meaning, between magical suggestion and "sense." There is (in Culler's terminology) a "convergence of meaning," but this convergence is two separate convergences: one on the level of the logic of the narrative, another on the level of magical initiation. On the level of storytelling, Shakespeare makes these two levels into a single dimension: what Macbeth "learns" about his own fate. But it is Macbeth's fate to have a destiny that is not reducible to the story of his own fate, nor reducible to his final comprehension of the "facts" of this fate. The fatal "remainder" here is what the gap between the two orders constantly fabricates in *Macbeth*: the persisting ability of the order of the miraculous to supply an excess of signification that the "narratological" and causal order is unable to cope with.

This discrepancy—between magical sense and sense—is not only there at the final showing of the drama, in its concluding pyrotechnics, but also there from the outset in the magical excess that Shakespeare pours into all appearing and all appearances. In the magical opening of *Macbeth*, already, Shakespeare wants the appearings to be appearances and to remain appearances. And this special effect is determined by the fortunate failure of appearances to make sense. An appearance that makes sense is not only an appearance but also sense. But in *Macbeth*, for the creation of the higher-order system of miraculous overbidding, appearances must not make sense—or not only make sense, not mainly make sense. If what was powerful about the appearances was their ability to somehow make sense, the subject perceiving them would not become intoxicated with the sensation of the magical but instead go about the business of merely pursuing the course of his meaning. Macbeth obviously does that too, and fatally; but that pursuit does not encompass all that operates through our sense of his fatality.

Meaning, convergence, and destiny thus function on two levels, in two orders: that of signification ("sense," the principle of narratological coherence) and that of the excess of signification (magic appearing, the miraculous, the other, the reign of appearances and apparitions).

In temporal terms, this means that we have two main temporalities: one where narratological sense can be produced and achieved through the cooperative efforts of hero, spectator, and the production of the units of narrative; another where sense itself is obstructed through the fact that appearances are "quicker" than their meaning. In this second temporality, time itself is warped, as is causation.

Baudrillard deals with this situation (the preeminence of appearances over meanings) by saying that things have time to really *appear* when they run faster than their causes.[52] The process of appearing dominates any event where things are extra-rapid, there being no time for entities to get reflected in themselves, to settle reflectively in a ponderous process of interrogation.[53] (As I pointed out in my introductory remarks, the processes of "slowing" and "speeding-up" need to be seen as interimplicative in *Macbeth*; in terms of Baudrillard's theorizing, the "slowing" of destiny is the tragic, its acceleration the magical.) And once again Baudrillard relates this motion of the fatal to the process of writing: things run faster than their causes not only in magical drama but also in magical moments of writing. Writing is in such a situation faster than the conceptual (and causal) aspect of its unfolding—a fact that is supremely apparent in the case of the extra-rapid writer William Shakespeare. Meaning tends to get a bit behind, to get "delayed." (Much traditional Shakespeare criticism, rather than wanting to focus and preserve this delay, wants to erase it; wishes to make Shakespearean meaning catch up with the spectacle of Shakespearean writing, coincide perfectly with it—wants the Shakespearean moment, in brief, to be an event.)

If meaning does not catch up with pure appearances in *Macbeth*, and if pure appearances converge on a separate level of suggestion, we are left with a quite "Manichaean" situation, where order faces order, where one order *defies* its other.[54] A "logical mutation" governs the difference.[55] Catastrophe is from this perspective nothing but the flooding effectuated by effects, the swamping and abolition of all causes. A crisis disorganizes causes; a catastrophe floods them.[56] Words, in this type of situation, start to function like things, defying the principles of any coherent syntax.[57] Words, as in dreams, do not in the final analysis point to their logical causes but to the dream itself: they tell the dreamer of dreaming. Such dreamwords achieve the extreme limit of what is possible in language through their nonsignifying banality[58]—a banality that the dreamer himself (we, Macbeth, critical theory, the audience, Shakespeare) can understand in terms of the miraculous, the highest possible order of elevation.

The subject, the hero, on such a threshold of initiation, comes to know "meanings" that are close to him but still outside him, tiny "cyclones" of signification where unprecedented accelerations of gravitation are quickly born.[59] Interested, now, in the surface appearances of things rather than in the crypts of their meanings, interested in the extra-rapid tracks where the surface displays the lineaments of its superficiality, the heroic subject finds that he likes the idea of pure chance and rationalist alibis, but that he prefers the infinitely cruel world where he is resorbed into the automatism of magic events—where he is part of their miraculous unfolding rather than part of his own subjectivist dilemma.[60] This type of preoccupation with the symbolic order of higher bidding is of course quite compatible with the sense of a quest for Truth in the name of metaphysical presence (the leitmotif of our previous inquiry); for while Truth in one sense is the sordid and subjectivist process (in *Macbeth*) of philosophically establishing oneself inside the political and servile court of one's own supreme identity, it is in another sense the arena of magic and enchantment: quite simply the promise that the Other makes.

In *Macbeth*, of course, truth is not merely truth, but truth facing truth. At this point of inquiry, one might say that magical truth faces moral truth, since the question of the murder of Duncan creates a tragic discrimination between murder as seen from the moral viewpoint and murder as seen from the magical viewpoint. The temptation of chance (1.3.144–45), I have mentioned, is a provisional temptation for Macbeth, a logical way out of the dilemma; but this is only so until it is quickly realized that chance is not magical at all. To leave someone else's death to mere chance is to relinquish intense involvement with the magical order. Not to have desired the death of a comrade is quite logical from the emotional and moral perspective; but from the perspective of the higher order of symbolic beauty, this "not" may amount to a sense of removal from the fatal world of pure appearances, and from the higher bidding going on there.[61]

* * *

These supplementary comments have been piloted, we have seen, by the notion of gambling; to "go" for the miraculous order of the symbolic is to gamble on it. Macbeth, clearly, is a gambler. But if gambling, as Baudrillard observes, is a supremely untheatrical event,[62] it is clear that the hero would hardly at all be a theatrically strong figure if his entire being were given over to gambling. What in fact always brings back Macbeth—to "reality," to the stage, to the sense of narrative order and causal mastery—is his aboriginal status as a heroic fighter. There is gambling in fighting too, but there is more to the fight, as we have seen, than its gamble. However much Macbeth gives himself over to the sense of the eruption of the pure object (prophecy, gold, Truth), and however much this magical object erases him as subject by shifting over the initiative to its own side, Macbeth still lingers in this world as subject: as fighter, as mind, as desire and consciousness. What is thus shown to us and staged is never simply a Macbeth who has passed over into the magical realm of the object, but a *subject* who is "aware" of this de-subjectivization. Indeed, if Truth, as metaphysical stone or miraculous mineral, inverts the relationship between the subject and the object (giving magic power over Macbeth instead of Macbeth power over magic), this very shift of power is staged not only from the viewpoint of the magical (where its subjective other does not count), but also from the viewpoint of the subject. There may well be an incompatibility between the otherness of the magical and the nonotherness of subjectivity, but Macbeth has to convey the sense of that incompatibility too—and that, paradoxically, preserves his dramatic status as subject. Moreover, the reversal (between subjectivity and objectivity) that is created by the magical object (prophetic Truth) itself comes over as something "subjective"—"subjective" because only subjects know what "power" is, and because the ascendancy that magic has over Macbeth is precisely a kind of subjective power.[63] (Shakespeare's use of the Weird Sisters is nowhere more effective than on this level of suggestion: that the unhuman, "objective" quality of magical enchantment is also "subjective"—therefore human; the witch hovers between the human and the nonhuman.)

Thus, no matter how far a theory of otherness plunges into the (magical) peripheries of otherness, one still always returns to the sense of power as a human dialectic, as the life-and-death matter of a desiring subject. If the mineral other (the seductive object as "exterior" to the subject) achieves mastery over the subject, the subject on the one hand gets cancelled as "subject," on the other hand once more becomes part of the dialectic of mastery and servitude. (This paradox applies also to "sovereignty," as I have argued earlier; "sovereignty" is "outside" dialectic, but at the same time it is pregnant with all the tensions that afflict dialectic.) As we move toward the conclusion of our efforts, therefore, we must once more recognize the fact that there is no place in the drama where Shakespeare really permits us to forget about Macbethian mastery or Macbethian servitude. Generally speaking this is so because there is no corner of the play that is not swept by the conflict between these two "states." Even "nonconflictual" and "nondialectical" spots in the play are put right where they are (instead of somewhere else) by the dialectical forces they subvert.

For the entire duration of the play, Macbeth continues to participate in the dialectical equivocation he has sought to end. He lasts in our recollections as contradiction itself: being both private and public, sublime and absurd, solemn and gay, taught and abandoned, divine and profane, despotic and subversive, credulous and sceptical, composed and distraught, poetic and vulgar, contemplative and headstrong, calculating and spontaneous, dreamy and wide-awake, invincible and doomed. The confounding of opposites, of mastery and servitude, is ultimately also a celebration of them. To pass beyond the phenomenology of dialectical contradiction is thus also to risk its most precise reinscription.

On the one hand, our whole being has been seized with dread, has trembled in every fiber of its being, and everything solid and stable has been shaken to its foundations; in this absolute melting-away of everything stable, absolute negativity has jeopardized consciousness and shaken its entire contents to the ground.

On the other hand, we hang out our banners. And we laugh a siege to scorn.

NOTES

Chapter 1

1. *The Tain of the Mirror: Derrida and the Philosophy of Reflection* (Cambridge and London: Harvard University Press, 1986). Abbreviated *TM* in parenthetical page references in the text. Gasché's book is one of the few accurate accounts of Derridean thinking.
2. See David Carroll, *Paraesthetics: Foucault, Lyotard, Derrida* (New York and London: Methuen, 1987), pp. 150–51.
3. Jacques Derrida, *The Truth in Painting*, trans. Geoff Bennington and Ian McLeod (Chicago and London: University of Chicago Press, 1987), p. 372.
4. Georges Bataille, *Inner Experience*, trans. Leslie Anne Boldt (Albany: State University of New York Press, 1988), p. 91; emphasis added.
5. (Rutherford, Madison and Teaneck, N.J.: Fairleigh Dickinson University Press).
6. Jean Baudrillard, *Selected Writings*, ed. Mark Poster (Cambridge and Oxford: Polity Press and Basil Blackwell, 1988), pp. 193–95.
7. Jean Baudrillard, *Les Stratégies fatales* (Paris: Bernard Grasset, 1983), p. 193.
8. Jacques Derrida, *Memoires for Paul de Man* (New York: Columbia University Press, 1986), p. 135.
9. Terence Hawkes, "Telmah," in *Shakespeare and the Question of Theory*, ed. Patricia Parker and Geoffrey Hartman (New York and London: Methuen, 1985), p. 318.
10. Ibid., p. 319.
11. Ibid., p. 330.
12. Ibid.
13. Ibid.
14. Ibid., p. 329
15. Ibid., pp. 330–31.
16. *Memoires*, p. 73.
17. Ibid., pp. 72–73.
18. Ibid., p. 135.
19. *What Is Called Thinking?* (New York: Harper & Row, 1968), p. 103.
20. Parker and Hartman, *Shakespeare and the Question of Theory*, pp. 8, 13, 16.
21. Ibid., p. 14.
22. Heidegger suggests that the Western "definition of Being [is] ruled by the view of presence," and he wants to think out this unthought presence (*What Is Called Thinking*, p. 103). Thus, in a sense, he does not want to remove presence from the center of the Western scenario, but think it. Yet Heidegger also disrupts presence. As Derrida suggests, Heidegger's "ontological difference"—that between Being and beings, or between the presence of the present and the present—is a difference that itself never by definition is present

219

(*Memoires*, p. 60). It is when this type of weak conception of central absence joins up with the central absence posited by Heidegger in thought (the "unthought" blackhole inside all thinking) that the Derridean transmutation can take place: the creation of the strong sense of central absence in presence. Here it is no longer a question of merely thinking into the "unthought" blackhole, but instead a question of refusing to believe that the central blackhole needs to be filled at all—that it actually *could* have a filling. Hence, Derrida can discuss "traces which themselves never occupy the form of presence" and "a present that will never have been present" (ibid., pp. 58, 59). The recollection of the present, in the form of a trace of it, does not shape itself as the tracing *of* the present, since the present, strictly speaking, is never fully "there." The present is so fragile, volatile, and mobile that "its" traces are as it were always "to come" (ibid., p. 58). This bizarre notion of "memory" and "the trace" is not entirely unimportant for the comprehension of *Macbeth;* for there, precisely, the hero considers the dreadful "traces" (in his mind) thrown from a murderous volition (in the "what is not" soliloquy) that strictly speaking never has been present—and strictly speaking never *can* be present.

23. *De l'esprit: Heidegger et la question* (Paris: Galilée, 1987), p. 147.
24. *Ulysse gramophone: deux mots pour Joyce* ["Ouï-dire de Joyce"] (Paris: Galilée, 1987), p. 108.
25. *What Is Called Thinking*, p. 119.
26. Ibid., p. 154.
27. Ibid., p. 118.
28. Ibid., p. 128.
29. Ibid., p. 178.
30. *Ulysse gramophone*, p. 80.
31. Ibid.
32. *What Is Called Thinking*, p. 76.
33. *De l'esprit*, p. 18 (translation mine).
34. Ibid., p. 41.
35. Derrida would like "to understand to what extent this [Heideggerian] privilege of the Questioning [of metaphysics and its "unthought" kernel] itself remains protected [from questioning]" (ibid., p. 25); "perhaps *Geist* is the name that Heidegger [unconsciously] gives . . . to this unquestioned possibility inside his Questioning" (ibid., p. 26; translation mine).
36. Ibid., p. 80.
37. Jacques Derrida, *Glas*, trans. John P. Leavey, Jr., and Richard Rand (Lincoln and London: University of Nebraska Press, 1986), p. 244.
38. Ibid., p. 240.
39. Ibid., p. 244.
40. During the course of a private meeting with Jacques Derrida in early December 1986, I broached the question of *Macbeth* as it relates itself to "mastery," "servitude," and other Hegelian notions. When we discussed the danger of psychologizing an understanding of the "metaphysics of presence" Derrida immediately dismissed that danger by questioning the relevance of defining *anything* as exclusively "psychological." No rigid opposition exists between the psychological and the nonpsychological. ("I am not sure I know what psychology is . . .".)
41. Derrida, *Glas*, p. 135.
42. Ibid., p. 136.
43. King Lear, Macbeth, *Indefinition, and Tragedy* (New Haven and London: Yale University Press, 1983), p. 97.

44. Ibid., p. 101.
45. Ibid., p. 96.
46. Ibid., p. 98.
47. Ibid., p. 97.
48. Ibid., p. 93.
49. Ibid., p. 94.
50. Ibid., p. 91.
51. Ibid., p. 94.
52. *If It Were Done: Macbeth and Tragic Action* (Amherst: University of Massachusetts Press, 1986), pp. 57, 59, 100.
53. Ibid., p.12.
54. Ibid., p. 9.
55. Ibid., p. 24.
56. See Richard B. Sewall, *The Vision of Tragedy* (New Haven: Yale University Press, 1959), p. 5.
57. Ibid.
58. *Shakespeare and the Common Understanding* (New York: The Free Press; London: Collier-Macmillan, 1967), p. 13.
59. *Shakespeare's Mature Tragedies* (Princeton: Princeton University Press, 1973), p. 207.
60. Sukanta Chaudhuri, *Infirm Glory: Shakespeare and the Renaissance Image of Man* (Oxford: Clarendon Press, 1981), p. 181.
61. *Shakespeare's Scepticism* (Brighton: Harvester Press, 1987), p. 219.
62. Ibid., p. 230.
63. Ibid., p. 235.
64. Ibid., p. 227.
65. *Infirm Glory*, p. 173.
66. *Carnival and Theater: Plebeian Culture and the Structure of Authority in Renaissance England* (New York and London: Methuen, 1985), p. 11.
67. Elmer Edgar Stoll, "Source and Motive in *Macbeth* and *Othello*." In *Shakespeare: Modern Essays in Criticism*, ed. Leonard F. Dean (New York: Oxford University Press, 1961), p. 286.
68. "Shakespeare and the Exorcists," in *After Strange Texts: The Role of Theory in the Study of Literature*, ed. Gregory S. Jay and David L. Miller (University, Ala.: University of Alabama Press, 1985) p. 102.
69. *Ambition and Privilege: The Social Tropes of Elizabethan Courtesy Theory* (Berkeley, Los Angeles, and London: University of California Press, 1984), p. 20.
70. *The Weak King Dilemma in the Shakespearean History Play* (Syracuse: Syracuse University Press, 1973), p. 5.
71. See M. D. H. Parker, *The Slave of Life: A Study of Shakespeare and the Idea of Justice* (London: Chatto & Windus, 1955), p. 15.
72. *The Tiger's Heart: Eight Essays on Shakespeare* (London: Chatto & Windus, 1970), p. 187.
73. Alan Dessen, *Elizabethan Stage Conventions and Modern Interpreters* (Cambridge and New York: Cambridge University Press, 1984), p. 7.
74. "Text against Performance in Shakespeare: The Example of *Macbeth*," in *The Power of Forms in the English Renaissance*, ed. Stephen Greenblatt (Norman, Ok.: Pilgrim Books, 1982), p. 51.
75. "The Deconstruction of Presence in *The Winter's Tale*," p. 7. Gary Taylor tries to strengthen the stage-oriented position by forwarding a special "response" theory: the "ordinary playgoer" is free from academic preconception

and reacts in "unison" with all other "ordinary" playgoers during the course of a performance. See *Moment by Moment by Shakespeare* (London: Macmillan, 1985), pp. 6–7.

76. *Shakespearean Meanings* (Princeton: Princeton University Press, 1968), p. vii.

77. *The Mirror up to Nature: The Technique of Shakespeare's Tragedies* (San Marino, Ca.: The Huntington Library, 1965), p. 182.

78. *Shakespeare and the Common Understanding*, p. 1

79. *The Slave of Life*, p. 11.

80. Some critics argue with Rabkin that the Shakespearean enigmas are "supralogical" and therefore "beyond philosophy" (*Shakespeare and the Common Understanding*, pp. 12–13). Deconstruction would not necessarily refute this idea, since deconstruction itself refutes philosophy—if by philosophy we mean a closed system of meaning. But if the negation of philosophy (favored by such criticism as Rabkin's) implies a return to some "prephilosophical" innocence and intuitionism, some Eden of tragic suggestion "preceding" philosophy, then deconstruction can hardly pick up the cue. Sewall forwards a similar notion, adopting Unamuno's conception of the tragic sense as a form of prephilosophy or subphilosophy: as something "primal" the tragic vision takes us back to the depths of an "original terror" antedating the conceptions of philosophical thought and religious truth. We here encounter "irrational" terror, "original un-reason" (*The Vision of Tragedy*, pp. 4–5). The trouble with this line of approach is that it quickly boils down to a mere terminological issue. There are plenty of thinkers who have argued that "prephilosophic" insight surpasses philosophic (post-Socratic) thought; yet these special thinkers eventually also become known as philosophers—for the simple reason that they too discuss issues of cosmic magnitude in terms of universality and truthful deep-structures. It is difficult to see how Shakespeare's tragic vision could be *reduced* to this notion of the "prephilosophic," since he so clearly was influenced by the New Philosophy of his day, notably that of Montaigne. As a man given to discursive outbursts of a philosophic kind, Shakespeare was not miraculously creating *ex nihilo*. The idea that we get at the "real" Shakespeare (the literary "thing-in-itself") by cleaning away all preexisting traces of philosophical preconceptions is itself a typically philosophical move, exemplified most radically by Descartes and Husserl.

81. See McElroy, *Shakespeare's Mature Tragedies*, p. 25.

82. *Shakespeare and the Idea of the Play* (London: Chatto & Windus, 1962), p. 83.

83. See Frances A. Yates, *Giordano Bruno and the Hermetic Tradition* (London: Routledge & Kegan Paul, 1964), p. 66.

84. Immanuel Kant, *The Critique of Judgement*, trans. James Creed Meredith (Oxford: Clarendon Press, 1957; 1986), pp. 177–78.

85. Thought and air coimplicated one another for the medieval mind. See Ruth Leila Anderson, *Elizabethan Psychology and Shakespeare's Plays* (Iowa City: University of Iowa Humanistic Studies, 1927), p. 30.

86. *Shakespeare's Theater of Presence: Language, Spectacle, and the Audience* (Lewisburg, Pa.: Bucknell University Press; London and Toronto: Associated University Presses, 1986), pp. 106–8, 114, 117.

87. "Servitude," in the metaphysical sense, is identified in Hegel's *Phenomenology of Spirit* (§§ 178–96). It is a mania for certainty, a metaphysically colored quest for absolutely reassuring truth, and as Derrida writes in his essay

on Bataille in *Writing and Difference* (Chicago: The University of Chicago Press, 1978), the servile condition arrives (as in *Macbeth*) at the time when the death-risking man (the quasi-pagan man of honor) no longer identifies fighting as the privileged realm for the production of meaning. This privileged realm now becomes mind. "The servant is the man who does not put his life at stake, the man who wants to conserve his life, wants to be conserved *(servus)*" ("From Restricted to General Economy: A Hegelianism without Reserve," p. 254). Cf. Alexandre Kojève, *Introduction to the Reading of Hegel: Lectures on the Phenomenology of Spirit*, trans. James H. Nichols, Jr. (Ithaca and London: Cornell University Press, 1980): "Through animal fear of death *(Angst)* the Slave experienced the dread of the Terror *(Furcht)* of Nothingness, of his nothingness. He caught a glimpse of himself as nothingness, he understood that his whole existence was but a 'surpassed,' 'overcome' *(aufgehoben)* death—a Nothingness maintained in Being" (pp. 47–48).

88. Although, as I stated by way of introduction, Derridean deconstruction is not reducible to the branch of criticism I have called "epistemological" deconstruction, there is nevertheless an undercurrent of pessimism that connects crucial aspects of the two movements. In a sense Derrida is working in a tradition attempting to overcome modern scepticism and modern defeatism (a tradition triggered by Hegel's rejection of the extreme sceptic as "Unhappy Consciousness"); yet the affirmative side of Derridean thinking is counterbalanced by a strain of implicit pessimism that sometimes permits us to view him as a latter-day sceptic. In any review of subjectivity as extreme scepticism, deconstruction thus risks losing its own (rather different) contours in its object of study.

89. *Playhouse and Cosmos: Shakespearean Theater as Metaphor* (Newark: University of Delaware Press; London and Toronto: Associated University Presses, 1985), p. 35.

90. Ibid.

91. Ibid., p. 137.

92. Ibid., p. 25.

93. Jonas Barish, *The Antitheatrical Prejudice* (Berkeley, Los Angeles, and London: University of California Press, 1981), pp. 56–57.

94. Ibid., p. 68.

95. Ibid., p. 76.

96. Ibid., p. 79.

97. Ibid., p. 89.

98. Ibid., p. 93.

99. Ibid., p. 94.

100. Ibid., p. 96.

101. *Shakespeare's Theater of Presence*, p. 107.

102. Ibid., p. 112.

103. *Role-Playing in Shakespeare* (Toronto, Buffalo, and London: University of Toronto Press, 1978), p. 190.

104. Ibid., p. 191.

105. The fact that Macbeth hovers between participation and nonparticipation, play and detachment, needs to be reviewed against the background of a complicated cultural, historical, and theatrical situatedness. There is simply no room for an extensive discussion of these contexts in the current study, but it is clear that such a discussion would have to take account of the difference between classical and medieval audience responses and of Shakespeare's abso-

lutely innovative treatment of the play metaphor in various dramas—notably those staging Player Kings of the flawed rule. In addition, such a discussion of sly withdrawal/nonwithdrawal in the player/hero would need to recognize the development of the traditional Vice ("Ambidexter" in *Cambyses*) into the yet more equivocating type of figure represented by Don Andrea in Kyd's *Spanish Tragedy*.

Chapter 2

1. See John L. Murphy, *Darkness and Devils: Exorcism and* King Lear (Athens, Ohio, and London: Ohio University Press, 1984), pp. 3ff.
2. *Macbeth*, ed. John Dover Wilson (Cambridge, London, and New York: Cambridge University Press, 1980; first published 1947), p. xix.
3. *The Heroic Idiom of Shakespearean Tragedy* (Newark: University of Delaware Press; London and Toronto: Associated University Presses, 1985), p. 172.
4. *Shakespeare's Theater of Presence*, p. 113.
5. "'Multiplying Villainies of Nature," in *Focus on* Macbeth, ed. John Russell Brown (London, Boston, and Henley: Routledge & Kegan Paul, 1982), p. 122.
6. Ibid., pp. 119–20.
7. *The Royal Play of* Macbeth (New York: Macmillan, 1950), p. 119.
8. See ibid., p. 129.
9. See ibid., pp. 104–5.
10. Ibid., p. 67. As John L. Murphy observes, the loss of self-presence during "demonic possession" is related to medically poignant slidings that today are investigated by neuroscience: "In a secular context, I find that certain contemporary studies in depth psychology concerned with 'multiple personality' and with 'splitting' suggest dramatic forms parallel to the exorcisings as presented by Harsnett and used in *King Lear*. . . . Much in this area is still obscure to our understanding but bodily effects in 1586 may have been startling in the extreme" (*Darkness and Devils*, p. 4).
11. (Cambridge: Cambridge University Press, 1969), p. xi.
12. Ibid., p. 28.
13. Ibid., p. 61.
14. See Marvin Rosenberg, "Macbeth and Lady Macbeth in the Eighteenth and Nineteenth Centuries," In Brown, *Focus on* Macbeth, p. 83.
15. See Gareth Lloyd Evans, "*Macbeth* 1946–80 at Stratford-upon-Avon," in Brown, *Focus on* Macbeth, pp. 96–97.
16. Ibid., p. 104.
17. Ibid., p. 105.
18. Ibid., p. 106.
19. Ibid., p. 108.
20. *Shakespeare and Tragedy* (London, Boston, and Henley: Routledge & Kegan Paul, 1981), p. 6.
21. Ibid., p. 4.
22. Ibid.
23. Ibid.
24. Ibid., p. 70.

25. Ibid., p. 69.
26. "*Hamlet:* Letters and Spirits," in Parker and Hartman, *Shakespeare and the Question of Theory,* p. 298.
27. Ibid.
28. Ibid.
29. The hyperontological sphere is the dimension where the ideological opposition between ontology and its other has been problematized. In a hyperontological zone, what is ontological has not just "disappeared"; rather, it has been taken so far, has been pressurized so much, that it is no longer possible to speak *either* of "the ontological" *or* of "the nonontological."
30. "Language and Action in *Macbeth,*" in Brown, *Focus on* Macbeth, p. 150.
31. *Macbeth,* the Arden Shakespeare (London and New York: Methuen, 1983; 1972). Abbreviated KM.
32. Samuel Johnson, *Johnson on Shakespeare,* ed. Walter Raleigh (London: Oxford University Press, 1952; 1908), p. 175.
33. There is a difference between the sense of circular closure in the two discourses (Shakespeare's and that of the interpolation). The interpolation obviously favors the notion of a tranquil ring, and Shakespeare's emphasis on triplicity in his own discourse might first seem to suggest that he is working with the traditional triadic structures of magic, religion, philosophy, and myth. But if we look closely at Shakespeare's text, we see that the structure "three" tends to be supplemented in order to give a "three-plus-one" movement. A curious "extra" comes to add itself to the economy at the point where this economy seems to have completed the circular orbit of its formula. It is only when the recipe is done that there is suddenly the introduction of additional material (4.1.64–67). The same pattern is conspicuous in the showing of the various "Apparitions." They are numbered from one to three: First Apparition, Second Apparition, and Third Apparition. But Macbeth, always pressing for the "extra," manages to extract a supplementary showing; yet this new apparition is not called "Fourth Apparition." Instead it stands as precisely that which it is: a curious addition *outside* the original triad. This "three-plus-one" movement can also be studied on a more verbally direct level: "Thrice the brinded cat hath mew'd. / Thrice, *and once* the hedge-pig whin'd" (4.1.1–2). The lunar "thirty-one" (4.1.7) faintly rehearses this numerical sliding but also neutralizes it by reintroducing the feeling of cyclical regularity.
34. Johnson, *Johnson on Shakespeare,* p. 175.
35. Falconers tamed birds by sewing up ("seeling") their eyelids (KM, 84).

Chapter 3

1. *Shakespeare and Tragedy,* p. 191.
2. Quoted by J. I. M. Stewart in "Steep Tragic Contrast: *Macbeth,*" in *Shakespeare: The Tragedies,* ed. Clifford Leech (Chicago and London: University of Chicago Press, 1965), p. 106.
3. Ibid., p. 108.
4. Ibid., p. 119.
5. Ibid., p. 114.
6. Muir argues that the eye-versus-hand imagery "is Shakespearian" (KM,

25); but it could be argued that the too-obvious Shakespearean stress here is exactly what looks suspicious. The passage contains the Shakespearean building blocks, but does it contain the Shakespearean way of assembling these blocks?

7. *Shakespeare and Tragedy*, p. 69.
8. See Bartholomeusz, *Macbeth and the Players*, p. 259.
9. "*Hamlet*: Letters and Spirits," p. 299.
10. *Shakespeare and Tragedy*, p. 69.
11. Ibid.
12. *Shakespeare's Tragic Practice* (Oxford: Clarendon Press, 1979), pp. 200–201.
13. Ibid., p. 201.
14. Ibid., p. 202.
15. Ibid., p. 201.
16. Ibid., p. 202. I should perhaps emphasize, here, that I am in favor of retaining the Folio punctuation. This is not the place to undertake a critique of the "emendation" currently institutionalized; all I can say at this moment, by way of a general remark, is that the grammatically "correct" punctuation that we now have is an ontologizing construct that spoils a number of crucial spacings in the text. The cryptoromantic and ultra-ontologizing "bank and shoal of time" instead of "bank and school of time" is another interesting "improvement"—especially from the viewpoint of a critique of metaphysical presence.
17. Ibid.
18. Ibid.
19. Ibid.
20. Ibid., p. 203.
21. It may be objected that in discussing a process of "absencing" in Macbeth, I am contradicting my main thesis: that the hero gradually shifts over into a quest for metaphysical presence. But matters cannot be oversimplified. It all very much depends on what we mean by "Macbeth." There certainly is *a* Macbeth who in the most alarming and conspicuous manner falls into a quest for presence. But the name "Macbeth" is never reducible to a presence: "other" Macbeths are operative "offstage." In addition, as I argue all along, the structural impossibility of (metaphysical) presence, of presence as *absolute* self-presence, ensures the production of an absent Macbeth by the production of a present one.
22. "Language and Action in *Macbeth*," p. 146.
23. Cf. "Thou sure and firm-set earth" (2.1.56).
24. Macbeth eventually makes his wife's melodramatic tone his own for a while: "Bring forth men-children only!" (1.7.73). Could it be argued that this tonal mimesis too is fragile?—that it too is not altogether convincing?
25. Calderwood's definition of the Derridean "supplement" involves "an excess added to a sufficiency, but paradoxically, because its presence implies a prior insufficiency, also a replacement of a lack" (*If It Were Done*, p. 57). This process, as I argue too, is true for the play as a whole. The general movement traces the paradox of the work of the "supplement." "Each fulfillment creates a lack to be filled," and the "fullness of final presence—the apparent closure of an end—fades even as it appears" (ibid., p. 69).
26. See the discussion of "*trace*" in Jacques Derrida, *Parages* (Paris: Galilée, 1986), p. 192.

Notes 227

Chapter 4

1. Jean-Paul Sartre, *Being and Nothingness: An Essay on Phenomenological Ontology*, trans. Hazel E. Barnes (London: Methuen & Co., 1958, 1981; French original 1943), p. 29. Emphasis added.

2. This statement does not mean that Shakespearean drama is reducible to subjectivity.

3. Hunter observes that the weak mid-career Macbeth who dominates many twentieth-century productions is a nineteenth-century creation (G. K. Hunter, *The New Penguin Shakespeare: Macbeth*, Harmondsworth: Penguin, 1967; 1983, pp. 35–36). As Garrick learned from criticism provided by spectators, a white-livered Macbeth is not a particularly convincing stage figure. (Shakespeare has of course ruled out the possibility of such a Macbeth by writing the heroic scenes of the opening act.) Garrick changed his interpretation and eventually realized the need for the modification: the intentions of Shakespeare, he states, would be disfigured by a reading that made Macbeth sink into "pusillanimity" in the spectral encounter (Willard Farnham, *Shakespeare's Tragic Frontier: The World of His Final Tragedies*, Berkeley and Los Angeles: University of California Press, 1950, p. 125). Macbeth was played at the Globe in 1611 (almost certainly by Richard Burbage) as one who encountered the Ghost with "a great passion of fear and fury" (Bartholomeusz, *Macbeth and the Players*, p. 68). The two reactions are interproductive. Fear and fury are not "opposites," not dialectically organized. Macbeth does not pass from the fury of act 1 to the fear of act 3. In the interval between mastery and servitude, courage does not pour out of him like tea out of a teapot. He is still full of courage when he encounters the Ghost—as he himself realizes (3.4.58–59, 98–105). To have the "fit" is not simply to *lack* courage; although Macbeth is no longer "a man" (3.4.107) in the sense of having normal human reactions, he is still "man" (3.4.98) in the sense of being manly and brave.

4. *Shakespeare's Tragic Frontier*, p.124.
5. *Shakespeare and Tragedy*, p. 196.
6. Cf. ibid., p. 197.
7. *Writing and Difference* abbreviated WD.
8. See Jonathan Goldberg, *James I and the Politics of Literature: Jonson, Shakespeare, Donne, and Their Contemporaries* (Baltimore and London: The Johns Hopkins University Press, 1983), p. 148.
9. See Charles Guignon, *Heidegger and the Problem of Knowledge* (Indianapolis: Hackett, 1983), pp. 17–18.
10. Ibid., pp. 18–19.
11. Quoted by Kenneth Muir (KM, 112). Emphasis added.
12. Dover Wilson, *Macbeth*, p. 134.
13. See ibid.
14. See KM, 79.
15. See ibid.
16. Andrew C. Bradley, *Shakespearean Tragedy: Lectures on Hamlet, Othello, King Lear, Macbeth* (London: Macmillan and Co., 1904; 1950), p. 386.
17. Banquo and Macbeth tend to be fighters on the ontodramatic level (cf. 3.4.103).
18. *The New Penguin Shakespeare: Macbeth*, p. 160.
19. *Macbeth*, p. xxvi.
20. Ibid., p. 134.

228   Notes

Chapter 5

1. Cf. Jacques Derrida, *D'un ton apocalyptique adopté naguère en philosophie* (Paris: Galilée, 1983), p. 19.
2. Cf. ibid., p. 83.
3. *Macbeth*, p. 106.
4. Ibid.
5. See ibid.
6. This tension is of course what Hegel, following the pattern of classical tragedies such as *Antigone*, schematized as the division between "divine law" (supervised by woman) and "human law" (supervised by the political male).
7. *What Is Called Thinking*, p. 185.
8. Ibid.
9. Ibid., p. 191.
10. Ibid.
11. "Language Most Shows a Man. . . .? Language and Speaker in *Macbeth*," in *Shakespeare's Styles: Essays in Honour of Kenneth Muir*, ed. Philip Edwards, Inga-Stina Ewbank, and G. K. Hunter (Cambridge, London, and New York: Cambridge University Press, 1980), pp. 68–69.
12. Derrida points out that a "confrontation" is often a subtle form of evasion; one "confronts" something unsettling (like deconstruction), and then one moves on to more serious business, or simply back to business-as-usual. Derrida makes this point when he meets the massive Freud community and when he confronts the equally massive Joyce establishment: Jacques Derrida, "Du tout," in *La carte postale: de Socrate à Freud et au-delà* (Paris: Flammarion, 1980), p. 533; and *Ulysse gramophone*, p. 95. Duncan confronts Macbeth in the politest possible manner, just as a controversial critic is "confronted" at a symposium; yet this politeness may be looked upon as a way of ignoring what is out-standing in the other—what troubles and upsets, producing the uncomfortable intuition of a more dangerous confrontation.
13. In the *Phenomenology of Spirit*, Hegel identifies woman as a crucial instrument in the creation of the modern, privatized self. She subverts the all-powerfulness of the pagan male by turning his political "wisdom [into] an object of derision": G. W. F. Hegel, *Phenomenology of Spirit*, trans. A. V. Miller (Oxford and New York: Oxford University Press, 1977), §475, p. 288. "Womankind—the everlasting irony of the community—changes by intrigue the universal end of the government into a private end, transforms its universal activity into a work of some particular individual" (ibid.). By suppressing this female irony, the state only preserves it and keeps it going as something of importance to evolution in general (ibid.). For significant commentary see Kojève, *Introduction to the Reading of Hegel*, p. 62, and Derrida, *Glas*, pp. 187–90.
14. *The Idea of Woman in Renaissance Literature: The Feminine Reclaimed* (Brighton: Harvester Press, 1986), p. 169.
15. Herman Rapaport, "Staging: Mont Blanc," in *Displacement: Derrida and After*, ed. Mark Krupnick (Bloomington: Indiana University Press, 1983), p. 68.
16. Ibid., p. 67.
17. Ibid., p. 68.
18. *Shakespeare and Tragedy*, p. 187.
19. *Macbeth*, p. 109.
20. *The Masks of Macbeth* (Berkeley, Los Angeles, and London: University

Notes 229

of California Press, 1978), p. 318. Hereafter abbreviated *MM*. This psychologization of Lady Macbeth seems to be a function of the very humanization of her character that Rosenberg calls attention to elsewhere. As modern culture appropriated Lady Macbeth, she gradually became *human:* a soft, secretly tender woman. In the Romantic age this psychologizing of Lady Macbeth was promoted by Coleridge in England and by Tieck in Germany—much to the surprise of Goethe and others (*MM*, 177). To this anthropocentric obsession with centering Lady Macbeth in a psyche that one could call her own there belongs such edifying acts of research as consulting psychiatrists in order to discover the true "nature" that triggers the bloodthirsty lady's conduct (*MM*, 172). It could be argued, of course, that all efforts to "humanize" Lady Macbeth and turn her into a naturalistic person do great damage to the tragedy as a whole. To say that much is not to endorse some crudely wicked Lady Macbeth, a ridiculous browbeating virago or siren-like personification of feminine evil. It is simply to realize, as Angela Pitt points out, that Lady Macbeth is the most terrifying female figure that Shakespeare ever created: *Shakespeare's Women* (Newton Abbot, London: David & Charles; Totowa, N.J.: Barnes & Noble, 1981), p. 70.

21. Dover Wilson, *Macbeth*, p. 155.
22. *Shakespearean Tragedy*, p. 57.
23. Ibid., pp. 58–64.
24. *The Moral Vision of Jacobean Tragedy* (Madison: University of Wisconsin Press, 1960), p. 20.

Chapter 6

1. Georges Bataille, *Visions of Excess: Selected Writings, 1927–1939*, trans. Allan Stoekl (Minneapolis: University of Minnesota Press, 1985), p. 118.
2. Ibid., p. 129.
3. Ibid., p. 120.
4. Ibid., pp. 128–29.
5. Ibid., p. 128.
6. Ibid., p. 120.
7. Ibid., p. 128.
8. Ibid., p. 172.
9. Lawrence Stone, *The Crisis of the Aristocracy 1558–1641* (Oxford: Clarendon Press, 1965), p. 584.
10. Ibid., p. 582.
11. Ibid., p. 500.
12. *Visions of Excess*, p. 119.
13. Ibid., p. 124.
14. Ibid.
15. Ibid.
16. The travail of the unit "full" can also be observed in "full of growing" (1.4.29) and "full so valiant" (1.4.54). The fulness of the growth-potential is housed inside the monarchial embrace that encircles and ontologizes it.
17. According to the classical exposition of dialectical recognition, it is of course the young man who tends to oppose the kind of firm state dialectic that old Siward represents. See Kojève, *Introduction to the Reading of Hegel*, p. 62.
18. See Marilyn French, *Shakespeare's Division of Experience* (London: Jonathan Cape, 1982), p. 242.

19. *Glas*, p. 244.
20. Ibid.
21. Ibid., p. 243.
22. Cf. Jacques Derrida, *Schibboleth* (Paris: Galilée, 1986), p. 63.
23. My use of the term "vanishing" is of course a poststructuralist use. It appears in its terminological poignancy already in Roland Barthes's S/Z (trans. Richard Miller; New York: Hill and Wang, 1985), where the migration of meanings (p. 14) is related to a theory of "vanishing" (p. 12). Generally speaking all such Continental theory falls back on Hegel's discussion of the struggle to death in the *Phenomenology of Spirit*, where the deathward risk involves an unbalancing of self-consciousness as presence: "there is nothing present in it which could not be regarded as a vanishing moment" (§187, p. 114).
24. See the discussion of the "pharmakon" in "Plato's Pharmacy," in Jacques Derrida, *Dissemination*, trans. Barbara Johnson (Chicago: University of Chicago Press; London: The Athlone Press, 1981), pp. 63–171.
25. "Antithesis in *Macbeth*," *Shakespeare Survey* 19 (1966): 30.
26. Fear is one of the most salient features of act 5: 5.1.21, 5.1.35, 5.1.42–43, 5.1.59, 5.1.76, 5.2.23, 5.3.3–17, 5.3.28, 5.3.36–39, 5.3.59, 5.4.2, 5.4.19, 5.5.31, 5.5.48, 5.7.1–9, 5.8.4, 5.8.18, 5.8.22. Fear, as the middle sections of the play (with their mania for certainty) showed, is related to metaphysical desire. Classically, as Robert C. Solomon points out, stoicism is a philosophy against fear, a system that denies what it cannot really master. See *In the Spirit of Hegel: A Study of G. W. F. Hegel's* Phenomenology of Spirit (New York and Oxford: Oxford University Press, 1983), p. 461.
27. Derrida, *Glas*, p.136.
28. Ibid.
29. (London: Sheed and Ward, 1985), p. 82.
30. The "geese" image is of course not in itself one of sovereign recklessness, as we perceive in its traditional usage in *Coriolanus* (1.4.34–37).

Chapter 7

1. Michael Long, *The Unnatural Scene* (London: Methuen, 1976), abbreviated US. Friedrich Nietzsche, *The Birth of Tragedy*, trans. Walter Kaufmann (New York: Vintage, 1967), abbreviated BT.
2. See David Norbrook, *Poetry and Politics in the English Renaissance* (London and Boston: Routledge & Kegan Paul, 1984), p. 244.
3. Jacques Derrida, *Margins of Philosophy*, trans. Alan Bass (Chicago: University of Chicago Press; Brighton: Harvester Press, 1982), p. 329.
4. Roland Barthes, *S/Z*, pp. 6–9.
5. Ibid., p. 14.
6. Ibid., p. 21.
7. Hearing, in *Macbeth*, is the convergence of its surplus and its lack. An analysis of that problematic would need to deal with units such as: "Macbeth! Macbeth! Macbeth!— / Had I three ears, I'd hear thee" (4.1.77–78).
8. *Shakespeare's Tragic Heroes: Slaves of Passion* (London: Methuen, 1962; first published 1930).
9. "Language and Action in *Macbeth*," p. 142.
10. Ibid., p. 143.
11. Terence Hawkes seems to be working against the "melodic" type of

music analogy when he focuses on jazz in his Shakespeare criticism. The strength of this approach does not seem to me to be the jazz metaphor as such, but the effort to suggest that orality too can destabilize normative conceptions of discourse: we do not always have to fight the phonocentric and glorify the graphocentric as soon as we wish to challenge plenary speech or expressivism. See *That Shakespeherian Rag: Essays on a Critical Process* (London and New York: Methuen, 1986), pp. 73–91. A student of mine once associated the violence of the language of *King Lear* with "rapping."
    12. "Language and Action in *Macbeth*," p. 142.
    13. Jacques Derrida, "Limited Inc.," *Glyph* 2 (1977): 216.
    14. Derrida, *Margins of Philosophy*, p. 325.
    15. *Shakespeare's Ghost Writers: Literature as Uncanny Causality* (New York and London: Methuen, 1987), p. 91.
    16. Ibid., pp. 88–90.
    17. Ibid., p. 90.
    18. Ibid., p. 95.
    19. Ibid.
    20. Ibid., p. 96.
    21. Ibid., p. 90.
    22. *The Pursuit of Signs: Semiotics, Literature, Deconstruction* (Ithaca: Cornell University Press, 1981), p. 174.
    23. Ibid.
    24. Ibid.
    25. Ibid., pp. 174–75.
    26. Ibid., p. 175.
    27. Ibid.
    28. Ibid., pp. 175–76.
    29. Baudrillard, *Les Stratégies fatales*, pp. 198–202.
    30. Ibid., p. 199; my translation.
    31. Ibid.
    32. Ibid., p. 201.
    33. Ibid., p. 199.
    34. Ibid., p. 200.
    35. Ibid.
    36. Why gold? Simply because Truth itself is gold for Macbeth: whether as dialectical recognition ("Golden opinions," 1.7.33) or as the summit of prophecy ("the golden round / Which fate and metaphysical aid doth seem / To have thee crown'd withal," 1.5.28–30). Gold is metaphysical, what Truth completes once it has come full circle: once it has crowned Macbeth. There is not *first* the possibility of the fulfillment of Truth/prophecy, and *then* the placing of the golden crown on Macbeth's head. On the contrary, the becoming-Truth of Macbeth *is* the crowning of him. The pure golden moment is the perfect convergence of two forces: the completion of Truth and the completion of Macbeth. Completion is itself golden here. When the circle of Truth is absolutely circular it is golden; when the circle/crown is absolutely circular it is gold. Monarchial blood, too, is always "golden blood" (2.3.110).
    37. Baudrillard, *Les Stratégies fatales*, p. 198.
    38. Ibid., p. 201.
    39. Ibid., p. 197.
    40. Ibid., p. 196.
    41. Ibid., p. 198.

42. Ibid., p. 197.

43. See *Hegel's Logic*, trans. William Wallace (Oxford: Clarendon Press, 1873; reprinted 1985): "Positive and negative . . . are at bottom the same. . . . In opposition, the different is not confronted by any other, but by its other" (p. 173). "Everything is opposite. . . . Contradiction is the very moving principle of the world" (p. 174). Being and Nothing are thus an absolute opposition as well as an absolute "unity" (p. 129).

44. *Les Stratégies fatales*, p. 206.

45. Ibid., p. 216.

46. Ibid., p. 224.

47. Ibid., p. 220.

48. For the "general other" it is enough that otherness is other; for the fatal other otherness has to be miraculous.

49. *Les Stratégies fatales*, p. 220.

50. Ibid., p. 219.

51. Ibid., p. 230.

52. Ibid., p. 231. This notion may be contrasted with my discussion in section 2.2 of "broken appearance." Baudrillard seems to be arguing that excessive speed enhances appearing, while I was saying that the excess of speed disrupted appearing. This surface contradiction on the level of theoretical rhetoric of course only hides the similarity of the two notions: when I spoke of the disruption of appearing, I meant the cancellation of appearing *as presence*. What was "left" of appearing, once speed had done its work, was for me thus a process of appearing without presence, a mode of appearing I called "vanishing." But when Baudrillard refers to "pure" appearing, he means exactly this: an appearing whose moment of visibility is so furtive that only the most apparent part of the appearing gets recorded or actualized. "Pure" appearing is already charged with the full measure of what I called "vanishing." Baudrillard's "pure appearing" is in fact a mode of *disappearing*. The excess of speed itself takes care of that. As my "falling star" example in section 2.2 tried to suggest, the experience of pure appearing (of our perceiving nothing but the "burst" into the apparent) is tied to the notion of the "immediate" vanishing of the sense of the possible presence of the appearing object.

53. Ibid., p. 238.

54. Ibid., p. 233.

55. Ibid., p. 221.

56. Ibid., p. 223.

57. Ibid., p. 221.

58. Ibid., p. 222.

59. Ibid.

60. Ibid., pp. 230–31.

61. Ibid., p. 230.

62. Ibid., p. 243.

63. The eruption of Baudrillard's "pure object" reverses the power relation between subject and object so that the object finds itself empowered by all the might of the subject (ibid., p. 198).

TERMINOLOGICAL USAGE

BEING. The notion of reality as something metaphysically centered; life conceived as founded on presence.

CUT. The re-marking of originary interstitial otherness; the trace and tracing of originary violence.

DECONSTRUCTION. A radical post-Nietzschean perspectivism that unmasks the imaginary stability of solid concepts and other metaphysical and ideological universals.

DESIRE. Not merely an emotion, the feeling of wanting something, but the human need to "negate" otherness, to voraciously make the other part of oneself [Hegel].

DIALECTIC. (1) Tug-of-war between binary opposites; "thesis-versus-antithesis"; (2) dialectical play caused by originary doubling; antithesis "preceding" thesis as its condition of possibility; (3) metaphysical orderliness through the work of symmetrically opposed notions. These three definitions correspond to (1) commonsensical thought (intuitionism), (2) Hegelian thought, and (3) Hegelianism as totalitarian system promoting closure; philosophy as dialectical reason.

DISSEMINATION. (1) Signification without foundational center; (2) the dispersal of foundational meaning.

EPISTEMOLOGICAL DECONSTRUCTION. Deconstructionism assuming that texts show the futility of knowing them or the world.

GAIETY. A sense of joy beyond the work of dialectical interaction and foundational meaning.

GENERAL ECONOMY. An organization or sense of reality promoting unconditional spending.

HYPERONTOLOGY. The ecstasy of ontology; the sphere where the transvaluation of ontological issues has not left us "without" ontology but in a zone of inquiry where ontologically oriented questions are free from narrow assumptions about foundational truth; a specific area of literary suggestion (in a text) where ontological forces are defeated by forces of greater intensity so that the "ontological ground" is displaced (rather than cancelled). The study of the hyperontological. The "trace" or remainder left by deconstruction between itself and its program. What is ontologically powerful without being ontologically true.

LOGOCENTRIC. Based on traditional systems of philosophic hierarchization (inside over outside, presence over nonpresence, domesticity over alterity, etc.).

LORD. See "Master" and/or "Lordship."

LORDSHIP. Any sense of philosophical mastery derived from the notion or experience of the dialectic of master-and-slave; a servile state [Nietzsche] in which being "master" is being as base and foolish as being "slave." The dialectical mode of being [Bataille].

MASTER. Man as winner in the fight to death for dialectical recognition ("golden opinions"); the one who knows everything of the nothingness of the fight to death (its infinite risk) but who does not (yet) know everything of the nothingness experienced in the absolute fear of death [Kojève]. The "first" man [Hegel].

MASTERY. (1) Control over meaning through the conscious or unconscious use of a philosophical attitude (dialectical thinking); (2) the activity or state of a Master (see "Master").

METAPHYSICS OF PRESENCE. (1) A philosophy of centeredness; (2) philosophy (the conscious or unconscious implementation of post-Platonic logic); (3) the convergence of (1) and (2) [Derrida].

MINERAL. An object possessing all initiative through its dominance over the subject/object dialectic it "should" belong to [Baudrillard]. The "mineral" is thus an "object" that is not an object.

NIHILATION. Action or creative forwardness that negates the given; the forward drive of human desire as a transcendental "negating" [Hegel/Kojève].

ONTOLOGY. (1) The study of (the philosophical notion of) Being; (2) the conscious or unconscious promotion of the notion of the preeminence of Being.

ONTODRAMATIC. Staging the dramatic conflict between the ontological and its other; dramatizing the play between what ontologizes, what de-ontologizes, and what hyperontologizes.

ONTO-THEOLOGY. The conscious or unconscious philosophic ideology of the West; the idealization of reality in relation to its possible truth-center [Heidegger].

ORIGIN. A transcendental (sense of a) beginning whose purity is a priori uncontaminated by powerful otherness and powerful difference.

PHARMAKON. A "supplement" whose effect is undecided and whose supplementarity is confusing [Derrida].

PHENOMENOLOGY. (1) The study of the pure objects of awareness [Husserl]; (2) Hegelian philosophy as absolute knowledge; (3) Hegelian thinking as the experimental discourse of the *Phenomenology of Spirit;* (4) the era of philosophical inquiry immediately preceding Heidegger and/or Derrida.

PHONOCENTRIC. Based consciously or unconsciously on the longstanding philosophical prejudice that automatically hierarchizes the oral and the written so that the latter always necessarily becomes secondary in relation to the former.

POLYSEMIA. The static and harmless "opposite" of dissemination; pluralism (of signification) in the weak (centered) sense.

SEDUCTION. A willing not monitored by a volitional subject [Baudrillard].

SELF-PRESENCE. (1) Ontological egocentricity; (2) the metaphysics of presence as operative in the cogito.

SERVITUDE. The activity, passivity, or state of a "Slave." See "Slave."

SLAVE. Man as loser in the protostruggle for human recognition; the one who has come "closer" to death than the Master by (paradoxically) *not* daring to go into the deathward struggle with the same degree of transcendental enthusiasm [Kojève]; man as inward nothingness rather than fighting nothingness; the postheroic level of human experience [Hegel]. One who conserves.

SOVEREIGN. See "Sovereignty."

SOVEREIGNTY. A state or situation involving emancipation from "lordship," from the servile dialectic of master-and-slave; a position where the aim is no longer a "project," no longer the production of heroic or post-heroic "meaning" [Bataille].

STRUGGLE TO DEATH. A type of "originary," quasi-pagan fighting, where each participant in the duel knows that death is more valuable than survival-in-defeat and that triumph involves the production of transcendental truth (social and philosophic status rather than biological privilege).

TRACE. The outline, spacing or persisting "remainder" where the profile of an entity merges with *and* emerges from the silhouette of its other.

TRANSCENDENTAL SIGNIFIED. An ultimate referent needed to create foundational truth by arresting the play of references; the godhead, truth.

TRUTH. Meaning as a philosophic absolute or transcendentally centered summit. Also: the truth of truth [Hegel].

UNHAPPY CONSCIOUSNESS. An ego agonizing over its less-than-divine status; selfhood as the antithesis of the miraculous; a person for whom the other must always be projected as an unreachable "beyond" (Hegel, *Phenomenology of Spirit,* § 217); the perpetual sense of the absence of self-completion (§ 218); an individual practicing a philosophy of renouncement and self-renouncement but determined not to *renounce* this philosophy—determined, thus, to be unhappy (§222); the ego that enjoys the feeling of its own wretchedness by constantly brooding over its structural impoverishment (§225).

VANISHING. A state, experience, or movement involving (the sensation of) release from centeredness and metaphysical presence; a process of appearing where the excess of speed in appearances dramatizes the vividness of appearing by making it "immediate" and "pure."

BIBLIOGRAPHY

Abel, Elizabeth, ed. *Writing and Sexual Difference.* Brighton: Harvester Press, 1982.

Abercrombie, Lascelles. "A Plea for the Liberty of Interpreting." In *Aspects of Shakespeare.* Oxford: Clarendon Press, 1933.

Adams, Hazard. *Philosophy of the Literary Symbolic.* Tallahassee: University Presses of Florida, 1983.

Adorno, Theodor W. *Against Epistemology—A Metacritique: Studies in Husserl and the Phenomenological Antinomies.* Translated by Willis Domingo. Cambridge: MIT Press, 1985. German original 1956.

Alexander, Peter. *Shakespeare's Life and Art.* London: James Nisbet and Co., 1939.

Allman, Eileen Jorge. *Player-King and Adversary: Two Faces of Play in Shakespeare.* Baton Rouge and London: Louisiana State University Press, 1980.

Altman, Joel B. *The Tudor Play of Mind: Rhetorical Inquiry and the Development of Elizabethan Drama.* Berkeley, Los Angeles, and London: University of California Press, 1978.

Anderson, Ruth Leila. *Elizabethan Psychology and Shakespeare's Plays.* Iowa City: University of Iowa Humanistic Studies, 1927.

Aristotle. *Poetics.* Translated by S. H. Butcher. New York: Hill and Wang, 1961.

Armstrong, William A. *Shakespeare's Typology: Miracles and Morality Motifs in Macbeth.* London: Westfield College, 1968.

Aronson, Alex. *Psyche and Symbol in Shakespeare.* Bloomington: Indiana University Press, 1972.

Babcock, Barbara. *The Reversible World: Symbolic Inversion in Art and Society.* Ithaca and London: Cornell University Press, 1978.

Bamber, Linda. *Comic Women, Tragic Men: A Study of Gender and Genre in Shakespeare.* Stanford: Stanford University Press, 1982.

Barber, C. L., and Richard P. Wheeler. *The Whole Journey: Shakespeare's Power of Development.* Berkeley, Los Angeles, and London: University of California Press, 1986.

Barish, Jonas. *The Antitheatrical Prejudice.* Berkeley, Los Angeles, and London: University of California Press, 1981.

Barrault, Jean-Louis. *Le Phénomène théâtral.* Oxford: Clarendon Press, 1961.

———. *Nouvelles réflexions sur le théâtre.* Paris: Flammarion, 1959.

Barthes, Roland. *Le plaisir du texte.* Paris: Seuil, 1973.

———. *S/Z.* Translated by Richard Miller. New York: Hill and Wang, 1974; 1985.

Bartholomeusz, Dennis. *Macbeth and the Players*. Cambridge: Cambridge University Press, 1969.

Bataille, Georges. *Inner Experience*. Translated by Leslie Anne Boldt. Albany: State University of New York Press, 1988.

———. *Visions of Excess: Selected Writings 1927–1939*. Translated by Allan Stoekl. Minneapolis: University of Minnesota Press, 1985.

Battenhouse, Roy W. *Shakespearean Tragedy: Its Art and Its Christian Premises*. Bloomington and London: Indiana University Press, 1969.

Baudrillard, Jean. *America*. Translated by Chris Turner. London and New York: Verso, 1988.

———. *De la séduction*. Paris: Galilée. 1979.

———. *The Ecstasy of Communication*. New York: Semiotext(e), 1987.

———. *The Mirror of Production*. Translated by Mark Poster. St. Louis: Telos Press, 1975.

———. *Selected Writings*. Oxford: Polity Press, 1988.

———. *Les stratégies fatales*. Paris: Bernard Grasset, 1983.

Bayley, John. *Shakespeare and Tragedy*. London, Boston, and Henley: Routledge & Kegan Paul, 1981.

Belsey, Catherine. *The Subject of Tragedy: Identity and Difference in Renaissance Drama*. London and New York: Methuen, 1985.

Bentley, Eric. *The Life of the Drama*. London: Methuen, 1965.

Berger, Harry Jr. "Text against Performance: The Example of *Macbeth*." In *The Power of Forms in the English Renaissance*, edited by Stephen Greenblatt, pp. 49–79. Norman, Ok.: Pilgrim Books, 1982.

Berkeley, George. *Philosophical Works*. London and Melbourne: Dent, 1985.

Berry, Ralph. *The Shakespearean Metaphor: Studies in Language and Form*. London: Macmillan, 1978.

———. *Shakespearean Structures*. London: Macmillan, 1981.

Bethell, S. L. *The Cultural Revolution of the Seventeenth Century*. London: Dennis Dobson, 1951.

———. *Shakespeare and the Popular Dramatic Tradition*. London: Staples Press, 1944.

Boas, Frederick S. *An Introduction to Stuart Drama*. London: Oxford University Press, 1946; 1969.

Bono, Barbara J. *Literary Transvaluation: From Vergilian Epic to Shakespearean Tragicomedy*. Berkeley, Los Angeles, and London: University of California Press, 1984.

Booth, Stephen. *King Lear, Macbeth, Indefinition, and Tragedy*. New Haven and London: Yale University Press, 1983.

Bradbrook, Muriel C. *The Artist and Society in Shakespeare's England: The Collected Papers of Muriel Bradbrook*. Vol. 1. Brighton: Harvester Press; Totowa, N. J.: Barnes & Noble, 1982.

———. *The Living Monument: Shakespeare and the Theatre of His Time*. Cambridge, London, New York, and Melbourne: Cambridge University Press, 1976.

Bradbury, Malcolm, and David Palmer, eds. *Shakespearean Tragedy*. London: E. Arnold. 1984.

Bibliography

Bradley, Andrew C. *Oxford Lectures on Poetry*. London: Macmillan, 1909.
———. *Shakespearean Tragedy: Lectures on* Hamlet, Othello, King Lear, Macbeth. London: Macmillan, 1950. First edition 1904.
Bradshaw, Graham. *Shakespeare's Scepticism*. Brighton: Harvester Press, 1987.
Brennan, Anthony. *Shakespeare's Dramatic Structures*. London, Boston, and Henley: Routledge & Kegan Paul, 1986.
Briggs, Julia. *This Stage-Play World: English Literature and Its Background 1580–1625*. Oxford and New York: Oxford University Press, 1983.
Bristol, Michael D. *Carnival and Theater: Plebeian Culture and the Structure of Authority in Renaissance England*. New York and London: Methuen, 1985.
Brook, G. L. *The Language of Shakespeare*. London: André Deutsch, 1976.
Brooke, Nicholas. *Horrid Laughter in Jacobean Tragedy*. London: Open Books, 1979.
———. "Language Most Shows a Man. . . ?: Language and Speaker in Macbeth." In *Shakespeare's Styles: Essays in Honour of Kenneth Muir*, edited by Philip Edwards, Inga-Stina Ewbank and G. K. Hunter. Cambridge: Cambridge University Press, 1980.
Brown, John Russell. *Discovering Shakespeare: A New Guide to the Plays*. London: Macmillan, 1981.
———, ed. *Focus on* Macbeth. London and Boston: Routledge & Kegan Paul, 1982.
Bullough, Geoffrey. "The Defence of Paradox." In *Shakespeare's Styles: Essays in Honour of Kenneth Muir*, edited by Philip Edwards, et al. Cambridge: Cambridge University Press, 1980.
———, ed. *Narrative and Dramatic Sources of Shakespeare*. Vol. 7. London: Routledge & Kegan Paul; New York: Columbia University Press, 1973.
Bulman, James C. *The Heroic Idiom of Shakespearean Tragedy*. Newark: University of Delaware Press; London and Toronto: Associated University Presses, 1985.
Burckhardt, Sigurd. *Shakespearean Meanings*. Princeton: Princeton University Press, 1968.
Burke, Peter. *The Renaissance Sense of the Past*. London: Arnold, 1979.
Bush, Geoffrey. *Shakespeare and the Natural Condition*. Cambridge: Harvard University Press, 1956.
Butler, Christopher. *Interpretation, Deconstruction, and Ideology: An Introduction to Some Current Issues in Literary Theory*. Oxford: Clarendon Press, 1984.
Cain, William E. *The Crisis in Criticism: Theory, Literature, and Reform in English Studies*. Baltimore and London: The Johns Hopkins University Press, 1984.
Calderwood, James L. *If It Were Done*. Amherst: University of Massachusetts Press, 1986.
———. *To Be Or Not to Be: Negation and Metadrama in* Hamlet. New York: Columbia University Press, 1983.
Campbell, Lily B. *Shakespeare's Tragic Heroes: Slaves of Passion*. London: Methuen, 1962. First published 1930.
Carlson, Marvin. *Theories of the Theatre: A Historical and Critical Survey, from the Greeks to the Present*. Ithaca and London: Cornell University Press, 1984.

Carroll, David. *Paraesthetics: Foucault, Lyotard, Derrida.* New York and London: Methuen, 1987.

Cassirer, Ernst. *The Individual and the Cosmos in Renaissance Philosophy.* Philadephia: University of Pennsylvania Press, 1973.

Certeau, Michel de. *Heterologies: Discourse on the Other.* Minneapolis: University of Minnesota Press, 1986.

Chambers, E. K. *Shakespeare: A Survey.* London: Sidgwick and Jackson, 1925; 1955.

———. *Shakespearean Gleanings.* London: Oxford University Press, 1944.

Charney, Maurice. *Hamlet's Fictions.* London: Routledge, 1988.

Chaudhuri, Sukanta. *Infirm Glory: Shakespeare and the Renaissance Image of Man.* Oxford: Clarendon Press, 1981.

Clemen, Wolfgang H. *The Development of Shakespeare's Imagery.* London: Methuen, 1969. First published 1951.

Coleridge, Samuel Taylor. *Shakespearian Criticism.* Edited by Thomas Middleton Raysor. 2 vols. London: Dent; New York: Dutton, 1960.

Colie, Rosalie L. *Shakespeare's Living Art.* Princeton: Princeton University Press, 1974.

Compagnon, Antoine, ed. *Colloques de Cerisy: Été 1977.* Paris: Union Générale d'Éditions, 1978.

Conley, Tom. "A Trace of Style." In *Displacement: Derrida and After,* edited by Mark Krupnick, pp. 74–92. Bloomington: Indiana University Press, 1983.

Cooke, Ann Jennalie. *The Privileged Playgoers of Shakespeare's London 1576–1642.* Princeton: Princeton University Press, 1981.

Coursen, H. R. *The Compensatory Psyche: A Jungian Approach to Shakespeare.* Lanham, Md., New York, and London: University Press of America, 1986.

Crane, Milton, ed. *Shakespeare's Art: Seven Essays.* Chicago and London: University of Chicago Press, 1973.

Culler, Jonathan. *On Deconstruction: Theory and Criticism after Structuralism.* London, Melbourne, and Henley: Routledge & Kegan Paul, 1983.

———. *The Pursuit of Signs: Semiotics, Literature, Deconstruction.* Ithaca: Cornell University Press, 1981.

Curry, Walter Clyde. *Shakespeare's Philosophical Patterns.* Baton Rouge: Louisiana State University Press, 1937.

Danby, John. *Shakespeare's Doctrine of Nature.* London: Faber, 1949.

Danson, Lawrence. *Tragic Alphabet: Shakespeare's Drama of Language.* New Haven and London: Yale University Press, 1974.

Dash, Irene G. *Wooing, Wedding, and Power: Women in Shakespeare's Plays.* New York: Columbia University Press, 1981.

Davies, Stevie. *The Idea of Woman in Renaissance Literature.* Brighton: Harvester Press, 1986.

———. *Renaissance Views of Man.* Manchester: Manchester University Press, 1978.

Davis, Robert Con, and Ronald Schleifer. *Rhetoric and Form: Deconstruction at Yale.* Norman: University of Oklahoma Press, 1985.

Bibliography

Dean, Leonard F., ed. *Shakespeare: Modern Essays in Criticism*. New York: Oxford University Press, 1961.

Deleuze, Gilles. *Nietzsche and Philosophy*. Translated by Hugh Tomlinson. London: The Athlone Press, 1983. French original 1962.

Derrida, Jacques. *La carte postale: de Socrate à Freud et au-delà*. Paris: Flammarion, 1980.

———. *Ciò che resta del fuoco / Feu la cendre*. Florence: Sansoni, 1984.

———. *De l'esprit: Heidegger et la question*. Paris: Galilée, 1987.

———. *Dissemination*. Translated by Barbara Johnson. Chicago: University of Chicago Press, 1981. French original 1972.

———. *D'un ton apocalyptique adopté naguère en philosophie*. Paris: Galilée, 1983.

———. *Glas*. Translated by John P. Leavey, Jr. and Richard Rand. Lincoln and London: University of Nebraska Press, 1986. French original 1974.

———. "Limited Inc: a b c. . . ." *Glyph* 2 (1977): 162–254.

———. *Margins of Philosophy*. Translated by Alan Bass. Chicago: University of Chicago Press, 1982. French original 1972.

———. *Of Grammatology*. Translated by Gayatri Chakravorty Spivak. Baltimore and London: The Johns Hopkins University Press, 1976. French original 1967.

———. *Otobiographies: L'enseignement de Nietzsche et la politique du nom propre*. Paris: Galilée, 1984.

———. *Parages*. Paris: Galilée, 1986.

———. *Positions*. Translated by Alan Bass. Chicago: University of Chicago Press, 1981. French original 1972.

———. *Schibboleth*. Paris: Galilée, 1986.

———. "Signature Event Context." *Glyph* 1 (1977): 172–97.

———. *Signéponge/Signsponge*. Translated by Richard Rand. New York: Columbia University Press, 1984.

———. *Speech and Phenomena: And Other Essays on Husserl's Theory of Signs*. Translated by David B. Allison. Evanston: Northwestern University Press, 1973.

———. *Spurs: Nietzsche's Styles / Éperons: Les styles de Nietzsche*. Chicago and London: University of Chicago Press, 1979. French original 1978.

———. *The Truth in Painting*. Translated by Geoff Bennington and Ian McLeod. Chicago and London: University of Chicago Press, 1987. French original 1978.

———. *Ulysse gramophone: Deux mots pour Joyce*. Paris: Galilée, 1987.

———. *Writing and Difference*. Translated by Alan Bass. Chicago: University of Chicago Press; London: Routledge & Kegan Paul, 1978. French original 1967.

Dessen, Alan C. *Elizabethan Drama and the Viewer's Eye*. Chapel Hill: University of North Carolina Press, 1977.

———. *Elizabethan Stage Conventions and Modern Interpreters*. Cambridge and New York: Cambridge University Press, 1984.

D'Hondt, Jacques, ed. *Hegel et la pensée grecque*. Paris: Presses Universitaires de France, 1974.

Dillon, Janette. *Shakespeare and the Solitary Man*. London: Macmillan, 1981.
Doran, Madeleine. *Endeavors of Art: A Study of Form in Elizabethan Drama*. Madison: University of Wisconsin Press, 1954.
Drakakis, John, ed. *Alternative Shakespeares*. London and New York: Methuen, 1985.
Driscoll, James P. *Identity in Shakespearean Drama*. Lewisburg, Pa.: Bucknell University Press; London and Toronto: Associated University Presses, 1983.
Dusinberre, Juliet. *Shakespeare and the Nature of Women*. London: Macmillan, 1975.
Duthie, George Ian. "Antithesis in *Macbeth*." *Shakespeare Survey* 19 (1966): 25–33.
———. *Shakespeare*. London: Hutchinson, 1951; 1959.
Eagleton, Terence. *Shakespeare and Society: Critical Studies in Shakespearean Drama*. London: Chatto & Windus, 1967.
Easlea, Brian. *Witch-Hunting, Magic and the New Philosophy: An Introduction to Debates of the Scientific Revolution 1450–1750*. Brighton: Harvester Press, 1980.
Easterling, Anja. *Shakespearean Parallels and Affinities with the Theatre of the Absurd in Tom Stoppard's "Rosencrantz and Guildenstern Are Dead."* Umeå: Umeå University Press, 1982.
Edwards, Philip. "Person and Office in Shakespeare's Plays." In *Interpretations of Shakespeare*, edited by Kenneth Muir, pp. 105–23. Oxford: Clarendon Press, 1985.
———. *Shakespeare and the Confines of Art*. London: Methuen, 1968.
———. *Shakespeare: A Writer's Progress*. Oxford and New York: Oxford University Press, 1986.
Edwards, Philip, et al., eds. *Shakespeare's Styles: Essays in Honour of Kenneth Muir*. Cambridge: Cambridge University Press, 1980.
Elliott, G. R. *Dramatic Providence in* Macbeth: *A Study of Shakespeare's Tragic Theme of Humanity and Grace*. Princeton: Princeton University Press, 1958.
Ellis, John M. *Against Deconstruction*. Princeton: Princeton University Press, 1989.
Ellis-Fermor, Una. *The Frontiers of Drama*. London: Methuen, 1964.
Ellrodt, Robert. "Self-Consciousness in Montaigne and Shakespeare." *Shakespeare Survey* 28 (1975): 37–50.
Empson, William. *Essays on Shakespeare*. Edited by David B. Pirie. Cambridge: Cambridge University Press, 1986.
———. *Seven Types of Ambiguity*. London: Chatto & Windus, 1949.
Enright, D. J. *Shakespeare and the Students*. London: Chatto & Windus, 1970.
Erickson, Peter. *Patriarchal Structures in Shakespeare's Drama*. Berkeley, Los Angeles, and London: University of California Press, 1985.
Evans, Bertrand. *Shakespeare's Tragic Practice*. Oxford: Clarendon Press, 1979.
Evans, Gareth Lloyd. "*Macbeth*: 1946–80 at Stratford-upon-Avon." In *Focus on* Macbeth, edited by John Russell Brown, pp. 87–110. London and Boston: Routledge & Kegan Paul, 1982.
Evans, Ifor. *The Language of Shakespeare's Plays*. London: Methuen, 1952.

Evans, Malcolm. *Signifying Nothing: Truth's True Contents in Shakespeare's Text*. Athens: University of Georgia Press, 1986.

Faas, Ekbert. *Tragedy and After: Euripides, Shakespeare, Goethe*. Kingston and Montreal: McGill-Queen's University Press, 1984.

Faber, Melvin D., ed. *The Design Within: Psychoanalytic Approaches to Shakespeare*. New York and London: Jason Aronson, 1970, 1983.

Farnham, Willard. *The Medieval Heritage of Elizabethan Tragedy*. Berkeley: University of California Press; Oxford: Blackwell, 1936.

———. *Shakespeare's Tragic Frontier: The World of His Final Tragedies*. Berkeley and Los Angeles: University of California Press, 1950.

Fekete, John. *The Critical Twilight: Explorations in the Ideology of Anglo-American Literary Theory from Eliot to McLuhan*. London: Routledge, 1977.

———, ed. *The Structural Allegory: Reconstructive Encounters with the New French Thought*. Manchester: Manchester University Press, 1984.

Felman, Shoshana, ed. *Literature and Psychoanalysis: The Question of Reading—Otherwise*. Baltimore and London: The Johns Hopkins University Press, 1982.

Felperin, Howard. " 'Tongue-Ties Our Queen?': The Deconstruction of Presence in *The Winter's Tale*." In *Shakespeare and the Question of Theory*, edited by Patricia Parker and Geoffrey Hartman, pp. 3–18. New York and London: Methuen, 1985.

Ferguson, Margaret W. "*Hamlet*: Letters and Spirits." In *Shakespeare and the Question of Theory*, edited by Patricia Parker and Geoffrey Hartman, pp. 292–309. New York and London: Methuen, 1985.

Ferguson, Margaret W., Maureen Quilligan, and Nancy J. Vickers, eds. *Rewriting the Renaissance: The Discourse of Sexual Difference in Early Modern Europe*. Chicago and London: University of Chicago Press, 1986.

Fergusson, Francis. *The Human Image in Dramatic Literature*. Garden City, N.Y.: Doubleday, 1957.

Fiedler, Leslie A. *The Stranger in Shakespeare*. New York: Stein and Day, 1972.

Fisch, Harold. *A Remembered Future: A Study in Literary Mythology*. Bloomington: Indiana University Press, 1984.

Fish, Stanley. *Self-Consuming Artifacts: The Experience of Seventeenth Century Literature*. Berkeley: University of California Press, 1972.

Flores, Ralph. *The Rhetoric of Doubtful Authority: Deconstructive Readings of Self-Questioning Narratives, St. Augustine to Faulkner*. Ithaca and London: Cornell University Press, 1984.

Foakes, R. A. "Image of Death and Ambition in *Macbeth*." In *Focus on Macbeth*, edited by John Russell Brown, pp. 7–29. London and Boston: Routledge & Kegan Paul, 1982.

Foster, Donald W. "*Macbeth's* War on Time." *English Literary Renaissance* 16 (1986): 319–42.

French, Marilyn. *Shakespeare's Division of Experience*. London: Cape, 1982.

Frye, Northrop. *Fools of Time: Studies in Shakespearean Tragedy*. Toronto: University of Toronto Press; London: Oxford University Press, 1967.

Funke, Lewis, and John E. Booth. *Actors Talk about Acting*. New York: Avon, 1961; 1967.

Furness, Horace Howard Jr. *Macbeth: New Variorum Edition*. New York: Dover, 1963.
Gadamer, Hans-Georg. *Hegel's Dialectic: Five Hermeneutical Studies*. Translated by P. Christopher Smith. New York and London: Yale University Press, 1976.

———. *Truth and Method*. London: Sheed and Ward, 1975; 1985.

Gandillac, Maurice de. "Hegel et le néoplatonisme." In *Hegel et la pensée grecque*, edited by Jacques D'Hondt. Paris: Presses Universitaires de France, 1974.
Garber, Marjorie, ed. *Cannibals, Witches, and Divorce: Estranging the Renaissance*. Baltimore and London: The Johns Hopkins University Press, 1987.

———. *Dream in Shakespeare: From Metaphor to Metamorphosis*. New Haven and London: Yale University Press, 1974.

———. *Shakespeare's Ghost Writers: Literature as Uncanny Causality*. New York and London: Methuen, 1987.

Garrick, David. *The Letters of David Garrick*. Edited by David M. Little and George M. Kahrl. 3 Vols. London: Oxford University Press, 1963.
Garvin, Harry R., ed. *Shakespeare: Contemporary Critical Approaches*. Lewisburg: Bucknell University Press; London and Toronto: Associated University Presses, 1980.
Gasché, Rodolphe. *The Tain of the Mirror: Derrida and the Philosophy of Reflection*. Cambridge and London: Harvard University Press, 1986.
Gillespie, Gerald. "Scientific Discourse and Postmodernity: Francis Bacon and the Empirical Birth of 'Revision.'" *Boundary Two* 7 (Winter 1979): 119–48.
Goldberg, Jonathan. *James I and the Politics of Literature: Jonson, Shakespeare, Donne, and Their Contemporaries*. Baltimore and London: The Johns Hopkins University Press, 1983.

———. "Speculations: *Macbeth* and Source." In *Post-Structuralist Readings of English Poetry*, edited by Richard Machin and Christopher Norris, pp. 38–58. Cambridge, London, and New York: Cambridge University Press, 1987.

Goldman, Michael. *Acting and Action in Shakespearean Tragedy*. Princeton: Princeton University Press, 1985.

———. "Language and Action in *Macbeth*," In *Focus on Macbeth*, edited by John Russell Brown, pp. 140–52. London and Boston: Routledge & Kegan Paul, 1982.

———. *Shakespeare and the Energies of Drama*. Princeton: Princeton University Press, 1972.

Gray, J. C., ed. *Mirror up to Shakespeare: Essays in Honour of G. R. Hibbard*. Toronto, Buffalo, and London: University of Toronto Press, 1984.
Greenblatt, Stephen, ed., *The Power of Forms in the English Renaissance*. Norman, Ok.: Pilgrim Books, 1982.

———. *Renaissance Self-Fashioning: From More to Shakespeare*. Chicago and London: University of Chicago Press, 1980.

———. "Shakespeare and the Exorcists." In *After Strange Texts: The Role of Theory in the Study of Literature*, edited by Gregory S. Jay and David L. Miller, pp. 101–23. University: University of Alabama Press, 1985.

Bibliography

Greer, Germaine. *Shakespeare*. Oxford and New York: Oxford University Press, 1986.

Greg, W. W. "Principles of Emendation in Shakespeare." In *Aspects of Shakespeare*. Oxford: Clarendon Press, 1933.

———. *The Shakespeare First Folio: Its Bibliographical and Textual History*. Oxford: Clarendon Press, 1955.

Gregson, J. M. *Public and Private Man in Shakespeare*. London and Canberra: Croom Helm; Totowa, N. J.: Barnes & Noble, 1983.

Groom, Bernard, and R. E. C. Houghton, eds. *Macbeth: The New Clarendon Shakespeare*. Oxford: Clarendon Press, 1939; 1975.

Grove, Robin. "Multiplying Villainies of Nature." In *Focus on Macbeth*, edited by John Russell Brown, pp. 113–39. London and Boston: Routledge & Kegan Paul, 1982.

Grudin, Robert. *Mighty Opposites: Shakespeare and Renaissance Contrairety*. Berkeley, Los Angeles, and London: University of California Press, 1979.

Guignon, Charles B. *Heidegger and the Problem of Knowledge*. Indianapolis: Hackett, 1983.

Gurr, Andrew. *The Shakespearean Stage 1574–1642*. Cambridge, London, and New York: Cambridge University Press, 1980.

Harbage, Alfred. *As They Liked It: An Essay on Shakespeare and Morality*. New York: Macmillan, 1947.

———. *Shakespeare and the Rival Traditions*. New York: Macmillan, 1952.

———. *Shakespeare without Words and Other Essays*. Cambridge: Harvard University Press, 1972.

Harland, Richard. *Superstructuralism: The Philosophy of Structuralism and Post-Structuralism*. London and New York: Methuen, 1987.

Harris, Victor. *All Coherence Gone: A Study in the Seventeenth Century Controversy over Disorder and Decay in the Universe*. London: Cass, 1966.

Hartman, Geoffrey H. *Saving the Text: Literature/Derrida/Philosophy*. Baltimore and London: The Johns Hopkins University Press, 1981.

———. "Tea and Totality: The Demand of Theory on Critical Style." In *After Strange Texts: The Role of Theory in the Study of Literature*, edited by Gregory S. Jay and David L. Miller, pp. 29–45. University: University of Alabama Press, 1985.

Harvey, Irene E. *Derrida and the Economy of Différance*. Bloomington: Indiana University Press, 1986.

Hauser, Arnold. *Mannerism: The Crisis of the Renaissance and the Origin of Modern Art*. London: Routledge, 1965.

Hawkes, Terence. *Shakespeare and the Reason: A Study of the Tragedies and the Problem Plays*. London: Routledge & Kegan Paul, 1964.

———. *Shakespeare's Talking Animals: Language and Drama in Society*. London: E. Arnold, 1973.

———. "Telmah." In *Shakespeare and the Question of Theory*, edited by Patricia Parker and Geoffrey Hartman, pp. 310–32. New York and London: Methuen, 1985.

———. *That Shakespeherian Rag: Essays on a Critical Process*. London and New York: Methuen, 1986.

———, ed. *Twentieth Century Interpretations of Macbeth: A Collection of Critical Essays*. Englewood Cliffs, N. J.: Prentice-Hall, 1977.

Hawkins, Harriett. *The Devil's Party: Critical Counter-Interpretations of Shakespearean Drama*. Oxford: Clarendon Press, 1985.

Hayles, N. Katherine. *The Cosmic Web: Scientific Models and Literary Strategies in the Twentieth Century*. Ithaca and London: Cornell University Press, 1984.

Hegel, Georg Wilhelm Friedrich. *Lectures on Aesthetics*. Translated by T. M. Knox. Oxford: Clarendon Press, 1979.

———. *Lectures on the Philosophy of World History: Introduction—Reason in History*. Translated by H. B. Nisbet. Cambridge, London, and New York: Cambridge University Press, 1975.

———. *Logic*. Oxford: Clarendon Press, 1985.

———. *The Phenomenology of Spirit [The Phenomenology of Mind]*. Translated by A. V. Miller. Oxford, New York, Toronto, and Melbourne: Oxford University Press, 1977. German original 1807; 1952.

———. *The Philosophical Propaedeutic*. Translated by A. V. Miller. Oxford: Basil Blackwell, 1986.

———. *The Philosophy of Mind [The Philosophy of Spirit]*. Translated by William Wallace; Boumann's Zusätze translated by A. V. Miller. Oxford: Clarendon Press, 1971. German original 1830; Zusätze 1845.

———. *The Philosophy of Right*. Translated by T. M. Knox. Oxford, London, and New York: Oxford University Press, 1967.

Heidegger, Martin. *Discourse on Thinking*. Translated by John M. Anderson and E. Hans Freund. New York and London: Harper & Row, 1966; 1969.

———. *Early Greek Thinking*. Translated by David Farrell and Frank A. Capuzzi. San Francisco, Cambridge, and New York: Harper & Row, 1975; 1984.

———. *On "Time and Being."* Translated by Joan Stambaugh. New York: Harper Torchbooks, 1972. German original 1969.

———. *What Is Called Thinking?* Translated by J. Glenn Gray. New York, San Francisco, Cambridge, and London: Harper & Row, 1968. German original 1954.

Heilbrun, Carolyn G. *Toward a Recognition of Androgyny*. New York, Hagerstown, San Francisco, and London: Harper Colophon, 1974.

Heinemann, Margot. *Puritanism and Theatre: Thomas Middleton and Oppositional Drama under the Early Stuarts*. Cambridge: Cambridge University Press, 1980.

Hernadi, Paul, ed. *The Horizon of Literature*. Lincoln and London: University of Nebraska Press, 1982.

Hirsh, James E. *The Structure of Shakespearean Scenes*. New Haven and London: Yale University Press, 1981.

Hollander, John. *The Untuning of the Sky: Ideas of Music in English Poetry 1500–1700*. Princeton: Princeton University Press, 1961.

Holloway, John. *The Story of the Night: Studies in Shakespeare's Major Tragedies*. London: Routledge & Kegan Paul, 1961.

Homan, Sidney. *Shakespeare's Theater of Presence: Language, Spectacle, and the Audience*. Lewisburg, Pa: Bucknell University Press; London and Toronto: Associated University Presses, 1986.

———. *When the Theater Turns to Itself: The Aesthetic Metaphor in Shakespeare.* Lewisburg, Pa.: Bucknell University Press; London and Toronto: Associated University Presses, 1981.
Honigmann, E. A. J. *Shakespeare's Impact on His Contemporaries.* London: Macmillan, 1982.
Horkheimer, Max. *Eclipse of Reason.* New York: Seabury Press, 1974. First published 1947.
Horowitz, David. *Shakespeare: An Existential View.* London: Tavistock, 1965.
Houston, John Porter. *The Rhetoric of Poetry in the Renaissance and Seventeenth Century.* Baton Rouge and London: Louisiana State University Press, 1983.
Howarth, Herbert. *The Tiger's Heart: Eight Essays on Shakespeare.* London: Chatto & Windus, 1970.
Howell, Wilbur Samuel. *Logic and Rhetoric in England, 1500–1700.* Princeton: Princeton University Press, 1956.
Hunter, G. K. *Dramatic Identities and Cultural Tradition: Studies in Shakespeare and His Contemporaries.* Liverpool: Liverpool University Press, 1978.
———, ed. *Macbeth: The New Penguin Shakespeare.* Harmondsworth: Penguin, 1967; 1983.
Hussey, Stanley S. *The Literary Language of Shakespeare.* London and New York: Longman, 1982.
Ide, Richard S. *Possessed with Greatness: The Heroic Tragedies of Chapman and Shakespeare.* London: Scolar Press, 1980.
James, Mervyn. *English Politics and the Concept of Honour 1485–1642.* Oxford: Past and Present, 1978.
Jardine, Lisa. *Still Harping on Daughters: Women and Drama in the Age of Shakespeare.* Brighton: Harvester Press, 1983.
Jay, Gregory S., and David L. Miller, eds. *After Strange Texts: The Role of Theory in the Study of Literature.* University: University of Alabama Press, 1985.
Johnson, Barbara. *The Critical Difference: Essays in the Contemporary Rhetoric of Reading.* Baltimore and London: The Johns Hopkins University Press, 1980.
Johnson, Samuel. *Johnson on Shakespeare: Essays and Notes Selected by Walter Raleigh.* London: Oxford University Press, 1925. First published 1908.
Jorgensen, Paul A. *William Shakespeare: The Tragedies.* Boston: Twayne, 1985.
Jourdan, Serena. *The Sparrow and the Flea: The Sense of Providence in Shakespeare and Montaigne.* Salzburg: Salzburg Studies in English, 1983.
Kahn, Coppélia. *Man's Estate: Masculine Identity in Shakespeare.* Berkeley, Los Angeles, and London: University of California Press, 1981.
Kaiser, Walter. *Praisers of Folly: Erasmus, Rabelais, Shakespeare.* Cambridge: Harvard University Press, 1963.
Kant, Immanuel. *The Critique of Judgement.* Translated by James Creed Meredith. Oxford: Clarendon Press, 1957; 1986.
Kantorowicz, Ernst H. *The King's Two Bodies: A Study in Medieval Political Theology.* Princeton: Princeton University Press, 1957.
Kastan, David Scott. *Shakespeare and the Shapes of Time.* Hanover, N. H.: University Press of New England, 1982.

Kaufmann, Walter. *Tragedy and Philosophy.* New York: Doubleday, 1968.

Kelso, Ruth. *The Doctrine of the English Gentleman in the Sixteenth Century.* Urbana: University of Illinois Studies in Language and Literature, 1929.

Kittredge, George Lyman. *Witchcraft in Old and New England.* Cambridge: Harvard University Press, 1929.

Knight, G. Wilson. *The Imperial Theme: Further Interpretations of Shakespeare's Tragedies Including the Roman Plays.* London: Oxford University Press, Humphrey Milford, 1931.

———. *Shakespearian Dimensions.* Brighton: Harvester Press; Totowa, N. J.: Barnes & Noble., 1984.

———. *The Wheel of Fire: Essays in Interpretation of Shakespeare's Sombre Tragedies.* London: Oxford University Press, Humphrey Milford, 1930; 1937.

Knights, L. C. *Explorations 3.* London: Chatto & Windus, 1976.

———. *Explorations: Essays in Criticism Mainly in the Literature of the Seventeenth Century.* London: Chatto & Windus, 1946.

———. *Further Explorations.* London: Chatto & Windus, 1965.

———. *How Many Children Had Lady Macbeth?: An Essay in the Theory and Practice of Shakespeare Criticism.* Cambridge: The Minority Press, 1933.

———. *Some Shakespearean Themes.* London: Chatto & Windus, 1959.

Koelb, Clayton. *The Incredulous Reader: Literature and the Function of Disbelief.* Ithaca and London: Cornell University Press, 1984.

Kofman, Sarah. *Lectures de Derrida.* Paris: Galilée, 1984.

Kojève, Alexandre. *Introduction to the Reading of Hegel: Lectures on the Phenomenology of Spirit.* Edited by Allan Bloom. Translated by James H. Nichols, Jr. Assembled by Raymond Queneau. Ithaca and London: Cornell University Press, 1969. French original 1947.

Kott, Jan. *Shakespeare Notre Contemporain.* Translated by Anna Posner. Paris: Julliard, 1962.

Kozikowski, Stanly J. "The Gowrie Conspiracy against James VI: A New Source for *Macbeth.*" *Shakespeare Studies* 13 (1980): 197–212.

Krook, Dorothea. *Elements of Tragedy.* New Haven and London: Yale University Press, 1969.

Krupnick, Mark, ed. *Displacement: Derrida and After.* Bloomington: Indiana University Press, 1983.

Layton, Lynne, and Barbara Ann Schapiro. *Narcissism and the Text: Studies in Literature and the Psychology of Self.* New York and London: New York University Press, 1986.

Leavis, F. R. *The Common Pursuit.* Harmondsworth: Penguin/Peregrine, 1962.

Leech, Clifford, ed. *Shakespeare's Tragedies and Other Studies in Seventeenth Century Drama.* London: Chatto & Windus, 1950.

———. *Shakespeare—The Tragedies: A Collection of Critical Essays.* Chicago and London: University of Chicago Press, 1965.

Lerner, Laurence. *Shakespeare's Tragedies: A Selection of Modern Criticism.* Harmondsworth: Penguin, 1963.

Macfarlane, Alan. *Witchcraft in Tudor and Stuart England: A Regional and Comparative Study.* London: Routledge & Kegan Paul, 1970.

Bibliography

Mack, Maynard Jr. *Killing the King: Three Studies in Shakespeare's Tragic Structure.* New Haven and London: Yale University Press, 1973.

Mahood, M. M. "Unblotted Lines: Shakespeare at Work." In *Interpretations of Shakespeare,* edited by Kenneth Muir, pp. 69–84. Oxford: Clarendon Press, 1985.

Manheim, Michael. *The Weak King Dilemma in the Shakespearean History Play.* Syracuse: Syracuse University Press, 1973.

Marchant, Robert. *A Picture of Shakespeare's Tragedies.* Clarborough: Brynmill, 1984.

Mason, H. A. *The Tragic Plane.* Oxford: Clarendon Press, 1985.

McElroy, Bernard. *Shakespeare's Mature Tragedies.* Princeton: Princeton University Press, 1973.

McGee, Arthur R. "*Macbeth* and the Furies." *Shakespeare Survey* 19 (1966): 55–67.

Mack, Maynard, and George de Forest Lord, eds. *Poetic Traditions of the English Renaissance.* New Haven and London: Yale University Press, 1982.

Maynell, Hugo A. *The Nature of Aesthetic Value.* London: Macmillan, 1986.

Melville, Stephen W. *Philosophy beside Itself: On Deconstruction and Modernism.* Minneapolis: University of Minnesota Press, 1986.

Merell, Floyd. *Deconstruction Reframed.* West Lafayette: Purdue University Press, 1985.

Moulton, Richard G. *Shakespeare as a Dramatic Artist.* Oxford: Clarendon Press, 1906.

———. *Shakespeare as a Dramatic Thinker.* New York and London: Macmillan, 1903; 1912.

Muir, Kenneth. "Image and Symbol in *Macbeth.*" *Shakespeare Survey* 19 (1966): 45–54.

———. *Shakespeare: Contrasts and Controversies.* Brighton: Harvester Press, 1985.

———. *Shakespeare's Tragic Sequence.* London: Hutchinson, 1972.

———. *The Sources of Shakespeare's Plays.* London: Methuen, 1977.

———, ed. *Interpretations of Shakespeare.* Oxford: Clarendon Press, 1985.

———, ed. *Macbeth: The Arden Edition.* London and New York: Methuen, 1951; University Paperback 1983.

Muller, René J. *The Marginal Self: An Existential Inquiry into Narcissism.* Atlantic Highlands, N. J.: Humanities Press, 1987.

Murphy, James J., ed. *Renaissance Eloquence: Studies in the Theory and Practice of Renaissance Rhetoric.* Berkeley, Los Angeles, and London: University of California Press, 1983.

Murphy, John L. *Darkness and Devils: Exorcism and King Lear.* Athens, Ohio, and London: Ohio University Press, 1984.

Murray, Patrick. *The Shakespearean Scene: Some Twentieth-Century Perspectives.* London and Harlow: Longmans, Green & Co., 1969.

Murray. W. A. "Why Was Duncan's Blood Golden?" *Shakespeare Survey* 19 (1966): 34–44.

Nevo, Ruth. *Shakespeare's Other Language.* New York and London: Methuen, 1987.

Nietzsche, Friedrich. *Beyond Good and Evil.* Translated by R. J. Hollingdale. Harmondsworth: Penguin, 1973.

———. *The Birth of Tragedy.* Translated by Walter Kaufmann. New York: Vintage Books, 1967.

———. *The Gay Science.* Translated by Walter Kaufmann. New York: Vintage Books, 1974.

———. *On the Genealogy of Morals.* Translated by Walter Kaufmann and R. J. Hollingdale. New York: Vintage Books, 1969.

Norbrook, David. *Poetry and Politics in the English Renaissance.* London and Boston: Routledge & Kegan Paul, 1984.

Norris, Christopher. *Deconstruction: Theory and Practice.* London and New York: Methuen, 1982.

———. "Post-Structuralist Shakespeare: Text and Ideology." In *Alternative Shakespeares*, edited by John Drakakis, pp. 47–66. London and New York: Methuen, 1985.

Nosworthy, James M. "Macbeth, Doctor Faustus, and the Juggling Fiends." In *Mirror up to Shakespeare: Essays in Honour of G. R. Hibbard*, edited by J. C. Gray, pp. 208–22. Toronto, Buffalo, and London: University of Toronto Press, 1984.

Nuttall, A. D. *A New Mimesis: Shakespeare and the Representation of Reality.* London and New York: Methuen, 1983.

Olson, Elder. *Tragedy and the Theory of Drama.* Detroit: Wayne State University Press, 1961.

Orgel, Stephen. *The Illusion of Power: Political Theatre in the English Renaissance.* Berkeley: University of California Press, 1975.

Ornstein, Robert. *A Kingdom for a Stage: The Achievement of Shakespeare's History Plays.* Cambridge: Harvard University Press, 1972.

———. *The Moral Vision of Jacobean Tragedy.* Madison: University of Wisconsin Press, 1960.

Palmer, D. J. "'A New Gorgon:' Visual Effects in *Macbeth*." In *Focus on Macbeth*, edited by John Russell Brown, pp. 54–69. London and Boston: Routledge & Kegan Paul, 1982.

Papageorgiou, Vasilis. *Euripides' Medea and Cosmetics.* Stockholm: Almqvist and Wiksell, 1986.

Parker, Patricia, and Geoffrey Hartman, eds. *Shakespeare and the Question of Theory.* New York and London: Methuen, 1985.

Patey, Douglas Lane. *Probability and Literary Form.* Cambridge: Cambridge University Press, 1984.

Patnaik, J. N. *The Aesthetics of New Criticism.* Atlantic Highlands, N. J.: Humanities Press, 1983.

Patrides, C. A., and Joseph Wittreich, eds. *The Apocalypse in English Renaissance Thought and Literature: Patterns, Antecedents and Repercussions.* Manchester and Dover: Manchester University Press; Ithaca: Cornell University Press, 1984.

Paul, Henry N. *The Royal Play of* Macbeth: *When, Why, and How It Was Written by Shakespeare.* New York: Macmillan, 1950.

Pearl, Valerie. *London and the Outbreak of the Puritan Revolution.* Oxford: Oxford University Press, 1961.

Peirce, Charles S. *Values in a Universe of Chance.* New York: Doubleday, 1958.

Pennington, Donald, and Keith Thomas, eds. *Puritans and Revolutionaries: Essays in Seventeenth-Century History Presented to Christopher Hill.* Oxford: Clarendon Press, 1978.

Pitt, Angela. *Shakespeare's Women.* Totowa, N. J.: Barnes & Noble; London: David & Charles, 1981.

Plant, Raymond. *Hegel.* London: Allen & Unwin, 1973.

Prior, Moody E. *The Drama of Power: Studies in Shakespeare's History Play.* Evanston, Ill.: Northwestern University Press, 1973.

———. *The Language of Tragedy.* New York: Columbia University Press, 1947.

Proser, Matthew. *The Heroic Image in Five Shakespearean Tragedies.* Princeton: Princeton University Press, 1965.

Quennell, Peter. *Shakespeare: The Poet and His Background.* Harmondsworth: Penguin, 1969. First published 1963.

Raab, Felix. *The English Face of Machiavelli: A Changing Interpretation 1500–1700.* London: Routledge, 1964.

Rabkin, Norman. *Shakespeare and the Common Understanding.* New York: The Free Press; London: Collier-Macmillan, 1967.

Rapaport, Herman. "Staging: Mont Blanc." In *Displacement: Derrida and After,* edited by Mark Krupnick, pp. 59–73. Bloomington: Indiana University Press, 1983.

Ribner, Irving. *Patterns in Shakespearian Tragedy.* London: Methuen, 1960.

Richardson, William J. *Heidegger: Through Phenomenology to Thought.* The Hague: Martinus Nijhoff, 1962.

Rigaud, N. -J., ed. *Le monstrueux dans la littérature et la pensée anglaises.* Aix-en-Provence: C.A.R.A., 1985.

Righter, Anne. *Shakespeare and the Idea of the Play.* London: Chatto & Windus, 1962.

Rorty, Richard. *Consequences of Pragmatism: Essays 1972–1980.* Brighton: Harvester Press, 1982.

———. *Philosophy and the Mirror of Nature.* Princeton: Princeton University Press, 1980.

———, ed. *The Linguistic Turn: Recent Essays in Philosophical Method.* Chicago and London: University of Chicago Press, 1967.

Rose, Gillian. *Dialectic of Nihilism: Post-Structuralism and Law.* Oxford: Basil Blackwell, 1984.

Rose, Mark. *Shakespearean Design.* Cambridge: Harvard University Press, 1972.

Rosenberg, Marvin. "Macbeth and Lady Macbeth in the Eighteenth and Nineteenth Centuries." In *Focus on Macbeth,* edited by John Russell Brown, pp. 73–86. London and Boston: Routledge & Kegan Paul, 1982.

———. *The Masks of Macbeth.* Berkeley, Los Angeles, and London: University of California Press, 1978.

Rossiter, A. P. *Angel with Horns and Other Shakespearean Lectures.* London: Longmans, 1961.

Rotman, Brian. *Signifying Nothing: The Semiotics of Zero.* London: Macmillan, 1987.

Ruegg, Maria. "The End(s) of French Style: Structuralism and Post-Structuralism in the American Context." *Criticism* 21 (Summer 1979): 189–216.

Ryan, Michael. "Deconstruction and Social Theory: The Case of Liberalism." In *Displacement: Derrida and After,* edited by Mark Krupnick, pp. 154–68. Bloomington: Indiana University Press, 1983.

Sacks, Elizabeth. *Shakespeare's Imagery of Pregnancy.* London: Macmillan, 1980.

Saintillan, Daniel. "Hegel et Héraclite." In *Hegel et la pensée grecque,* edited by Jacques D'Hondt. Paris: Presses Universitaires de France, 1974.

Sanders, Wilbur. *The Dramatist and the Received Idea: Studies in the Plays of Marlowe and Shakespeare.* Cambridge: Cambridge University Press, 1968.

Sartre, Jean-Paul. *Being and Nothingness: An Essay on Phenomenological Ontology* Translated by Hazel E. Barnes. London: Methuen, 1958; 1981.

Schaper, Eva, ed. *Pleasure, Preference and Value: Studies in Philosophical Aesthetics.* Cambridge: Cambridge University Press, 1983.

Schmid, Herta, and Aloysius Van Kesteren, eds. *Semiotics of Drama and Theatre.* Amsterdam and Philadelphia: John Benjamins Publishing Company, 1984.

Schmidgall, Gary. *Shakespeare and the Courtly Aesthetic.* Berkeley, Los Angeles, and London: University of California Press, 1981.

Schoenbaum, S. *Shakespeare and Others.* Washington: The Folger Shakespeare Library, 1985.

Schwartz, Murray M., and Coppélia Kahn, eds., *Representing Shakespeare: New Psychoanalytic Essays.* Baltimore and London: The Johns Hopkins University Press, 1980.

Schwindt, John. "Luther's Paradoxes and Shakespeare's God: The Emergence of the Absurd in Sixteenth-Century Literature." *Modern Language Studies* 15 (Autumn 1985); 6–9.

Scott, Charles E. *The Language of Difference.* Atlantic Highlands, N. J.: Humanities Press, 1987.

Scragg, Leah. "Deconstructing Shakespeare?" *Critical Quarterly* 28 (Autumn 1986): 102–108.

Searle, John R. "Reiterating the Difference: A Reply to Derrida." *Glyph* 1 (1977); 198–208.

Selden, Raman. *Criticism and Objectivity.* London: George Allen & Unwin, 1984.

Sewall, Richard B. *The Vision of Tragedy.* New Haven: Yale University Press, 1959.

Sharratt, Bernard. *The Literary Labyrinth: Contemporary Critical Discourse.* Brighton: Harvester Press; Totowa, N. J.: Barnes & Noble, 1984.

Shumaker, Wayne. *The Occult Sciences in the Renaissance.* Berkeley, Los Angeles, and London: University of California Press, 1972.

Bibliography

Siegel, Paul N. *Shakespearean Tragedy and the Elizabethan Compromise*. Lanham, Md., New York, and London: University Press of America, 1983.

Siemon, James R. *Shakespearean Iconoclasm*. Berkeley and London: University of California Press, 1985.

Sinfield, Alan. *Literature in Protestant England 1560–1660*. London: Croom Helm, 1982.

Slights, Camille Wells. *The Casuistical Tradition in Shakespeare, Donne, Herbert, and Milton*. Princeton: Princeton University Press, 1981.

Smidt, Kristian. *Unconformities in Shakespeare's History Plays*. London: Macmillan, 1982.

Snyder, Susan. *The Comic Matrix of Shakespeare's Tragedies: Romeo and Juliet, Hamlet, Othello, and King Lear*. Princeton: Princeton University Press, 1979.

Soellner, Rolf. *Shakespeare's Patterns of Self-Knowledge*. Columbus: Ohio State University Press, 1972.

Solomon, Robert C. *In the Spirit of Hegel: A Study of G. W. F. Hegel's Phenomenology of Spirit*. New York and Oxford: Oxford University Press, 1983.

Speaight, Robert. *Nature in Shakespearian Tragedy*. London: Hollis and Carter, 1955.

Spivack, Bernard. *Shakespeare and the Allegory of Evil*. New York: Columbia University Press, 1958.

Sprague, Arthur Colby. *Shakespeare and the Actors: The Stage Business in His Plays (1660–1905)*. Cambridge: Harvard University Press, 1945.

Spurgeon, Caroline F. E. *Shakespeare's Imagery and What It Tells Us*. Cambridge: Cambridge University Press, 1968. First published 1935.

Stace, W. T. *The Philosophy of Hegel*. New York: Dover, 1955. First published 1924.

Stallybrass, Peter. "*Macbeth* and Witchcraft." In *Focus on* Macbeth, edited by John Russell Brown, pp. 189–209. London and Boston: Routledge & Kegan Paul, 1982.

Staten, Henry. *Wittgenstein and Derrida*. Oxford: Basil Blackwell, 1985.

Stauffer, Donald A. *Shakespeare's World of Images: The Development of His Moral Ideas*. Bloomington and London: Indiana University Press, 1966. First edition 1949.

Steiner, George. *Antigones*. Oxford: Clarendon Press, 1986. First published 1984.

———. *The Death of Tragedy*. London: Faber and Faber, 1961.

Stewart, J. I. M. *Character and Motive in Shakespeare: Some Recent Appraisals Examined*. London, New York, and Toronto: Longmans, Green & Co., 1949.

———. "Steep Tragic Contrast: *Macbeth*." In *Shakespeare: The Tragedies*, edited by Clifford Leech. Chicago and London: University of Chicago Press, 1965.

Stoll, Elmer Edgar. "Source and Motive in *Macbeth* and *Othello*." In *Shakespeare: Modern Essays in Criticism*, edited by Leonard F. Dean, pp. 282–93. New York: Oxford University Press, 1961.

Stone, Lawrence. *The Causes of the English Revolution 1529–1642*. London: Routledge, 1972.

———. *The Crisis of the Aristocracy 1558–1641*. Oxford: Oxford University Press, 1965.

Stroud, Barry. *The Significance of Philosophical Scepticism*. Oxford: Clarendon Press, 1984.

Styan, J. L. *The Shakespeare Revolution: Criticism and Performance in the Twentieth Century*. Cambridge, London, New York, and Melbourne: Cambridge University Press, 1977.

Summers, Joseph H. *Dreams of Love and Power: On Shakespeare's Plays*. Oxford: Clarendon Press; London and New York: Oxford University Press, 1984.

Sypher, Wylie. *Four Stages of Renaissance Style: Transformations in Art and Literature 1400–1700*. Garden City, N. Y.: Doubleday, 1955.

Taylor, Gary. *Moment by Moment by Shakespeare*. London: Macmillan, 1985.

———. *To Analyze Delight: A Hedonist Criticism of Shakespeare*. Newark: University of Delaware Press, 1985.

Tempera, Mariangela. "Lo spazio simbolico delle 'Weird Sisters' nel *Macbeth*." In *Macbeth dal testo alla scena*, edited by Mariangela Tempera, pp. 77–89. Bologna: Cooperativa Libraria Universitaria Editrice, 1982.

———, ed. *Macbeth dal testo alla scena*. Bologna: Cooperativa Libraria Universitaria Editrice, 1982.

Tennenhouse, Leonard. *Power on Display: The Politics of Shakespeare's Genres*. New York and London: Methuen, 1986.

Thomas, Vivian. *The Moral Universe of Shakespeare's Problem Plays*. Totowa, N. J.: Barnes & Noble, 1987.

Tindemans, Carlos. "Coherence and Focality: A Contribution to the Analysability of Theatre Discourse." In *Semiotics of Drama and Theatre*, edited by Herta Schmid and Aloysius Van Kesteren, pp. 127–34. Amsterdam and Philadelphia: John Benjamins Publishing House, 1984.

Thorpe, Willard. *The Triumph of Realism in Elizabethan Drama 1558–1612*. Princeton: Princeton University Press, 1928.

Traversi, Derek. *An Approach to Shakespeare*. London: Hollis and Carter, 1969.

Trousdale, Marion. *Shakespeare and the Rhetoricians*. London: Scolar Press, 1982.

Turner, Robert Y. *Shakespeare's Apprenticeship*. Chicago and London: University of Chicago Press, 1974.

Tymieniecka, Anna-Teresa, ed. *The Existential Coordinates of the Human Condition: Poetic—Epic—Tragic*. Dordrecht, Boston, and Lancaster: D. Reidel, 1984.

Ulmer, Gregory L. "Op Writing: Derrida's Solicitation of Theoria." In *Displacement: Derrida and After*, edited by Mark Krupnick, pp. 29–58. Bloomington: Indiana University Press, 1983.

Van den Berg, Kent T. *Playhouse and Cosmos: Shakespearean Theater as Metaphor*. Newark: University of Delaware Press; London and Toronto: Associated University Presses, 1985.

Van Laan, Thomas F. *Role-Playing in Shakespeare*. Toronto, Buffalo, and London: University of Toronto Press, 1978.

Verene, Donald Phillip. *Hegel's Recollection: A Study of Images in the Phenomenology of Spirit*. Albany: State University of New York Press, 1985.

Viswanathan S. *The Shakespeare Play as Poem: A Critical Tradition in Perspective.* Cambridge and New York: Cambridge University Press, 1980.

Walker, Roy. *The Time is Free: A Study of* Macbeth. London: Andrew Dakers, 1949.

Watson, Curtis Brown. *Shakespeare and the Renaissance Concept of Honor.* Princeton: Princeton University Press, 1960.

Weimann, Robert. "Shakespeare und Luther: von neuzeitlicher Autorität und Autor-Funktion." *Shakespeare Jahrbuch* 120 (1984): 7–24.

Weinsheimer, Joel C. *Gadamer's Hermeneutics: A Reading of* Truth and Method. New Haven and London: Yale University Press, 1985.

Wells, Robin Headlam. *Shakespeare, Politics and the State.* London: Macmillan, 1986.

Wells, Stanley. *Re-Editing Shakespeare for the Modern Reader: Based on Lectures Given at the Folger Shakespeare Library, Washington, D.C.* Oxford: Clarendon Press, 1984.

Wells, Susan. *The Dialectic of Representation.* Baltimore and London: The Johns Hopkins University Press, 1985.

West, Robert H. *Reginald Scot and Renaissance Writings on Witchcraft.* Boston: Twayne, 1984.

Whigham, Frank. *Ambition and Privilege: The Social Tropes of Elizabethan Courtesy Theory.* Berkeley, Los Angeles, and London: University of California Press, 1984.

Whitaker, Virgil K. *The Mirror Up to Nature: The Technique of Shakespeare's Tragedies.* San Marino, Ca.: The Huntington Library, 1965.

White, R. S. *Innocent Victims: Poetic Injustice in Shakespearean Tragedy.* Newcastle: Tyneside Free Press, 1982.

Wickham, Glynne. "Hell-Castle and Its Door-Keeper." *Shakespeare Survey* 19 (1966): 68–74.

Wilson, Harold S. *On the Design of Shakespearian Tragedy.* Toronto: University of Toronto Press; London: Oxford University Press, 1957.

Wilson, John Dover, ed. *Macbeth: The Works of Shakespeare.* Cambridge, London, New York, New Rochelle, Melbourne, and Sydney: Cambridge University Press, 1980. First published 1947.

Yates, Frances A. *Giordano Bruno and the Hermetic Tradition.* London: Routledge & Kegan Paul, 1964.

Zeeveld, W. Gordon. *The Temper of Shakespeare's Thought.* New Haven and London: Yale University Press, 1974.

INDEX

Abridgment. See Cuts
Absolute monarchy, 110, 153
Abyss, 83
Acceleration, 22, 62, 69, 215–16
Achilles' heel deconstruction, 26
Active servitude, 108, 111
Actresses, 138
Aesthetic idea, 44
Agony, 102, 126, 176
Air, 44, 89, 94, 96
Ambition, 80–82, 94
Analytical philosophy, 35
Androgyny, 93
Anesthesia, 105–6
Anguish, 98–100, 123, 171
Angulation, 176, 179
Anthropocentricity, 129
Antitheatricalness, 48–50
Antony and Cleopatra, 20, 38, 212
Apollo versus Dionysus, 188–205
Aporia, 19
Architechtonics, 26
Armor, 170, 184
Arrogance, 101, 178
Asceticism, 36. See also Unhappy Consciousness
Asides, 78
Automatization, 89

Babyhood, 142, 143
Barthes, Roland, 191, 230 n.23
Bartholomeusz, Dennis, 56
Bataille, Georges, 10, 14, 20, 33, 155–58, 165, 173
Baudrillard, Jean, 22, 209–17, 232 nn. 52 and 63
Bayley, John, 57–58, 66, 77, 81, 88, 108, 143
Belongingness, 32, 197
Berger, Harry, 41
Boiling, 71–72

Bonelessness, 142, 144
Booth, Stephen, 36, 37, 53
Boundary situation, 38
Bradley, Andrew C., 117
Bradshaw, Graham, 39
Breast, 142–44
Brightness, 151
Bristol, Michael, 39
Broken appearance, 59–63
Brooke, Nicholas, 133
Brutalization, 98
Bulman, James, 53
Burning, 12, 13, 61, 138, 139, 141

Calderwood, James, 37, 38, 226 n.25
Campbell, Lily, 198
Cartesianism, 20, 21, 27, 46, 110
Catastrophe, 216
Causality, 37, 78, 80, 82, 84, 209–17
Centripetalism, 32, 33
Chanting, 71
Charles II, 140
Chaudhuri, Sukanta, 39
Chiasmos, 75
Childlessness, 141
Cinders, 13
Clearness, 115–22
Cognitivism, 35, 36
Coleridge, Samuel Taylor, 228–29 n.20
Comic relief, 127
Compression, 178
Concentricity, 105
Conservation, 156
Conventions, 39, 40, 64, 103
Convergence. See Discursive convergence
Conversationalism, 30
Conviction, 92–93
Cooking. See Boiling
Coriolanus, 9

257

Cosmetics, 185
Counter-reading, 25, 26, 208
Craftsmanship, 73–74
Crossing. See Chiasmos
Crowning, 111–14
Culler, Jonathan, 208, 214
Cultural code, 152
Curvature, 74
Cuts, 68–76, 119–21, 204, 206

Daggers, 79, 94–97
Damnation, 87–89
Davies, Stevie, 143
Deceleration. See Slowing
Demonic possession, 49, 52, 55
Demonic recipe, 70–71
Density, 204–5
Dependency, 142
Deprivation, 143
Derrida, Jacques: and Bataille, 155, 165; and Calderwood, 37; and confrontation, 228n.12; and H. W. Fawkner, 10, 220n.40; and Hegel, 12–14, 33–34, 36, 165, 211, 222–23n.87; and Heidegger, 27, 32, 35, 219–20n.22; and method, 19; and ontology, 20–23, 28–36, 42, 108
Descartes, René. See Cartesianism
Dialectical fallacy, 37. See also Polyphony
Dilution, 105
Dionysus. See Apollo versus Dionysus
Discursive convergence, 208, 214
Distrust, 150
Domestication, 22, 32, 126–28
Doubling. See Originary duplication
Dramatic conventions. See Conventions
Drink, 125, 153, 167–72
Drugs, 168–71
Duthie, G. I., 173

Egocentricity, 105, 110
Elizabeth I, 138, 139, 140, 158
Empiricalness, 34, 35, 123, 136, 186
Epistemology, 27, 28, 35
Evans, Bertrand, 85–86
Exhaustion, 189–90
Exorcism, 52, 54, 224
Expenditure, 70, 155–65

Fainting, 57
Faking, 184
Falconry, 76, 225n.35
Falling star. See Meteor
Family dialectic, 142, 146
Farnham, Willard, 107
Fatigue, 186, 189–90
Fawkes, Guy, 139
Felperin, Howard, 27
Ferguson, Margaret W., 58, 80
Fits, 55, 56, 83, 94, 99, 112
Flatness, 134
Folio, 146
Forgiving, 54
Freedom, 47, 48, 177
Fury, 107

Gadamer, Hans-Georg, 175
Gaiety, 176–84, 205
Garber, Marjorie, 206–7
Garrick, David, 57, 77, 203, 227n.3
Gasché, Rodolphe, 19, 22
Geese, 179–80, 230n.30
General economy. See Expenditure
Generic rules, 58
Generosity, 138
Gestalt, 176
Ghost scene, 67, 90, 106, 112, 116
Gloating, 102, 105
Globe-making, 47
Glory, 156
Glover, Mary, 55
Gold, 210, 231n.36
Goldman, Michael, 68, 88, 204
Grace, 151
Greek tragedy, 131
Greenblatt, Stephen, 40
Greg, W. W., 24
Grove, Robin, 54, 192
Guarding, 33
Guignon, Charles, 110
Gunpowder Plot, 139, 140

Hallucination, 79, 95, 108. See also Ghost scene
Hamlet, 24, 38, 43, 58, 80, 108, 120
Hawkes, Terence, 24, 25, 230–31n.11
Healing. See Originary healing
Hearing, 196–97, 230n.7
Hegel, G. W. F.: and centeredness, 33; and ending philosophy, 42; and

Index

freedom, 36; and mastery, 9–10, 155, 220 n.40; and originary contradiction, 22, 232 n.43; and reflection, 19; and reversibility, 12–14; and sacrifice, 177; and servitude, 222–23 n.87; and the Unhappy Consciousness, 13–14, 211; and vanishing, 230 n.23; and woman, 228 n.13
Heidegger, Martin, 19–21, 27–35, 42, 110, 133, 219–20 n.22
Hell, 127–28
Heroic self-presence, 65–68
Heroic vanishing, 68
History, 40, 41, 46, 47, 115, 138, 140
Holinshed, Raphael, 135, 149
Homan, Sidney, 46, 49, 53
Horror, 98–108
Housekeeping, 126
Howarth, Herbert, 40
Humanism, 11
Humility, 101
Hunter, G. K., 227 n.3
Husbandry, 146, 160–62. *See also* Expenditure
Hypnosis, 56, 106, 160, 178
Hysteria, 54

Ideology, 11, 12, 14, 26, 129
Imagination, 104
Incalculability, 117–18
Individualism, 110
Induction, 82
Initiation, 212
Instrumentalism, 126, 145
Integrationism, 110
Intensity, 189–90
Intentionality, 22, 77–85, 132, 145
Interpolation, 73
Intimacy, 125
Inwardization, 108, 111, 192
Irony, 128, 141, 228 n.13

James I, 52, 55, 110, 153, 158, 159
Jesuits, 52, 128–29, 153
Johnson, Samuel, 71, 116
Joining, 75
Joyce, James, 28
Judaism, 11, 12

Kant, Immanuel, 44
King John, 120

King Lear, 39, 45, 230–31 n.11
Kojève, Alexandre, 9, 222–23 n.87, 228 n.13, 229 n.17

Lacan, Jacques, 143
Laughter, 169–71, 177–78, 205, 218
Leavis, F. R., 58
Light, 22
Liquefaction, 71
Long, Michael, 188–90

McElroy, Bernard, 39
McKellen, Ian, 57, 177
Macready, William Charles, 57
Magic, 214–17
Manheim, Michael, 40
Measure for Measure, 151
Medicine. *See* Pharmakon
Meditative thinking, 21
Melodrama, 88
Metaphysics of reflection. *See* Reflection
Meteor, 63, 232 n.52
Method, 19, 23
Metonymy, 183
Middleton, Thomas, 121
Mimicry, 71
Mineral, 209–10, 217
Miraculousness, 187, 211–17
Mourning, 163
Muir, Kenneth, 69, 73
Multiplication, 71, 74–75
Music. *See* Polyphony; Rosenberg, Marvin

Neoplatonism, 44
Neutralization, 137, 149
Nietzsche, Friedrich, 14, 27, 32, 36, 42, 188–90
Nostalgia, 34
Nuclear eye, 104

Oedipus, 207–9
Olivier, Laurence, 57, 77, 79, 112, 178, 179, 203–4
Ontological relief, 127
Optimism, 13
Originary duplication, 22, 23
Originary healing, 75
Originary reduction, 106–7
Originary repulsion, 84, 88

Originary wounding, 75
Ornstein, Robert, 152
Overbidding, 213
Overcrowding, 62
Overstatement, 165

Pain, 55
Palliative, 106
Paranoia, 112
Parker, M. D. H., 43
Passion, 198
Passive servitude, 108
Patriarchalism, 92
Paul, Henry N., 54–55
Perfection, 114–15, 123, 135
Perspectivism, 14
Pessimism, 223 n.88
Pharmakon, 167, 169, 170, 171
Phenomenological presence, 69
Phonocentricity, 29, 230–31 n.11
Pitt, Angela, 228–29 n.20
Plato, 46
Plenary speech, 195–97, 204, 230–31 n.11
Plot, 58, 147, 148
Pluralism. See Polyphony
Poison. See Drink; Drugs; Pharmakon
Politeness, 60, 133, 137, 138
Polyphony, 191–95, 201
Polysemia, 191
Positivism, 40, 92, 135–36, 145
Pragmatism, 85, 87, 154
Precipice. See Abyss
Privatization, 48
Prop. See Stage prop
Propositional truth, 19
Pseudodiagnosis, 92
Pseudohorror, 100–106
Psychoanalysis, 88, 209–12
Psychological realism, 77–78, 134
Psychologism, 220, 228–29 n.20
Punctuation, 226 n.16
Puritanism, 49

Question of Being, the. See Heidegger, Martin

Rabkin, Norman, 39, 43, 222 n.80
Radioactivity, 64–65, 92
Rapaport, Herman, 143
Realism, 78

Recitation, 57
Recognition, 9, 33
Reflection, 19–22
Reformation, the, 212
Rehearsing, 56
Relaying, 62
Relief, 127, 129
Renouncement. See Sacrifice
Representedness, 110
Repulsion. See Originary repulsion
Resonance. See Polyphony; Rosenberg, Marvin
Responsibility, 77
Reversibility, 12–14, 21
Rex Inutilis, 135
Rhubarb, 169–70
Richard III, 82
Righter, Anne, 43
Romances, the, 212
Rosenberg, Marvin, 145, 153, 188, 191–203
Rümelin, Gustav, 78

Sacrifice, 12, 13, 33, 165, 177, 184–85
Sadism, 109
Sartre, Jean-Paul, 98–100, 177
Scepticism, 47
Schopenhauer, Arthur, 188, 190
Scofield, Paul, 57
Screening, 207
Seeling, 76
Semiotics, 211
Sensuality, 35, 36, 103
Servile anguish. See Anguish
Servile presence, 68
Servile vanishing, 68
Sewall, Richard, 222 n.80
Sewing, 76
Sex-anthropology, 92
Sexuality, 125, 143, 172
Simulacrum, 175, 184–85
Sincerity, 49
Sleep, 105–6, 125, 162
Slowing, 21–23, 215
Socrates, 46
Sovereignty, 155–57, 164–87
Stage directions, 72
Stage history, 56
Stage prop, 143
Staging, 88, 94
Stewart, J. I. M., 78

Index

Stoll, Elmer Edgar, 39, 40, 78
Strangulation, 74
Structure-thinking, 41
Subjectivization, 104
Sublimity, 173, 211, 218
Supplementarity, 120, 167, 169–71, 186, 211
Surplus value, 137
Symbolic order, 214, 216

Taylor, Gary, 221–22 n.75
Technicism, 19
Telephonetics, 29, 31
Terrorism, 129
Theatricality, 45–48, 94, 100, 110
Thematic criticism, 149
Thickening, 21, 62, 151–52. See also Density
Tieck, Ludwig, 228–29 n.20
Tillyard, E. M. W., 39
Time, 22, 117, 171, 174, 186, 193–94, 215
Tone, 124–25, 128
Transcendental signified, 25, 26, 32
Transgression, 206, 209
Trick picture, 175–76
Triplicity, 225 n.33
Trust, 150
Tyranny, 153

Unanswerability, 53

Uncrowning, 112
Unhappy Consciousness, 13, 14, 211–12
Unjoining, 75
Un-knowledge, 186
Unstaging, 50, 51
Unthinkability, 24–25, 27, 31–32, 89, 92, 99, 106
Unworthiness, 65–66
Utility, 158

Value judgements, 11
Van den Berg, Kent, 47, 48
Vanishing, 59–68, 123, 124, 230 n.23
Van Laan, Thomas, 50
Verdi, Giuseppe, 191
Voluptuousness, 154

Wantonness, 161
Whigham, Frank, 40
Whitaker, Virgil, 43
Williamson, Nicol, 57
Wilson, John Dover, 24, 52, 68, 69, 119–21, 130, 207
Wit, 29
Wounding. See Originary wounding

Yes-saying, 28, 29
Youth, 229 n.17

Zones, 64